Tactics for TOEIC®

Listening and Reading Test

Grant Trew

IIBC

OXFORD
UNIVERSITY PRESS

Contents

Introduction

The TOEIC test

The TOEIC (Test of English for International Communication) test is an English language proficiency test for non-native English speakers. More than 5,000 corporations and institutions in over 60 countries use the TOEIC test, with nearly five million people registering to take it each year.

The TOEIC test measures the everyday listening and reading skills of people working in an international workplace environment. The scores indicate how well people can communicate in English with others in business, commerce, and industry. The test does not require specialized knowledge or vocabulary beyond that of a person who uses English in everyday work activities.

The TOEIC Listening and Reading test has recently been redesigned. Some question types remain the same, while some have been replaced with authentic tasks that test a broader range of sub-skills. The score scale and the range of difficulty tested have not changed so scores on both forms of the test are comparable. The redesigned test provides useful information for test takers, allowing them to make informed decisions regarding job recruitment, placement, and further training.

Test format

The material in this book reflects the changes made to the TOEIC Listening and Reading test in 2006. The overall timing and number of test parts and questions remain the same but some significant changes have been made to the individual parts of the test. The table below outlines the major changes in the test.

Listening Comprehension (45 minutes) 100 items

Part	**TOEIC**	**New TOEIC**
1	Photographs (20 questions)	Photographs (10 questions)
2	Question-Response (30 questions)	Question-Response (30 questions)
3	Short Conversations (30 questions) 30 conversations with 1 question each	Conversations (30 questions) 10 conversations with 3 questions each
4	Short Talks (20 questions)	Talks (30 questions) 10 talks with 3 questions each

Reading Comprehension (75 minutes) 100 items

Part	TOEIC	New TOEIC
5	Incomplete Sentences (40 questions)	Incomplete Sentences (40 questions)
6	Error Recognition (20 questions)	Text Completion (12 questions)
7	Reading Comprehension (40 questions)	Reading Comprehension (48 questions) • Single passages: 28 questions 7–10 reading texts with 2–5 questions each • Double passages: 20 questions 4 pairs of reading texts with 5 questions per pair

TOEIC test preparation

Learners who are preparing to take any of the TOEIC test components (Listening and Reading, Speaking, or Writing) generally do best when they are familiar with the test format. A thorough understanding of test directions and task requirements allows the test taker to focus fully on demonstrating his or her language proficiency. Because the TOEIC test is a proficiency test that assesses a wide range of language, test takers who have become familiar with the TOEIC test format should concentrate on improving their overall language skills.

Tactics for TOEIC Listening and Reading Test

About this course

Tactics for TOEIC® Listening and Reading Test is designed specifically to develop the test-taking and language skills that you will need to do well on the Listening and Reading test. It is endorsed by Educational Testing Service (ETS) and contains authentic ETS test questions.

Student's Book

The Student's Book is divided into four cycles of seven units. Each unit covers one part of the test and follows a clear and consistent format. The main sections of each unit and the key test-taking and linguistic skills it develops are listed below:

A Focus (25–40 minutes)

This section provides input on language and test-taking skills that will help you when you take the TOEIC test. It features a number of "Test tips" that provide important information on the conventions of the test and advice on how to approach them. Three activities in this section exemplify and give direct practice of the key points covered:

1. Language building These activities aim to build vocabulary and grammatical knowledge that is relevant to the section and to the test as a whole.

- Improve vocabulary and grammar
- Develop understanding of language in use

2. Test tactic These activities relate directly to one or more of the unit's "Test tips" and give immediate practice and reinforcement of test-taking skills, such as time management and dealing with the listening tasks more efficiently and effectively.
(Note: Part 7 features an additional Test tactic instead of a Language building activity.)

- Learn how to manage your time carefully
- Process information more efficiently

3. Tactic practice These activities focus directly on the Test tactic and/or Language building tasks covered in the unit. They aim to further contextualize and reinforce the tactics introduced in the unit.

Understanding natural English
This feature, which appears just before the mini-tests, focuses on two important challenges learners face in the Listening part of the test. Firstly, it aims to draw attention to one of the main factors that prevents learners from understanding spoken English – the fact that some sounds change or are dropped altogether, and that some words can sound completely different to how they are spelled. These short gap-fill listening activities exemplify and explain these differences. Secondly, the new TOEIC test features speakers from the United States, Canada, Britain and Australia. To help learners become familiar with these accents, each of the sentences in this section will be spoken by speakers from three different countries.

- Become aware of the sound changes that occur in spoken English
- Become familiar with the different native-speaker accents used in the Listening test

B Mini-test (10–20 minutes)
The mini-tests provide practice of each part of the test under timed conditions similar to those on the TOEIC test. They also help to reinforce the language and test-taking skills covered in the unit. Roughly half of the questions will focus on the tactics covered in the unit, while the rest are a random selection of question types appropriate to the test part. The tapescripts and explanatory answers in the Tapescripts and Answer Key booklet allow learners to analyze correct and incorrect answer choices.

The mini-tests help learners to:
- become more familiar with the test format, instructions and question types
- practice under test conditions
- reinforce language skills and test tactics

C Learn by doing/Grammar practice/Vocabulary practice/ Reading in action
In different parts of the course the name and form of this section varies slightly, but the overall purpose is the same – to extend language learning beyond the test context and show how it can be applied in different contexts and/or used in the real world. This makes the language more memorable and gives a broader understanding of how it is actually used. The communicative activities included in this section are often accompanied by "Activity files" at the back of the book which provide additional language and information needed to complete the task.

Learn by doing (20–30 minutes): Listening
Parts 1–4
These activities aim to provide further practice which is relevant to the test part and the focus of the unit. They encourage the learner to become more familiar with the language through a variety of communicative oral tasks, including pair conversations, role plays, short presentations, and communicative games.

Grammar/Vocabulary practice (10–15 minutes): Reading Parts 5 and 6
These activities aim to reinforce and recycle the grammar or vocabulary point covered in the unit, including for example, phrasal verbs, adjectives, adverbs, etc.

Reading in action (20–30 minutes): Reading Part 7
These activities aim to reinforce the reading tasks found in Part 7 of the test (dealing with forms, letters, e-mails, etc.). They go a step further by including a task in which the information gained is used to create a response, for example completing a letter or orally checking a schedule, etc.

D Further practice (Homework for Parts 1–4)
These activities provide additional focused practice. They typically involve the learner in writing test questions or texts similar to the ones found in the test, using English-language newspapers, magazines, or their own ideas.

- Develop understanding of language in use
- Build vocabulary and grammar
- Extend reading skills

Word lists and Quizzes
Building an extensive vocabulary is an important way to improve your language skills. To help you accomplish this, the most challenging vocabulary from each unit is listed, defined, and exemplified at the back of the book. These words are organized by unit to allow for easy reference after class; or they may be used to prepare for a lesson. To help learners understand and remember the vocabulary, the word list for each unit includes one or two quizzes for further practice. All the words from the word list are also included in an alphabetical list at the back of the book, for easy access at any time.

TOEIC practice tests
Two complete practice tests are included in the pack. Each test contains authentic ETS test questions, and includes a tapescript and an explanatory key. There is also a score conversion table to allow test takers to get an estimated TOEIC test score.

The practice tests can be used as pre- and post-tests for the course. Alternatively, individual test parts or blocks of questions can be used as additional practice material during the course.

Tapescripts and answer key
Tapescripts and an explanatory answer key for Units 1–28 are provided in a separate booklet.

How to use this book

The text was specifically written to suit a variety of course lengths and styles. Two possible approaches to using the material are suggested below:

Approach 1: Fixed courses

- For fixed courses of 40 to 45 hours in length, go through each cycle, Units 1–7, Units 8–14, Units 15–21, and Units 22–28, in the order presented.
- For courses of less than 30 hours, do the units which focus on the Listening test (Units 1–4, Units 8–11, Units 15–18, Units 22–25) and the units which focus on Reading Part 7 of the test (Units 7, 14, 21, 28) in class, and assign the units which deal with Reading Parts 5 and 6 of the test (Units 5–6, Units 12–13, Units 19–20, Units 26–27) for homework.
- For courses of less than 20 hours, follow the procedure for courses of less than 30 hours, but do only section A (Language building) and section B (Mini-test) of the units assigned for class work.

Approach 2: Short/Flexible courses
For a very short or flexible course of study or if you wish to practice only specific parts of the test, it is recommended that teachers do all the relevant test parts in the first cycle of units before moving on to the next cycle. The reason for this is that the tactics and language focus of the earlier units tend to be more general and are applicable across test parts.

TOEIC test general strategies

This course has been designed to provide you with specific strategies to help you deal with each part of the test. In addition, there are some more general strategies that will help you prepare for and take the test.

Overall test strategies

Plan your time carefully
Make sure you allow enough time to attempt all the questions. Don't spend too much time on any one question. Work quickly and if you do not know the answer to a question, come back to it later.

Don't leave any questions unanswered – make your "best guess"
If you aren't sure of the correct answer, eliminate any answers you think are wrong, then choose the answer that looks best from the remaining choices. Wrong answers are not penalized, and even a blind guess gives you a 25–33% chance of getting the right answer. If you can eliminate even one wrong answer, your chance of success increases significantly.

Don't spend too much time on the instructions for each part of the test
Become familiar with the test format. Knowing what to expect before you take the test will allow you to spend more time on the questions themselves.

Use the order of the questions as a guide
Except for questions dealing with the general situation or the main idea, the answers in the reading or listening test will often be presented in the same order as the questions. This means the answer to the first question may appear early in the passage, the second question will come after that, and so on.

Become aware of the features that can make incorrect answer choices attractive
Being aware of the forms that some incorrect answer choices take can help you choose the right answer.

Listening strategies

Answer the questions as quickly as you can
Mark the answers as soon as you are sure, and then begin to focus on the next questions.

Prepare for the next question
Before each question is played, preview the answer choices or picture, and try to predict as much as you can about what you are going to hear and what you need to listen for. The more you can predict, the easier the task will be. This applies to all listening parts of the test, except for Part 2. (Approaches to Part 2 are covered in more detail in the relevant units.)

Reading strategies

Check the time regularly
Time management is an important part of doing the reading test and you need to monitor exactly how much time you spend on each section to make sure you don't run out of time. You should spend no more than about 60–90 seconds on each Part 7 question and no more than about 30–45 seconds on each Part 5 and 6 question. This will allow you some time to check your answers at the end.

Read the questions first
In Part 7 move immediately to the questions and focus on what you need to answer.

Answer the easy questions first
You do not have to answer the questions in the order they appear in the test so answer the easy questions first, then come back later and answer the remaining questions (or make your best guess at them).

Study strategies

Build your vocabulary
This is an important factor in doing well on the TOEIC test. To help you build and improve your vocabulary, here are some suggestions:

- keep a vocabulary notebook of all the new words you come across, including the sentence you see them in
- study the word lists in this book and do the quizzes
- read, read, read!

Study outside of class
Making big improvements on the TOEIC test requires you to significantly improve your knowledge of English. To do this in a reasonable amount of time you must be prepared to follow up on your class lessons with additional study at home. At the end of each unit there is a "Further Study" section that gives tips to help you expand and reinforce what you learned in class.

*Learn to **use** English*
The TOEIC test measures your ability to understand English as it is used in everyday work and life situations. The more capable and comfortable you are in using natural English, both spoken and written, the better you will do on the TOEIC test. Make an effort to use English to communicate as much as you can and your score will improve much faster than if you just study test items, grammar, and vocabulary.

1 Listening Test Part 1 Photographs

A

Focus: Using the photo to predict what you will hear

As soon as this section starts, pick out the main theme of the first photograph and start to predict the type of statements you may hear.

unit 1

Test tip

Focus on nouns and verbs

Most distractors in the TOEIC test Part 1 involve the wrong noun or verb. Brainstorm nouns and verbs related to the picture before you listen. Focus on them while listening.

1 Language building: Brainstorm vocabulary for the focus

Match the nouns and verbs with pictures 1–3. You can use them more than once.

Nouns			Verbs		
people	briefcase	meal	eat	sit	type
screen	family	keyboard	hold	look	discuss

1

Nouns	Verbs

2

Nouns	Verbs

3

Nouns	Verbs

Follow up: Add at least two more nouns and verbs to each picture, then compare your lists with a partner.

unit 1

Test tip

Scan the instructions quickly to make sure you understand what is required.

2 Test tactic: Predict possible statements before you listen

Read the information in the box below. Then using the words from Activity 1, write two sentences about each of the pictures 1–3. Read your sentences to your partner.

Many statements in Part 1 will take one of the following forms.

1. The (man/woman/people/thing) **is** / **are** *doing* (something).
   e.g. *The man* ***is working*** *on the computer.*
2. The (man/woman/people/thing) **has** / **is** / **are** (something/ somewhere).
   e.g. *The man* ***has*** *a briefcase.*
   The family ***are*** *at the table.*

Test tip

Predict the statement type

Most statements are about:

a) The activity, e.g. *The man is writing an email.*

b) The general situation, e.g. *The meal is ready.*

c) Spatial relationships (e.g. *next to, near, across from*, etc.)

Follow up: Listen to the correct answer choice for each picture. After each listening discuss with your partner how close your predictions were.

3 Tactic practice

For each picture 1–4, you will have two minutes to brainstorm vocabulary and predict possible statements about them with your partner.

Then you will hear the correct statement for each picture. After each one, pause the audio and discuss with your partner how close your predictions were.

1

2

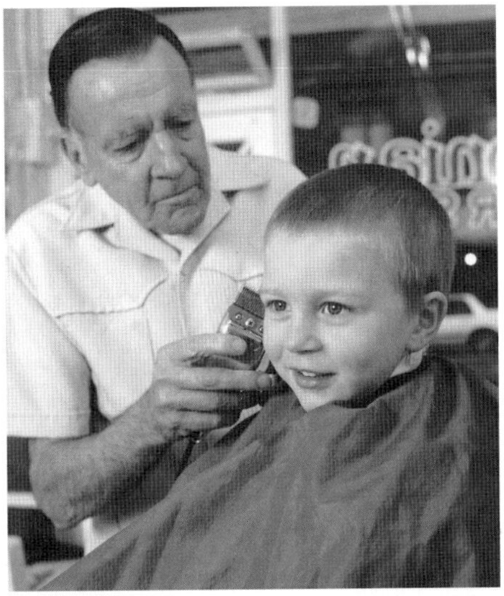

3

4

Understanding natural English

Tactics checklist

☑ Brainstorm possible nouns/verbs.

☑ Predict possible statements.

Understanding natural English

In natural spoken English, sounds are sometimes changed, combined and dropped. Listen to these sentences spoken naturally and write in the missing words.

The .... discussing something.

The .... at the table.

B Mini-test

Now practice what you have learnt at the actual test speed with questions 1–8.

Use any time available to skim the first pictures before the listening starts. After that you will have exactly 5 seconds between each question to mark your answer and focus on the next picture.

1

2

3

4

5

6

7

8

1	Ⓐ	Ⓑ	Ⓒ	Ⓓ	5	Ⓐ	Ⓑ	Ⓒ	Ⓓ
2	Ⓐ	Ⓑ	Ⓒ	Ⓓ	6	Ⓐ	Ⓑ	Ⓒ	Ⓓ
3	Ⓐ	Ⓑ	Ⓒ	Ⓓ	7	Ⓐ	Ⓑ	Ⓒ	Ⓓ
4	Ⓐ	Ⓑ	Ⓒ	Ⓓ	8	Ⓐ	Ⓑ	Ⓒ	Ⓓ

C Learn by doing: Writing stories

A Choose one of the pictures below, brainstorm vocabulary and write a three-sentence story about it. Look at the examples in the box first. Which picture do they describe?

Vocabulary (nouns and verbs)		**Sentences**
table	point	*They are sitting at the table.*
computer	discuss	*They are looking at the woman.*
document	sit	*The woman is pointing at the whiteboard.*
presentation	look at	

1

2

3

4

B Read one of your sentences to your partner. Your partner must guess which picture you chose.

Follow up: Re-write the three sentences you wrote in A above. Change one word (noun or verb) in two of the sentences so that they are wrong. Read the three sentences to a different partner and ask them to choose the correct sentence.

D Further study

Find an interesting picture and write three sentences about it. Change one word (noun or verb) in two of the sentences to test on your classmates in the next lesson.

Go to word list and quiz page 170.

2 Listening Test Part 2 — Question-Response

A

Focus: Thinking about the meaning of factual questions

Think carefully about what the question is actually asking for. Some answers may closely relate to the topic in the question, but not answer it directly.

Test tip

Answers in the TOEIC test do not always answer the question directly
Listen for answers with related details or explanations.

Test tip

Often the question and answer will be different tenses
Don't expect the tense always to be the same, e.g. the answer to a future or present question may explain something in the past.

Test tip

The focus in Part 2 is on meaning
Listen for key words (nouns/verbs/question words) to help you avoid distractors and find the correct answer choice.

Test tip

Watch out for common distractors
Being familiar with the ways incorrect answer choices may distract you can help you to make a good choice.

1 Language building: Focus on meaning in *Wh-* questions

Match each question 1–3 with two answers from a–f.

1. What are you doing on Sunday?
2. Who is going to represent them at the meeting?
3. How did you get to the airport?

a I heard Miller was chosen.
b I always go to my brother's house.
c Mary gave me a lift.
d They haven't decided yet.
e Oh, I didn't. My trip was put off until next week.
f Actually, I don't have any plans.

Follow up: Write two more answers for each question. Read them to your partner and ask them which question 1–3 they are the answer to.

2 Test tactic: Focus on the key words and avoid common distractors

Focus on the key words

Listen to sentence 1 and write number 1 next to three key words or phrases as you hear them. Compare your words with your partner's, and then make an appropriate answer for the question.

Why?	When?	rest	get	company	last birthday ......
How?	What?	come	improve	class	TOEIC score ......

Now do the same for the next two sentences.

Avoid common distractors

A Read the information in the box carefully. It shows examples of the ways in which the choices on the test may be incorrect.

A. Same word – unrelated meaning

If you hear the same word in the question and the answer choices, be careful! It could be a distractor.

Q. Has the sale improved profits?
A. Yes, it is for sale.

B. Related subject – doesn't answer the question

The test may use words that relate to one of the key words in the question, but don't actually answer the question.

Q. Where can I buy a cheap air conditioner?
A. I agree that it's very cheap.

C. Similar sound – different/unrelated word

Sometimes the incorrect choices use words that sound similar to the ones in the recording.

Q. Have you met the new staff?
A. No, it's not the same stuff.

B Read questions 1–3 and underline the key words. Then read the two incorrect distractors for each question and mark the type A–C from the box on page 13.

1. What did the customer cancel his contract for?	C	*He says he can sell it quite cheaply.* (*cancel* sounds like *can sell*)
	☐	*My customers live in Boston.*
2. Why did you buy a new car?	☐	*No, traffic can be terrible in this city.*
	☐	*Yes, my wife usually drives the car.*
3. How are they going to ship the documents?	☐	*Have you seen the notice about the shop?*
	☐	*I just love ocean cruises.*

Follow up: Think of a correct answer choice for each of the questions, and then compare your answers and new sentences with your partner.

Tactics checklist

Remember:

☑ Listen for key words and focus on meaning.

☑ Don't expect the form of the answer to be the same as the question.

☑ Listen for common distractors.

3 Tactic practice

You will hear six Part 2 questions. After each question pause the audio. Tell your partner the key words you heard. As soon as the answer choices start, stop speaking, and mark your answer choice.

1	Ⓐ	Ⓑ	Ⓒ	4	Ⓐ	Ⓑ	Ⓒ
2	Ⓐ	Ⓑ	Ⓒ	5	Ⓐ	Ⓑ	Ⓒ
3	Ⓐ	Ⓑ	Ⓒ	6	Ⓐ	Ⓑ	Ⓒ

Understanding natural English

In natural spoken English, sounds are sometimes changed, combined and dropped. Listen to these sentences spoken naturally and write in the missing words.

.... leave your last company?

.... get for your last birthday?

B Mini-test

Now practice what you have learnt at the actual test speed with questions 1–12.

You will have 5 seconds at the end of each item to make your choice. You must then be ready to listen to the next question.

1	Ⓐ	Ⓑ	Ⓒ	7	Ⓐ	Ⓑ	Ⓒ
2	Ⓐ	Ⓑ	Ⓒ	8	Ⓐ	Ⓑ	Ⓒ
3	Ⓐ	Ⓑ	Ⓒ	9	Ⓐ	Ⓑ	Ⓒ
4	Ⓐ	Ⓑ	Ⓒ	10	Ⓐ	Ⓑ	Ⓒ
5	Ⓐ	Ⓑ	Ⓒ	11	Ⓐ	Ⓑ	Ⓒ
6	Ⓐ	Ⓑ	Ⓒ	12	Ⓐ	Ⓑ	Ⓒ

C Learn by doing: Factual questions

Role play: Student A use the information below.
Student B look at Activity file 2 on page 162.

Student A

You just received the following fax from the director of your company. Unfortunately, your fax machine is broken and **some of the words are unclear.**

Task

- Work with your partner and write out the questions you will ask him or her.
- Call him or her up, apologize for the problem and ask the questions to get the information you need.

Fax Message

Important

Re: August 14 meeting

Mr. Carson,

I am writing to let you know that I will be arriving on (1) [illegible].
I am flying with United Airlines and my plane is scheduled to land at (2) [illegible]. Could you arrange my hotel for me?

The main purpose of my visit is (3) [illegible] Accuron Line of watches. We have had many complaints about water damage. We must discuss (4) [illegible]. Please invite (5) [illegible] and [illegible] also.

Barton Donovan.

Useful language

Opening

I'm sorry to bother you Mr. Donovan, but I'm afraid we couldn't read your fax properly.

Closing

Thanks very much. That's all the information I need. I will take care of this right away.

D Further study

Write down one of the questions you asked Mr. Donovan, and then make up your own answer and two other Part 2 type distractors to test other students in your next lesson.

Go to word list and quiz page 170.

unit 2

3 Listening Test Part 3 Conversations

A

Focus: Skimming to predict the context before listening

The questions and answer choices in this part of the test can help you predict what you are going to hear. Using the time available to skim them before listening will help you to identify the key parts of the conversation.

Test tip

Predicting the context of the conversation can make the listening easier

Use the key information in the answer choices to make a rough guess about what you are going to hear.

unit 3

1 Language building: Paraphrasing

Match the statements 1–4 with those with a similar meaning a–d.

1.	You can run it with an AC adapter	a	The adapter is missing
2.	Look to see if they have the item	b	Buy the part
3.	The part wasn't included	c	Check the parts stock
4.	Purchase an adapter	d	You can plug it into a socket
5.	....	e	Provide a replacement
6.	....	f	The label is incorrect
7.	....	g	It's an expensive model

Follow up: Now listen to three more statements, 5–7, and match them with the remaining three phrases with a similar meaning in e–g.

2 Test tactic: Pick out key words to predict the context

A Skim the questions and answer choices and underline key words (10–15 seconds per item). Compare with a partner and discuss what the conversation may be about. Try to predict who and where the speakers are.

1. What does the woman want to do?
   (A) Buy batteries for her CD player
   (B) Purchase an adapter
   (C) Have a missing part replaced
   (D) Check the part is in stock

2. What does the man tell her?
   (A) It doesn't run on batteries.
   (B) The label is incorrect.
   (C) The adapter isn't included.
   (D) She should buy another model.

3. What does the man offer to do?
   (A) Order the item
   (B) Check the box label
   (C) Give her a new model
   (D) Include the adapter

B Focus on the answer choices as you listen. Mark the best answer. Guess if you aren't sure, and then move on to the next question.

1	Ⓐ	Ⓑ	Ⓒ	Ⓓ
2	Ⓐ	Ⓑ	Ⓒ	Ⓓ
3	Ⓐ	Ⓑ	Ⓒ	Ⓓ

Tactics checklist

☑ Use the time before the listening to predict the context.

☑ Think of other ways to say the answer choices.

☑ Answer quickly.

Understanding natural English

In natural spoken English, sounds are sometimes changed, combined and dropped. Listen to these sentences spoken naturally and write in the missing words.

.... visit the Taylorville branch?

.... send these packages?

3 Tactic practice

Now listen to two more conversations. Before each conversation begins, use the time to predict the context with your partner, and think of other ways to say the answer choices.

1. What are the speakers discussing?
- (A) The weather in Taylorville
- (B) A meeting with clients
- (C) The fee for some repairs
- (D) A visit to a branch office

2. What is the problem?
- (A) The head office air conditioner is broken.
- (B) Bill cannot do the job.
- (C) Karl is busy all next week.
- (D) The Taylorville office is closed.

3. What does the man suggest?
- (A) Going to the head office on Tuesday
- (B) Changing the air conditioning unit
- (C) Asking someone else to do the job
- (D) Delaying the trip to Taylorville

4. How does the man feel about their new training program?
- (A) It is not as good as the old one.
- (B) It is an improvement on their previous one.
- (C) It does not have any practical value.
- (D) It is full of useful ideas.

5. What did the woman ask the man about?
- (A) How many trainees attended
- (B) A package she needs
- (C) The trainees' practical skills
- (D) Comments from the participants

6. What did some trainees criticize?
- (A) There were too many ideas.
- (B) There was no opportunity for feedback.
- (C) The training was too theoretical.
- (D) It was hard to say anything in the session.

1	Ⓐ	Ⓑ	Ⓒ	Ⓓ	4	Ⓐ	Ⓑ	Ⓒ	Ⓓ
2	Ⓐ	Ⓑ	Ⓒ	Ⓓ	5	Ⓐ	Ⓑ	Ⓒ	Ⓓ
3	Ⓐ	Ⓑ	Ⓒ	Ⓓ	6	Ⓐ	Ⓑ	Ⓒ	Ⓓ

Understanding natural English

B Mini-test

Now practice what you have learnt at the actual test speed with questions 1–12.

Use any time available to skim the questions and answer choices before the first listening starts. When you finish answering the questions about one conversation, immediately start previewing the questions for the next conversation.

1. What does the man want the woman to do?
- (A) Visit some customers
- (B) Send some packages
- (C) Attend a meeting
- (D) Give him some names

2. What is the man's problem?
- (A) He cannot find the post office.
- (B) He has to buy a present.
- (C) He does not know the woman's address.
- (D) He is late for a meeting.

3. What does the woman request?
- (A) A list of addresses
- (B) The time of a delivery
- (C) The location of a meeting
- (D) A map of the city

4. What does the woman want?
- (A) To share a ride
- (B) To go shopping
- (C) To borrow Eric's car
- (D) To look at new cars

GO ON TO THE NEXT PAGE

5. What is the woman's problem?
   (A) She has missed the bus.
   (B) Her car is broken.
   (C) She is late for work.
   (D) She does not know the area well.

6. What will the man do?
   (A) Visit the woman's company
   (B) Show the woman to the bus stop
   (C) Repair the woman's car
   (D) Drive the woman to the central office

7. What does the man suggest the woman should do?
   (A) Visit the theater
   (B) Move her vehicle
   (C) Lock her car
   (D) Enter the building

8. What does the woman ask?
   (A) Directions to a city park
   (B) Assistance reading a sign
   (C) Information about a theater
   (D) The location of available parking

9. Why was the sign not visible?
   (A) It was around a corner.
   (B) It had fallen over.
   (C) It was hidden by a tree.
   (D) It was behind a van.

10. What is the problem with the man's watch?
   (A) It needs a new battery.
   (B) The glass is broken.
   (C) It does not keep time correctly.
   (D) It is expensive to repair.

11. What will cause a delay?
   (A) There is a problem with the battery.
   (B) A strap must be ordered.
   (C) New watches have not yet arrived.
   (D) The watch must be sent out of town.

12. When will the watch finally be ready?
   (A) On Monday
   (B) On Tuesday
   (C) On Wednesday
   (D) On Thursday

1	Ⓐ	Ⓑ	Ⓒ	Ⓓ	7	Ⓐ	Ⓑ	Ⓒ	Ⓓ
2	Ⓐ	Ⓑ	Ⓒ	Ⓓ	8	Ⓐ	Ⓑ	Ⓒ	Ⓓ
3	Ⓐ	Ⓑ	Ⓒ	Ⓓ	9	Ⓐ	Ⓑ	Ⓒ	Ⓓ
4	Ⓐ	Ⓑ	Ⓒ	Ⓓ	10	Ⓐ	Ⓑ	Ⓒ	Ⓓ
5	Ⓐ	Ⓑ	Ⓒ	Ⓓ	11	Ⓐ	Ⓑ	Ⓒ	Ⓓ
6	Ⓐ	Ⓑ	Ⓒ	Ⓓ	12	Ⓐ	Ⓑ	Ⓒ	Ⓓ

C Learn by doing: Requests

A Complete the two conversations using the words in the box.

I'll do it	Any time will be fine
Sure	Do you think I could
Would you mind	Sure, no problem
	Would that be alright

A: .... mailing these packages for me?
B: .... When do they have to arrive?
A: They need to be delivered by Tuesday at the latest.
B: OK, ... this afternoon.

C: .... borrow your camera? Mine is broken.
D: .... When do you want it?
C: How about Saturday afternoon? ....?
D: Yeah, of course. ....

Follow up: Practice the conversations.

B Make similar conversations with your partner using situations 1–4 below. First, look at the useful expressions in the box and read the *Culture note*.

More common request phrases	Response phrases
Would you mind (helping me with these files)? Are you by any chance (driving down to the central office)? I wonder if you would mind (moving your car)?	Of course. Certainly. Sorry, (I'm using it on the weekend). I'm afraid I can't (right now). Sorry, I'm really busy. Maybe (Bob) could give you a hand.

1. Ask your partner to help you make some copies (you need them for a meeting in one hour).
2. Ask to borrow your partner's calculator (yours is at home).
3. Ask your partner for some help moving some boxes (the courier is going to pick them up in 15 minutes).
4. Ask your partner for a ride home (your car is in the shop).

unit 3

Culture note

If you don't know the person well, start your request with:
Excuse me ... or
I'm sorry to bother you, but ...

Follow up: With your partner, write down one of the conversations you had. Then write three Part 3 type questions (no answer choices) for your conversation. Join up with another pair, read out the conversation as naturally as possible, and ask them the questions you wrote.

D Further study

Think of an actual request you made recently, or imagine one you might make, and write the conversation in English. Write three questions (you don't need to make answer choices) to test your classmates in the next lesson.

Go to word list and quiz page 171.

4 Listening Test Part 4 Talks

A

Focus: Skimming to predict the context before listening

The questions and answer choices in this part of the test can help you predict what you are going to hear. Use the time available to skim through them before listening to help you to identify the key parts of the talk.

Test tip

The TOEIC test often uses different words in the answer choices and the recording

Before you listen try to imagine other ways the answer choice might be said.

Test tip

Note key words

Picking out the key words from the answer choices will help you to predict what you will hear, and focuses you on what you have to listen for.

1 Language building: Paraphrasing

Match each of the underlined words and phrases in the announcements below with the word or phrase with the closest meaning from the list a–e. The first one has been done for you.

May I have your attention.

I am sorry to announce that the ferry service to the Fairport Islands will be interrupted (1) ....d.... due to engine problems. Ticket holders may get a refund (2) .... immediately (3) .... The shuttle bus back to the train station should be here in about 20 minutes and in the meantime, we will be serving complimentary (4) .... beverages (5) ....

a without delay
b money returned
c drinks
d ~~stopped~~
e free

2 Test tactic: Pick key words and predict the context

A Skim the questions and answer choices in 1–3 and underline the key words (10–15 seconds per item). Then compare with a partner and discuss which of the situations A–C you think the talk will be about.

1. Where is this announcement being made?
   (A) At a train station
   (B) At an airport
   (C) At a bus station
   (D) At a coffee shop

2. What is the problem?
   (A) A ticket counter has closed.
   (B) Some construction work has been canceled.
   (C) A bus service has been interrupted.
   (D) Passengers have been refused a refund.

3. What may people wishing to go to Darby do?
   (A) Go directly to Darby by bus
   (B) Cross the Evanston Bridge
   (C) Take the 3:55 bus
   (D) Take a bus to another station and then a train

A A TV news report about road construction

B A tourist information report on new travel routes

C An announcement about a change in transportation services

Test tip

Answer the questions as soon as you hear the answer

Do not wait for the voice to tell you. Answer quickly, then use the 35–40 seconds between conversations to skim the next questions.

Tactics checklist

☑ Use the time before the listening to predict the context.

☑ Think of other ways to say the answer choices.

☑ Answer quickly.

Understanding Natural English

In natural spoken English, sounds are sometimes changed, combined and dropped. Listen to these sentences spoken naturally and write in the missing words.

We apologize .... inconvenience.

Check the documents .... typos.

B Focus on the answer choices in A 1–3 as you listen. Mark the best answer. Guess if you aren't sure, and move on to the next question.

1	Ⓐ	Ⓑ	Ⓒ	Ⓓ
2	Ⓐ	Ⓑ	Ⓒ	Ⓓ
3	Ⓐ	Ⓑ	Ⓒ	Ⓓ

3 Tactic practice

Listen to two more talks. Before each talk begins, with a partner take one minute to predict the context and think of other ways to say the answer choices.

1. What is the main purpose of this announcement?
   (A) To discuss the history of Arabella
   (B) To outline ways to get to Arabella
   (C) To make Arabella sound attractive to visitors
   (D) To describe Arabella's local music

2. What was Arabella originally?
   (A) A cultural center
   (B) A center for sailing events
   (C) A resort island
   (D) A trading center

3. When is the Caribbean Carnival held?
   (A) In mid-October
   (B) During the winter holidays
   (C) During the March break
   (D) At the end of April

4. Why was the meeting called?
   (A) To announce a schedule change
   (B) To move the deadline
   (C) To discuss the image files
   (D) To answer any questions

5. When does the project have to be finished?
   (A) By tomorrow
   (B) By Thursday
   (C) In five days
   (D) In a week

6. What are Beth and Howard asked to do?
   (A) Finalize the image files
   (B) Check for typos
   (C) Ask questions
   (D) Write the address labels

1	Ⓐ	Ⓑ	Ⓒ	Ⓓ	4	Ⓐ	Ⓑ	Ⓒ	Ⓓ
2	Ⓐ	Ⓑ	Ⓒ	Ⓓ	5	Ⓐ	Ⓑ	Ⓒ	Ⓓ
3	Ⓐ	Ⓑ	Ⓒ	Ⓓ	6	Ⓐ	Ⓑ	Ⓒ	Ⓓ

Understanding natural English

unit 4

B Mini-test

Now practice what you have learnt at actual test speed with questions 1–12.

Use any time available to skim the questions and answer choices before the first listening starts. When you finish answering the questions about one talk, immediately start previewing the questions for the next talk.

1. Where is the announcement taking place?
   (A) In a college classroom
   (B) At a company board meeting
   (C) At a computer conference
   (D) In a department store

2. What is the main purpose of the announcement?
   (A) To summarize sales volumes
   (B) To suggest areas for research
   (C) To advertise a product
   (D) To outline a business plan

GO ON TO THE NEXT PAGE

3. What is suggested about the EL401 standard desktop computer?
   (A) It has become less popular.
   (B) It has risen in price.
   (C) It is popular with college students.
   (D) It is exceptionally reliable.

---

4. According to the announcement, why should discarded items be put in bags?
   (A) To keep city streets clean
   (B) To reduce waste collection costs
   (C) To make materials safe to handle
   (D) To avoid attracting hungry animals

5. On what day are leaves and grass collected?
   (A) On Tuesday
   (B) On Wednesday
   (C) On Thursday
   (D) On Friday

6. By what time should bags be placed outside?
   (A) By 7:00
   (B) By 7:30
   (C) By 8:00
   (D) By 8:30

---

7. Who most likely is making this announcement?
   (A) An automobile salesperson
   (B) A police officer
   (C) A weather reporter
   (D) An insurance company representative

8. According to the announcement, what should drivers do in poor weather conditions?
   (A) Adjust their driving to road conditions
   (B) Listen to the weather report
   (C) Plan the shortest possible route
   (D) Pull into the side of the road

9. When are listeners invited to contact an Auto and Marine agent?
   (A) When roads are blocked
   (B) When safety tips are unclear
   (C) When a vehicle needs maintenance
   (D) When a mobile telephone is not working

---

10. What is the purpose of this announcement?
    (A) To announce some important computer improvements
    (B) To apologize for some incorrect information
    (C) To explain the cause of a computer system failure
    (D) To describe how to send company e-mail

11. What has caused a problem?
    (A) The installation of computer games
    (B) The opening of an infected file
    (C) The failure to install company software
    (D) The sharing of computer passwords

12. What are computer users reminded to do?
    (A) Keep a record of all passwords
    (B) Open attachments only from familiar senders
    (C) Install a better security system
    (D) Purchase new computers

1	Ⓐ	Ⓑ	Ⓒ	Ⓓ	7	Ⓐ	Ⓑ	Ⓒ	Ⓓ
2	Ⓐ	Ⓑ	Ⓒ	Ⓓ	8	Ⓐ	Ⓑ	Ⓒ	Ⓓ
3	Ⓐ	Ⓑ	Ⓒ	Ⓓ	9	Ⓐ	Ⓑ	Ⓒ	Ⓓ
4	Ⓐ	Ⓑ	Ⓒ	Ⓓ	10	Ⓐ	Ⓑ	Ⓒ	Ⓓ
5	Ⓐ	Ⓑ	Ⓒ	Ⓓ	11	Ⓐ	Ⓑ	Ⓒ	Ⓓ
6	Ⓐ	Ⓑ	Ⓒ	Ⓓ	12	Ⓐ	Ⓑ	Ⓒ	Ⓓ

C Learn by doing: Announcements

A Match the beginnings of the sentences 1–4 with the appropriate endings a–d to complete the announcement.

c **1.** Excuse me everyone, ...

a **2.** I'm afraid that today's class is canceled ...

d **3.** The class will be rescheduled ...

b **4.** If you are unable to attend on that day, ...

a ... because Mr. Phillips is off with the flu today.

b ... please speak to Mr. Phillips in his office on Monday. Thank you.

c ... could I have your attention, please.

d ... for next Wednesday at 2:00.

B Now practice reading this announcement to your partner.

Follow up: With a partner, take turns to make announcements using the notes below.

Change to meeting room
The room for the sales meeting has been changed.
The new meeting space is room 401.
The meeting start time is 3:15.

Collecting gift money
We are collecting money for Shelley's wedding gift.
Give money to Sam or Helen by Friday.
Also, we would like gift suggestions.

Farewell party
After work there will be a farewell party for Tom.
It will be held at the Nightshift Café.
If you need directions, please get a map from Jim.

unit 4

Culture note

When giving news to groups of customers it is common to start with:
May I have your attention, please.

If the news is unpleasant, say:
I am sorry to tell you ... or *I am afraid I have to announce that ...* .

If you are requesting something, say *please*.

Thank the customers at the end.
Thank you for your attention.

D Further study

Think of an announcement you have made or an event that would require a similar announcement. Prepare to make this announcement in the next lesson.

Go to word list and quiz page 171.

5 A

unit 5

Reading Test Part 5 — Incomplete Sentences

Focus: Identifying the part of speech
Using your time wisely

Parts of speech (nouns, verbs, etc.) are a commonly tested feature. This unit will help you identify the part of speech you need quickly and efficiently.

Test tip

First decide what part of speech is needed

Recognizing the part of speech (noun, verb, adjective, etc.) that is needed to fill the blank can help you to choose the correct answer.

Test tip

Find the answer choices of the correct type

Once you know what you are looking for, skim the answer choices to find it. This can help you to eliminate wrong answers.

Grammar note

Use suffixes (word endings) to help identify the part of speech, e.g.
-ed / *-ing* / *-ful* / *-le* (adjective)
-ly (adverb)
-ment (noun)

1 Language building: Know what you are looking for (main parts of speech)

A Read sentences 1–6 and note the part of speech of the word that is missing (noun, verb, adjective or adverb). Compare your ideas with a partner and think of a word that would fit.

1. The guests were amazed by the ...... statues in the garden. [ ]
2. Ms. Watkins was ...... pleased with her retirement present. [ ]
3. While Jane was at college, she ...... to her sister every week. [ ]
4. The project team found it very difficult to hide their ...... over the rejection. [ ]
5. The report suggested there was an immediate need to improve cost .... [ ]
6. The delegates seemed to find the presentation very .... [ ]

B The complete questions are shown below. Quickly skim the answers to find the part of speech you noted above.

1. The guests were amazed by the ...... statues in the garden.
   (A) color
   (B) colorful
   (C) colors
   (D) colorfully

2. The rise in steel prices has resulted in a ...... increase in our production costs.
   (A) considerably
   (B) consideration
   (C) considerable
   (D) considers

3. While Jane was at college, she ...... to her sister every week.
   (A) writing
   (B) written
   (C) write
   (D) wrote

4. The project team found it very difficult to hide their ...... over the rejection.
   (A) disappoint
   (B) disappointing
   (C) disappointedly
   (D) disappointment

5. I heard that the board gave our project proposal a very ...... review.
   (A) favor
   (B) favorable
   (C) favoring
   (D) favorably

6. The delegates seemed to find the presentation very ....
   (A) interests
   (B) interest
   (C) interesting
   (D) interestingly

2 Test tactic: The 2-pass method

The 2-pass method is a way to help you use your time more effectively. Go through the questions twice. On the first pass, quickly answer the easy questions. On the second pass, go back and spend a bit more time on the more challenging questions. In total, spend no more than about 30 seconds on a question. The exercise below helps you practice the 2-pass method.

First pass: Answer the easy questions – 1:00 minute (maximum 10 seconds per question)

Take one minute to read the six sentences below. Choose the best answer to each one. If you don't know the answer within 10 seconds, move on to the next question.

1. Ms. Jennings suggests we ...... our sales profits by simplifying our distribution system.
   (A) to increase
   (B) increase
   (C) increases
   (D) increasing
2. To ...... an outside call, please dial "9", then the number you wish to reach.
   (A) ring
   (B) telephone
   (C) reach
   (D) place
3. What time does the courier come ...... the office in the evenings?
   (A) with
   (B) on
   (C) by
   (D) for
4. If shipping costs are not fully covered, ... for delivery will be the responsibility of the recipient.
   (A) pay
   (B) payment
   (C) paid
   (D) to pay
5. ...... an emergency, press the red alarm button.
   (A) In case of
   (B) When
   (C) If
   (D) Due to
6. The director was very ...... in the quality of his accommodations.
   (A) disappointed
   (B) disappointment
   (C) disappointing
   (D) disappoints

Second pass: Answer the challenging questions – maximum 20 seconds per question

Go back and answer the questions you didn't answer on the first pass. If you don't know the answer within 20 seconds, guess and move on. Answer as quickly as possible, but don't leave any questions unanswered.

3 Tactic practice

A Read sentences 1–4, decide the part of speech of the missing word, and think of a word that would fit. Compare your ideas with your partner.

1. It has long been .... that small downturns in the US economy can have a global impact.
2. The sales clerk .... charged me twice for the light bulbs I bought.
3. Due to disappointing sales, the money .... for new computers was unavailable.
4. The city welfare fund collects donations to aid the local .... ; including underprivileged citizens.

Test tip

Manage your time wisely

Answer the easy questions first, very quickly. After you have answered all the easy ones come back and spend a maximum of 20 seconds each on the rest.

Test tip

Try to predict answers

On the first pass, try to think of possible answers before you look at the answer choices.

Test tip

Don't waste time on questions you don't know

Spending more than 30 seconds on a Part 5 question probably won't help you find the answer. If you don't know the answer, guess and move on.

Tactics checklist

☑ Determine the part of speech that fits the blank.

☑ Look for answer choices with the correct part of speech.

☑ Think of words that might fit before you look at the answer choices.

☑ Use the 2-pass method to answer quickly. If you aren't sure, guess and move on.

unit 5

B Choose the correct answer for sentences 1–4 on page 25.

1. (A) know
   (B) known
   (C) knowing
   (D) knows

2. (A) mistake
   (B) mistook
   (C) mistaken
   (D) mistakenly

3. (A) require
   (B) requires
   (C) requiring
   (D) required

4. (A) needing
   (B) needful
   (C) need
   (D) needy

B Mini-test

Now apply what you have learnt at the actual test speed with questions 1–12.

> Recommended Time: 6 minutes (or less)
> Try using the 2-pass method to help you make the most of the time available. Try to spend no more than about 30 seconds on each item. If you don't know the answer, guess and move on.

1. Young adults who are ...... with their use of credit may find themselves in trouble sooner than they expect.
   (A) careless
   (B) uncaring
   (C) carelessly
   (D) uncared

2. The attorney was warned against trying to ...... the young witness.
   (A) influential
   (B) influence
   (C) influentially
   (D) influencing

3. Inexperienced investors are ...... to enter this new market with caution.
   (A) advice
   (B) advisory
   (C) advised
   (D) advising

4. The journalist refused ...... the federal investigator the names of his sources.
   (A) tell
   (B) told
   (C) telling
   (D) to tell

5. All the components for Hanson scooters are ...... right here in this state.
   (A) to manufacture
   (B) manufactures
   (C) manufacturing
   (D) manufactured

6. The ...... is likely to have serious repercussions in future negotiations.
   (A) incident
   (B) incidence
   (C) incidentally
   (D) incidental

7. Doan Trang was selected to ...... the company at the annual conference.
   (A) represent
   (B) representing
   (C) representative
   (D) representational

8. Customers requesting a refund must be prepared to wait ...... 4–6 weeks for the request to be processed.
   (A) rough
   (B) roughly
   (C) rougher
   (D) roughest

9. The plot of the movie is too ...... ; its conflicts are either forced or simplistic.
   (A) predict
   (B) predictable
   (C) predicting
   (D) predictability

10. Adam Antoniotti is generally considered to be one of the most ...... designers in the fashion industry today.
   (A) impression
   (B) impressively
   (C) impressive
   (D) impressing

11. Mr. Yamada is ...... that the consultant's recommendation will help the situation.
   (A) convince
   (B) convinced
   (C) conviction
   (D) convincing

12. To enter information on the spreadsheet you will ...... a cell by clicking on it and then type your data.
   (A) select
   (B) selecting
   (C) to select
   (D) selection

unit 5

C Vocabulary practice

A Read sentences 1–10 and note the part of speech of the word that is missing. Use the abbreviations: noun (n), verb (v), adjective (adj), adverb (adv).

1. The owner of the largest factory in town was a very .... (adj) member of the town council.
2. John's skill in quickly and .... (   ) solving the problem saved his company thousands of dollars and avoided weeks of lost production.
3. The rich businessman made thousands of dollars of .... (   ) to help medical research each year.
4. The salesman made many promises to try to .... (   ) the manager to purchase his company's product.
5. The inspector stared .... (   ) at the components on the moving belt.
6. An .... (   ) person always sees the good side of any situation.
7. The fact that Mary graduated from a famous university was a .... (   ) advantage when she started job hunting.
8. Regular exercise and a good diet can .... (   ) your health and fitness.
9. We hired a motorcycle .... (   ) to deliver the package by hand.
10. Can you .... (   ) ways in which we can improve the work–life balance in our department?

B Note the part of speech for each of the following words. If you aren't sure, confirm the meaning with a classmate or look in the word list on page 172.

efficiently		intently		improve		suggest		courier	
influential		optimistic		donations		convince		significant	

C Now put each word into the sentence above that it best fits.

Go to word list and quiz page 172.

6 Reading Test Part 6 — Text Completion

A

Focus: Using context to choose the correct verb form and meaning

In the TOEIC test you will be asked to distinguish between different verbs as well as different forms of the same verb. This unit will help you to find clues in the questions and choose the correct answer choice.

unit 6

Test tip

Choose the correct verb form

Some questions provide four options that feature different tenses of the same verb. Look at the sentence (and the rest of the passage if necessary), then decide what tense is required, and then choose the correct option.

1 Language building: Present/Past tense verb forms

Present tense verb forms

Read the information about verb forms below. Then complete sentences 1–4 by using the correct present tense form of the verb.

Present simple	**Present continuous**
base form (*he/she/it* + s) (Happens regularly or always true) e.g. *Our summer interns work very hard.* *She works in the main office.*	*am/is/are* + verb + *ing* (Happening right now and not finished yet) e.g. *I am waiting to see the doctor.* *He is waiting till her birthday to buy the present.*

1. They often .... (play) golf with their customers on Saturday.
2. I was just informed that the parts .... (still/sit) on the ship waiting to be unloaded.
3. The customer .... (sign) his name on the insurance form as we speak.
4. Mary .... (work) as a cashier in the bank on Wilkins Street.

Past tense verb forms

Read the information about the verb forms below. Then complete sentences 5–8 by using the correct past tense form of the verb.

Past simple An action or actions completed in the past		**Past continuous**
(+) base form + *ed* or irregular past e.g. I installed the software. They brought the package yesterday.	(-) *did not* + base form e.g. The repair person did not fix the problem.	*was/were* + base form + *-ing* (past action that continued for a period of time when another action interrupted it.) e.g. *He was driving slowly.* *They were working in the office when the power went off.*

5. The workers .... (stand) around waiting for the manager to arrive for over an hour.
6. I .... (work) in the back when the customer arrived.
7. I .... (drop) Sally off at the bus stop more than an hour ago.
8. They .... (not/go) to the conference.

Follow up: With your partner, compare your answers to questions 1–8, and pick out the word(s) in the sentence that told you what the verb form should be.

2 Test tactic: Use clues to choose the correct word

A Read the text and decide if the missing verb should be in present or past form. Circle the words of the text that helped you identify the correct tense. Then with a partner guess the words that could go in each blank.

Test tip

Sometimes the sentence may not give enough information to choose the correct answer

In this case look at the rest of the text to find the correct option. These questions can test both grammatical and vocabulary knowledge.

All first-year engineering students (1) .... the story of Herbert Mansfield when they enter university.	1 ☑ Present ☐ Past
Before his invention of the steam converter in 1903, Herbert (2) .... as a design engineer for a manufacturing company.	2 ☐ Present ☐ Past
He (3) .... in a small, tidy, very average house outside Billington.	3 ☐ Present ☐ Past
He (4) .... at the National Institute before receiving his degree in engineering.	4 ☐ Present ☐ Past
It wasn't until several years later that he (5) .... the invention that would change the world.	5 ☐ Present ☐ Past
Many of the most influential scientists still (6) .... it to be the greatest breakthrough of the century.	6 ☐ Present ☐ Past
Currently the city (7) .... a monument to this very important individual.	7 ☐ Present ☐ Past

B Complete the text using the verbs in the box. Did you guess correctly?

made	believe	lived	studied	is building	worked	learn

C Look at the sentences below. Look for clues in the sentences around each blank to help you decide which word is correct.

1. In the winter the mountain trails are icy and dangerous. Travelers are encouraged to move .... along the marked paths.

(A) rapidly (B) cheerfully (C) carefully (D) perilously

2. The reports weren't distributed .... the first part of the presentation. They were made available at the end.

(A) after (B) while (C) during (D) until

3. After several hours of discussion the deal was still not signed. The main problem was the .... Due to the budget, the purchase would need to be postponed.

(A) quality (B) price (C) size (D) weight

4. It wasn't the largest company. It was, ... , one of the most highly respected in the field.

(A) furthermore (B) therefore (C) additionally (D) however

D *Follow up:* Compare your answers with your partner and explain which words gave you clues to the answers.

3 Tactic practice

Read the sentences for questions 1–3, decide which tense is needed and think of a word that would fit. Compare your ideas with a partner. Then quickly choose the correct answer.

Questions 1–3 refer to the following letter.

Tactics checklist

☑ Choose the correct verb form.

☑ If there are no clues in the sentence, look to the rest of the text.

Re: Diesel generator – Order No. B90008

Dear Mr. Johnson,

I am writing to complain about the large diesel generator that we .... from you.

1. (A) receive
(B) received
(C) are receiving
(D) to receive

Upon unpacking the equipment, we found the width of the mounting brackets to be almost 8 inches longer than we had .... in our design specifications.

2. (A) noted
(B) informed
(C) talked
(D) spoken

These will have to be replaced immediately as the generator must be installed by the end of the week.

Furthermore, the unit was sent without an instruction manual for the main control unit. Please send this out in the same shipment as the correct mounting bracket.

It is vital that we receive these parts by Tuesday. Late delivery .... our own installation schedule.

3. (A) affects
(B) affected
(C) will affect
(D) has affected

Yours sincerely,

Thomas Hardings

Thomas Hardings
Director

B Mini-test

Now apply the *Test tactics* at the actual test speed with questions 1–12.

> Recommended Time: 9 minutes (or less)
> Try using the 2-pass method to help you make the most of the time available. Try to spend no more than about 30–45 seconds on each item. If you don't know the answer, guess and move on.

Questions 1–3 refer to the following letter.

Mr. Robert Cheung
Sea Dragon Shipping
372 Clementi Ave 2#03–149A
SINGAPORE
120356

March 23

Dear Mr. Cheung,

We have been .... by one of our clients, Mikra Electronics, Jakarta, of a

1. (A) written
(B) reported
(C) informed
(D) said

possible shipping problem.

Specifically, the SS *Liberty Star*, due to arrive in Jakarta on March 22, ...

2. (A) failed
(B) fails
(C) failing
(D) fail

to arrive as scheduled.

This vessel was carrying a consignment (B/L 8974) for our client; we would like to know why the vessel has been .... and when it is expected to arrive.

3. (A) delayed
(B) replaced
(C) done
(D) repaired

A prompt reply would be appreciated in this matter.

Yours sincerely,

Emerson Filho

Emerson Filho

unit 6

GO ON TO THE NEXT PAGE

Questions 4–6 refer to the following memo.

Memorandum

To: Alvin Kurosawa, Vancouver Branch Manager

From: Melville Bromwich, Accounting Section

Alvin,

I am just .... to confirm that my colleague Tom Brooks and I will be

4. (A) write
(B) writing
(C) written
(D) to write

in Vancouver at the end of next week for the annual expenses audit. Could you please ask one of your employees to arrange our accommodation? We are planning to arrive on the 14th and .... on the 19th.

5. (A) left
(B) leaving
(C) had left
(D) leave

With the changes in deadlines, we are likely to be extremely busy.
So .... I don't think we will be able to find time to take in a hockey game

6. (A) whereas
(B) therefore
(C) however
(D) moreover

as you had previously suggested.

Thanks in advance for any assistance with the hotels. We are looking forward to seeing you next week.

Yours truly,

Mel

Questions 7–9 refer to the following letter.

Mr. Niels Kirstein
Olaf and Bohr Furnishings
Kristianiagade 19
2100 Copenhagen
Denmark

Dear Mr. Kirstein,

Your delivery of 150 hardwood table and chair sets (order# DH4589) ....

7. (A) arrives
(B) arrived
(C) will arrive
(D) arrive

this morning, but unfortunately, when we opened them we discovered that there is one leg missing from .... table.

8. (A) each
(B) all
(C) some
(D) any

Obviously we will need this problem corrected as soon as possible. We would appreciate it if you could .... the missing 150 legs to our warehouse by this

9. (A) to send
(B) sending
(C) send
(D) have been

Friday, August 16, at the latest.

I look forward to hearing from you in the next day or so.

Yours sincerely,

Alfred Axely

Alfred Axely
Purchasing Director

GO ON TO THE NEXT PAGE

Questions 10–12 refer to the following letter.

Dr. Barbara Nguyen
Family Medical Group
2825 Quebec St., Ste. 41
Denver, CO 80207

RE: Repair order #2089—P29 micro-video camera

Dear Ms Nguyen,

I am writing to you regarding the micro-video camera you .... with us

10. (A) left
(B) were leaving
(C) leave
(D) will leave

for repairs.

After thoroughly inspecting it, I must inform you that it will take approximately one week longer to repair than we originally thought. When we .... the inner

11. (A) cleaning
(B) were cleaning
(C) clean
(D) have cleaned

workings as part of the maintenance procedure, we found that the shutter was slightly bent and the lens was damaged. We do have the lens .... stock, but

12. (A) in
(B) for
(C) on
(D) at

the shutter will need to be ordered from the manufacturer in Germany.

I would appreciate if you could call me to confirm that you wish us to proceed with the repairs.

Yours sincerely,

Colin Bowie

Colin Bowie

unit 6

C Grammar practice

Read three short texts and put the verbs in the correct tense.

1. **Business letter**

Dear Mr. Jones,

I am writing in connection with the article you (1) ……….. (write) that appeared in this month's American Engineer. Our company (2) ……….. (make) parts for the aerospace industry and we think that your invention meets our specifications. Would you be able to meet with one of our design engineers next month? Currently we (3) ………..(work) on a project related to your research and we might be interested in licensing your design.

unit 6

2. **Complaint letter**

Last month your company (1) ……….. (put) in new automatic doors on our warehouse. Since then we have twice had problems with the motors. In the first case, they didn't (2)……….. (open) when the operator (3) ……….. (press) the button and we had to call in a mechanic to fix them. In the second case, the doors suddenly closed when a truck (4) ……….. (come) into the garage. This (5) ……….. (delay) the delivery of an important consignment of goods.

3. **E-mail**

Sally,

Have you been told that Jack Benson (1) ……….. now ……….. (work) on the Dorfin Project? As you know, he previously (2)……….. (manage) our Texas outfit, but he (3) ……….. just ……….. (arrive) this morning from Dallas and (4) ……….. (need) accommodation near the office.

Go to word list and quiz page 173.

7 Reading Test Part 7 — Reading Comprehension

A

Focus: Scanning the questions to decide which ones to answer first

It is essential to make the best use of your time in Part 7. Looking at the questions before you read will help you to find exactly what information you need. This will also help you to decide which questions to answer first. In this unit you will concentrate on the type of question you should first answer – specific information questions.

Test tip

Look at the questions first

To save time, do not start reading the passage until you know exactly what you need to find.

Test tip

Answer questions in the most efficient order

Some question types are easier to answer than others. Answering the easiest questions first will give you information that will help you answer the difficult ones more quickly.

unit 7

1 Test tactic: Answer easier questions first

Look at the list of question types below. The numbers indicate the order in which you should do them to make best use of your time.

1. **Specific information (positive)**
   These are the easiest and quickest to find the answer for. Do these first.
   - *According to the author, who will use x?*
   - *Where did x come from?*
   - *Who will benefit from this change?*
2. **Vocabulary questions**
   (See Unit 14)
   These should be answered quickly. If you don't know the word or words, guess and move on.
   - *The word "x" in paragraph 1 line 3 is closest in meaning to ...*
3. **Main idea/inference questions**
   (See Unit 14)
   Doing the previous question types first will help prepare you for these.
   - *What is the **purpose** of this memo?*
   - *Why is Mr. Jones writing this letter?*
   - *What **can be said/inferred** about...?*
   - *Who might read this advertisement?*
4. **Specific information (negative)**
   (See Unit 21)
   These can be the most time-consuming. Leave them till last, when you may have already got information to help you with the answers.
   - *Which of the following is NOT true?*
   - *Which of the following positions is NOT available?*

For each question below mark in the box the number of the question type. The first one has been done for you.

1. What is this notice mainly about? [3]
2. Where might you see this notice? [ ]
3. By when must you give notice in order to get the maximum refund? [ ]
4. What will happen if you withdraw prior to the second lesson? [ ]
5. Which of the following is NOT true? [ ]
6. The word "constitute" in paragraph 4, line 1, is closest in meaning to ... [ ]

Test tip

Pick out 'key words' (nouns and verbs) in the question

This will help you to quickly understand what you need to look for in the passage.

2 Test tactic: Answer specific information questions (positive) first

A Circle the specific information questions from the list below.

1 At what time does the club open?

2 The word "robust" in paragraph 1, line 2, is closest in meaning to

3 What is the price of the guitar?

4 Who might reply to this advertisement?

5 Where did the man buy his bicycle?

6 How long should the man wait for a reply?

7 What can be inferred about the woman's job?

B Look at the specific information questions below. First, underline the key words in the question and answer choices. Then scan the passage below to find the sentence that answers the question.

1. When is the latest that notice can be given in order to get the maximum refund?

(A) Five days before the first lesson

(B) After the first lesson but before the second

(C) Before the second class but after the first

(D) Just after the second lesson

2. What must people who want a refund on a fitness program do?

(A) Give their instructor notice that they can not attend

(B) Provide a medical reason for the request

(C) Give back their gym and pool passes

(D) Give notice prior to the mid-point of the program

Follow up: Compare your answers with your partner.

Summer program refund policy

The effective date of the withdrawal/cancellation is the date the withdrawal notice is received by the center, regardless of the date the participant stopped attending the class.

Withdrawal requests from all registered courses must be made before the second class is held. If the request is received 5 business days prior to the first class, the amount refunded will be the full amount, less the refund administration fee ($25.00). If the request is received after the first class, but before the second class, the amount refunded will be the full amount, less the cost of the first class and less the admin fee ($25.00). From the second lesson onwards, no refunds/credits will be issued.

If there is a medical reason for the request, it must be received prior to the mid-point of the program. Refunds for sports and fitness programs will NOT be processed until ALL gym and pool passes have been returned.

Please note that advising an instructor or not attending a program will not constitute a notice of withdrawal.

Cash/check remittances will be refunded by check. Please allow our office 4 to 6 weeks to process your refund. Credit card refunds will go back on the original card.

unit 7

Tactics checklist

- ☑ Don't read. Look at the questions first.
- ☑ Do the specific questions first.
- ☑ Pick out the key words in the questions.
- ☑ Scan the passage for the key words/ideas, then choose the best answer choice.

3 Tactic practice: Specific information

Use the tactics you have practiced to answer the following questions.

1. For whom is this letter intended?
   (A) Alberto Romero
   (B) Benjamin Weintraub
   (C) John Teirney
   (D) Alex Andreas

2. What kind of job does the applicant want?
   (A) Human resources
   (B) Advertising
   (C) Marketing
   (D) Sales

3. Where did Mr. Romero want to work?
   (A) In Britain
   (B) In North America
   (C) In Eastern Europe
   (D) In Asia

Questions 1–3 refer to the following letter.

Alberto Romero
3254 Turney Road
Garfield Heights
OH 44125
USA

Dear Mr. Romero,

This letter is to thank you for your application to join our international sales team. Unfortunately, we must inform you that due to the large number of highly-qualified applicants that applied for the position of Eastern European sales representative, we have already filled all the positions that were advertised in the May issue of the *Human Resources Bulletin*.

As you know, administrative and marketing positions in our European and Asia-Pacific offices regularly become available during the year and we would welcome your application for future international postings.

Yours truly,

Alex Andreas

p.p. Benjamin Weintraub
Human Resources Manager
London Office
John Teirney & Sons Ltd.

B Mini-test

Now apply what you have learnt at the actual test speed with questions 1–12.

> Recommended Time: 12 minutes (or less)
> Try to spend no more than about 60 seconds on each item; if you don't know the answer, guess and move on. If you have time at the end review any answers you weren't sure about.

Questions 1–3 refer to the following advertisement.

Printing for your personal & small business needs

Gaines Bros Printing

A commitment to quality and service since 1959

New opening hours:
Monday to Saturday from 9 A.M. to 7 P.M.

- Business Forms
- Business Cards
- Envelopes
- Folders
- Letterhead
- Menus
- Full Color Printing
- Graphic Design
- Digital Copying
- Invitations
- Graduation and Wedding Announcements

June-only special offers:

- **Order 10 sets of letterhead and get matching envelopes at a 50% discount**
- **Place an order worth over $100 and receive 2 business cards or invitations for the price of 1**
- **Make a purchase over $250 and you will receive a voucher worth 10% off your next order during the coming year**

Order by phone, fax or in person.

555–3467 • FAX 555–3478

458 Notting Drive Unit 119 • Alansburg

1. Who would NOT be a potential customer for this company?
(A) A couple planning a wedding
(B) A major corporation
(C) A local real estate agent
(D) A restaurant in need of new menus

2. What could customers who spend $150 get?
(A) A 10% discount
(B) Double the number of invitations
(C) A discount on envelopes
(D) Two free sets of business cards

3. What will happen from July 1?
(A) The time the shop opens will change.
(B) Fax orders will not be allowed.
(C) Discount vouchers will become invalid.
(D) No bonus will be given for large letterhead orders.

GO ON TO THE NEXT PAGE

Questions 4–6 refer to the following notice.

Welcome to the Groveland library service

We would like to invite all Groveland residents to become members of the public library system.

Interested applicants should follow the procedure below to receive their library card promptly and make use of the full range of facilities.

Please complete the accompanying personal information form and submit it to the applications desk in any of the Groveland branch libraries or to your local ward office community service desk.

Within two working days (Monday–Friday) of the application being submitted:

- You will receive a library barcode number via e-mail (enabling you to place reservations and access online databases before collecting your card).
  Note: You will require a PIN to place reservations and to access your record online. Please note that the default PIN number is the last four digits of your telephone number. If you would prefer to specify a different number please do so on the application form.
- Your card will be available for collection at the branch library you have nominated.

If you are under the age of 18, we require a parent or guardian's signature on a permission letter (Form 103) which will need to be brought into the library when you are collecting your card.

4. Who would be most interested in this notice?
(A) Members of the public library
(B) Staff at the applications desk
(C) People who wish to borrow books
(D) All residents of Groveland

5. What will NOT be possible two working days after submitting the application?
(A) Reserving books
(B) Picking up a card
(C) Checking book availability online
(D) Changing a PIN number

6. According to the notice, what special condition applies to children?
(A) They need an adult to collect their card.
(B) They must wait until they are 18.
(C) They must bring proof of age.
(D) They must sign a form.

Questions 7–9 refer to the following notice.

Online water/sewer payment

Welcome to the Worthwood Water/Sewer Account Payment System. You can now pay your bill online via credit card using the most secure online payment system available.

Please enter your Worthwood Water/Sewer account number below, then click "Submit". Your account number can be found in the upper left-hand corner of your bill. If you do not know your account number, please call 555-8375.

If your door has been tagged for non-payment, you must call 555-0874 to stop termination of water service.

Please do not use this Web site if your payment is intended for overdue sewer charges related to sewer certification. If you recently received a notice about unpaid sewer charges, please follow the payment instructions on the notice.

Sewer payments can be mailed to Division of Water, P.O. Box 139012, Worthwood, South Dakota 57248. Payments must be received by Feb 16.

A two dollar ($2.00) or two percent (2%) processing fee (whichever is GREATER) will be added to your payment.

All general inquiries should be addressed to the Information Section, Worthwood Public Works Section, P.O. Box 138976, Worthwood, South Dakota 57248, or call 555-2378 (ext. 124).

7. Who would be most interested in this notice?
(A) People who need sewer certification
(B) People who don't wish to pay additional processing charges
(C) People who want to pay by computer
(D) People who wish to receive a Water/Sewer account number

8. How can customers find their account number?
(A) By calling 555-0874 for information
(B) By clicking a button on the Web site
(C) By checking the corner of their bill
(D) By looking on their sewer certificate

9. What must people with overdue sewer bills do?
(A) Call the Division of Water
(B) Pay an additional processing fee
(C) Address their inquiries to the Information Section
(D) Follow the instructions given

GO ON TO THE NEXT PAGE

Questions 10–12 refer to the following agenda and letter.

Walken Student Empowerment Conference

Schedule of Events

Thursday, November 10

2:00 P.M.	Open Registration – *Walken University Park*
3:30 P.M.	Welcome and Introductions by Dean Alison Murret– *Griffen Hall*
4:15 P.M.	First speaker: Harry Lothian – *St. Exupery Auditorium* Chair of Economics, Senior Student Advisor "Transition from lecture hall to boardroom"
5:00 P.M.	Main speaker: Horst Van Buren – *St. Exupery Auditorium* Chairman of Alliance Department Stores "Making your way in the real world – struggles and successes"
6:00 P.M.	Reception with Horst Van Buren – *Vimy Atrium*
7:00 P.M.	Dinner at the Brownville Inn

Dear Mr. Van Buren,

I would like to take this opportunity to thank you for the very interesting and motivational talk at our conference last Thursday. I am sure the students found it particularly inspirational as they prepare to make their way in the working world.

Thank you also for the generous award donation that you made and for agreeing to present the grand prize during the reception after your talk.

I am sure I speak for the rest of the faculty and the student council when I say we would be honored if you would consider speaking at future conferences.

With sincerest appreciation and best wishes,

Yours,

Alison Murret

Alison Murret

10. For whom was the conference probably intended?
(A) High school students applying for university
(B) Students who will soon graduate from university
(C) Former university students who are now working
(D) Company workers taking university night school courses

11. What is suggested about Mr. Van Buren?
(A) He has spoken at the university before.
(B) He is a teacher of economics.
(C) He attended Walken University as a student.
(D) He has given some money to the university.

12. In the letter, the word "rest" in paragraph 3, line 1 is closest in meaning to
(A) relaxation
(B) gathering
(C) remainder
(D) excess

C Reading in action

A You are Sam Hong, the branch manager for Sea Star Shipping in Singapore. Read the notice your company has recently sent you and answer questions 1–4.

> **Notice**
>
> Recent weather conditions have caused delays of up to three days in some of our shipping contracts. Because of this, we anticipate complaints about late delivery from our customers.
>
> Our official policy is that we are not responsible for any costs resulting from failure to meet delivery schedules due to bad weather. This is clearly stated in all our shipping contracts.
>
> To assist customers with especially time-sensitive deliveries, we can offer a special 50% discount on Express air freight costs. Especially valued customers may be offered a 15% discount on their next order.

unit 7

1. What problem does this company have?
2. How much will Sea Star pay to customers who may have extra costs due to the delay?
3. What can the company do for customers who need quick delivery?
4. What bonus can the company offer important customers?

B One hour ago you received the following letter from the agent for MegaCo, one of your largest customers. Read the letter, then discuss the situation with your partner. Say what you think Mr. Hong should do. Then complete the reply to the letter of 16 February on page 44.

> 16 February
>
> Mr. Hong,
>
> We were informed that the heavy seas have delayed the delivery of product shipment SD1278 to San Francisco by an estimated three days.
>
> This is an extremely time-sensitive shipment for our customer, and because of this we will have to pay late penalties of approximately $7,500 per day.
>
> I am writing to inform you that we hold you responsible for these and any additional fees resulting from your failure to deliver as per our shipping contract.
>
> I look forward to hearing from you soon.
>
> Martha Rogers

Culture note

When refusing or giving bad news you should first apologize, e.g.

I am very sorry, but...

I'm afraid (that)...

You may then wish to offer an alternative, e.g.

Because (you are such an important customer) we are prepared to (offer you)...

Dear Ms Rogers,

We received your letter of 16 February concerning consignment number (**1**) …………….. .

We are very sorry for the unfortunate delays to your shipment, but I am afraid that we are not responsible for any (**2**) …………………………………………………………. due to (**3**) ……………………………………………. . This is clearly stated in your (**4**) ……………………………….. .

As you are a valued customer, however, we would like to assist you as much as possible in making the delivery to (**5**) …………………………….. on time. We are prepared to offer you a special (**6**) …………………………….. . In addition to this we will give you a (**7**) …………………………….. off the costs of your next order.

Please let us know as soon as possible about your intentions.

Yours sincerely,

Sam Hong

unit 7

D Further study

Write a short report on how you handled the delayed shipping problem. Be prepared to describe what you did in your next lesson.

Go to word list and quiz page 174.

Part 1
Photographs

Focus: Listening for the correct verb

Many of the incorrect answer choices in this section feature an inappropriate verb for the situation. This section will concentrate on identifying the sentence with the verb that best describes what is seen in the picture.

unit
8

Test tip

Listen carefully to check that the verb relates to the picture

Echo the sentence silently as you listen and compare the verb used with what you see in the picture.

1 Language building: Present continuous/present simple

A Look at the list of verbs and make possible sentences about each of the pictures using the present continuous or present simple tense. The first one is done for you.

1

2

study → They are studying in the library.
read → They're all ...
sit → The students ...
stand → Nobody ...
revise → They ...

run → The highway runs under the overpass.
run → The overpass ...
be (a sign) → There is ...
be (cars) → There ...
divide (a guardrail) → A guardrail ...

B Listen to four correct sentences about these pictures. Listen carefully, and after each one pause the audio and try to echo as much of the sentence as possible. Decide with a partner which picture you think the sentence matches.

Follow up: Make up one new sentence for each picture. You may use different verbs. Ask your partner to echo your sentence and choose the correct picture.

Test tip

Select answers quickly

As you listen, hold your pencil over the answers. Try to echo the sentences. If you think a sentence is possibly correct, keep your pen on that answer choice. Don't move it until you hear a better choice. Answer quickly and move on to the next question.

2 Test tactic: Select an answer quickly

A Listen to three sentences describing the pictures. When you have listened to all the sentences, choose an answer quickly.

1. (A) ☐
(B) ☑
(C) ☐

there are some cups on the table

2. (A) ☑
(B) ☐
(C) ☐

the boy is talking on the phone

B Now write two sentences to describe the following pictures.

Example: *The woman is holding a coffee cup.*

1

2

C You will hear four sentences describing each picture. After each sentence, pause the audio and tell your partner the verbs you heard, then mark below whether you think it is correct or wrong.

1

(A) ☐ Correct ☐ Wrong
(B) ☐ Correct ☐ Wrong
(C) ☐ Correct ☐ Wrong
(D) ☐ Correct ☐ Wrong

2

(A) ☐ Correct ☐ Wrong
(B) ☐ Correct ☐ Wrong
(C) ☐ Correct ☐ Wrong
(D) ☐ Correct ☐ Wrong

Follow up: With your partner compare the sentences you first made and the correct sentence.

3 Tactic practice

Use the tactics you have practiced for the next three photographs. You will have one minute to a) brainstorm vocabulary and b) predict possible sentences with your partner. Then listen to and echo (silently) the answer choices, and as you listen, tick whether you think it is correct, maybe correct, or wrong.

Tactics checklist

☑ Listen carefully for verbs.

☑ As you listen, echo the sentences. Keep your pen over sentences that are possibly correct.

1

(A) ☐ Correct ☐ Maybe correct ☐ Wrong
(B) ☐ Correct ☐ Maybe correct ☐ Wrong
(C) ☐ Correct ☐ Maybe correct ☐ Wrong
(D) ☐ Correct ☐ Maybe correct ☐ Wrong

2

(A) ☐ Correct ☐ Maybe correct ☐ Wrong
(B) ☐ Correct ☐ Maybe correct ☐ Wrong
(C) ☐ Correct ☐ Maybe correct ☐ Wrong
(D) ☐ Correct ☐ Maybe correct ☐ Wrong

Understanding natural English

In natural spoken English, sounds are sometimes changed, combined and dropped. Listen to these sentences and write in the missing words.

.... folding the newspaper.

The .... riding his horse by the sea.

3

(A)	☐ Correct	☐ Maybe correct	☐ Wrong
(B)	☐ Correct	☐ Maybe correct	☐ Wrong
(C)	☐ Correct	☐ Maybe correct	☐ Wrong
(D)	☐ Correct	☐ Maybe correct	☐ Wrong

Follow up: Compare your answers with your partner, explain your reasons, and say what you remember hearing.

Understanding natural English

B Mini-test

Now practice what you have learnt at the actual test speed with questions 1–8.

Use any time available to skim the first pictures before the listening starts. After that you will have exactly 5 seconds between each question to mark your answer and focus on the next picture.

1

2

3

4

5

6

7

8

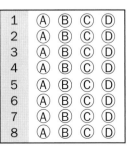

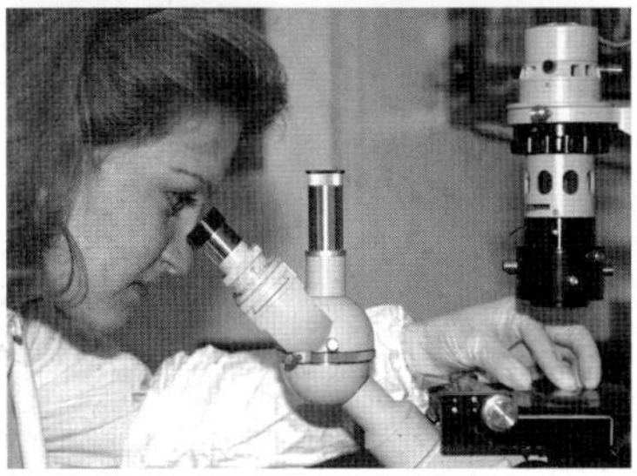

1	Ⓐ	Ⓑ	Ⓒ	Ⓓ
2	Ⓐ	Ⓑ	Ⓒ	Ⓓ
3	Ⓐ	Ⓑ	Ⓒ	Ⓓ
4	Ⓐ	Ⓑ	Ⓒ	Ⓓ
5	Ⓐ	Ⓑ	Ⓒ	Ⓓ
6	Ⓐ	Ⓑ	Ⓒ	Ⓓ
7	Ⓐ	Ⓑ	Ⓒ	Ⓓ
8	Ⓐ	Ⓑ	Ⓒ	Ⓓ

unit 8

C Learn by doing: Picture bingo

Student A: Look at Activity file 8a on page 162.

Student B: Look at Activity file 8b on page 163.

Choose one of the words on your bingo card in the Activity file, then pick a picture you think relates to that word. Tell your partner the picture number and ask them to make a sentence about the picture. There are some words to help you below. Listen to your partner's sentence and, if you hear the word, you can mark it off on your bingo card. Take turns until one person has marked off all their words. Bingo! They are the winner.

1

2

3

4

5

6

1.	family	road	**2.**	passenger	get into	**3.**	car	woman
	mother	walk		taxi	take		boats	door
	father	lift		suit	travel		dock	sit
	children	hold		street			men	open
4.	customers	outdoors	**5.**	boy	ground	**6.**	old man	push
	water	drink		gate	wear		bicycle	walk
	glasses	sit		hat	open		lake	going fishing
	table	sip		sweater	walk		sun	wear
	café	enjoy		snow	stand		cap	shine

D Further study

Find three pictures from newspapers or magazines. Write Part 1 type statements (one correct answer, three that are close but wrong) to test your classmates in the next lesson. The incorrect answers should include correct subject or object words, but incorrect verbs.

Go to word list and quiz page 175.

9 Listening Test Part 2 — Question-Response

A

Focus: Becoming familiar with different ways of answering direct questions
Becoming aware of similar-sounding words

In this part of the test, you will often hear direct questions. The correct answer will not usually be an answer with *yes*, *no* or *don't know*, and will often be in a different tense.

Test tip

Often direct questions will not be answered with *yes*, *no* or *don't know*

Look for options that use different words to express these meanings.

Test tip

Often the question and answer choice will be different verb tenses

Do not expect the grammar of the question to match the answer.

Example

Are you going tonight? → I've made other plans.

Test tip

Distractors using the same (or similar-sounding) words are common in Part 2

Be careful when choosing responses that use the same or similar-sounding words.

1 Language building: Choosing the correct answer

Choose two correct answers for each question.

a. Is Mr. Clemens coming to the presentation?

b. Did she say when she would be available?

c. Could you help Laura to prepare the documents?

d. Do you think they would mind if I came along?

1. She thinks she'll be free later today.
2. No. Everyone has been invited.
3. Unfortunately, he's on holiday then.
4. Sure. Where is she?
5. You should probably call them first.
6. No, I forgot to ask her.
7. Sorry, I have to help Michael.
8. Yes, but he'll be a few minutes late.

Follow up: Now listen to four more responses and match each one to questions a–d above.

1. a. b. c. d.
2. a. b. c. d.
3. a. b. c. d.
4. a. b. c. d.

2 Test tactic: Look out for same or similar-sounding words

A Look at the following questions and responses. Mark the correct response and circle any SAME or SIMILAR-SOUNDING words used in the distractors.

1. Are you going to the party tonight?
   (A) Yes, it's tonight.
   (B) No, he's departing tomorrow.
   ✓ (C) I haven't decided yet.
2. Have you handed in the report yet?
   (A) I've already reported it.
   (B) I put it on her desk yesterday.
   (C) I thought it was very handy.
3. Could you rearrange the venue for me?
   (A) Yes, it's new.
   (B) Sure. Is the meeting room better?
   (C) No, I didn't arrange it.
4. You called Simon back, didn't you?
   (A) No, I don't have his number.
   (B) Yes, I gave it back.
   (C) No, we call him David.

B Now compare your answers with your partner.

Test tip

Short-term memory is important

Repeat each response in your head and check if it answers the question or has same word/similar sound distractors.

unit 9

Follow up: Now listen to five more questions. Repeat each response as you hear it, and mark whether it is correct, or wrong with a same word or wrong with a similar-sounding distractor. Then compare your answer with your partner's.

1. Is this the last stop?	(A)	☐ Correct	☐ X – Same word	☐ X – Similar sound
	(B)	☐ Correct	☐ X – Same word	☐ X – Similar sound
	(C)	☐ Correct	☐ X – Same word	☐ X – Similar sound
2. Did you call the customer back?	(A)	☐ Correct	☐ X – Same word	☐ X – Similar sound
	(B)	☐ Correct	☐ X – Same word	☐ X – Similar sound
	(C)	☐ Correct	☐ X – Same word	☐ X – Similar sound
3. You're working tomorrow, aren't you?	(A)	☐ Correct	☐ X – Same word	☐ X – Similar sound
	(B)	☐ Correct	☐ X – Same word	☐ X – Similar sound
	(C)	☐ Correct	☐ X – Same word	☐ X – Similar sound
4. Can you remember the details?	(A)	☐ Correct	☐ X – Same word	☐ X – Similar sound
	(B)	☐ Correct	☐ X – Same word	☐ X – Similar sound
	(C)	☐ Correct	☐ X – Same word	☐ X – Similar sound
5. You read through the notes, didn't you?	(A)	☐ Correct	☐ X – Same word	☐ X – Similar sound
	(B)	☐ Correct	☐ X – Same word	☐ X – Similar sound
	(C)	☐ Correct	☐ X – Same word	☐ X – Similar sound

Tactics checklist

☑ Don't always expect *Yes/No* responses.

☑ Be careful of same/similar-sounding words.

☑ Verb tenses may be different.

3 Tactic practice

You will hear six question-response questions. After each question, pause the audio and repeat the response to your partner. Then mark your answer choice and compare your answers with your partner.

1	Ⓐ	Ⓑ	Ⓒ	4	Ⓐ	Ⓑ	Ⓒ
2	Ⓐ	Ⓑ	Ⓒ	5	Ⓐ	Ⓑ	Ⓒ
3	Ⓐ	Ⓑ	Ⓒ	6	Ⓐ	Ⓑ	Ⓒ

Understanding natural English

In natural spoken English, sounds are sometimes changed, combined and dropped. Listen to these sentences spoken naturally and write in the missing words.

I'm .... go after work.

Are you .... wait for Mark?

B Mini-test

Now practice what you have learnt at the actual test speed with questions 1–12.

You will have 5 seconds at the end of each item to make your choice.
You must then be ready to listen to the next question.

1	Ⓐ	Ⓑ	Ⓒ	7	Ⓐ	Ⓑ	Ⓒ
2	Ⓐ	Ⓑ	Ⓒ	8	Ⓐ	Ⓑ	Ⓒ
3	Ⓐ	Ⓑ	Ⓒ	9	Ⓐ	Ⓑ	Ⓒ
4	Ⓐ	Ⓑ	Ⓒ	10	Ⓐ	Ⓑ	Ⓒ
5	Ⓐ	Ⓑ	Ⓒ	11	Ⓐ	Ⓑ	Ⓒ
6	Ⓐ	Ⓑ	Ⓒ	12	Ⓐ	Ⓑ	Ⓒ

C Learn by doing: Checking information

A Complete the questions and responses by choosing the correct items from the boxes.

1. A: .... the **printer paper** kept in the **storeroom**?
B: .... next to the photocopier.

Is	Does	That's	No, it's

2. A: This is your **bag**, ... ?
B: Thanks. I .... looking for that.

was	isn't it	were	am not

3. A: The new **boss** seems really **nice**, ... ?
B: .... , but I heard he can be very **strict** too.

doesn't he	isn't he	He does	He will

4. A: .... show me how to use the **photocopier**?
B: .... , it's really easy.

Could you	Do you	Of course	I'm afraid

5. A: The **meeting** begins at **2:30**, ... ?
B: ...., it's starting **now**.

doesn't it	didn't it	Probably	Actually

6. A: .... that the last **report**?
B: ....

Were	I'll think about it	Was	I think so

B Now make similar conversations by replacing the words in bold in sentences 1–6 above with the following words.

1. key/boss's office?
2. calculator
3. accountant/friendly/rude
4. fax machine
5. presentation/11:30/after lunch
6. box

Follow up: Ask your partner some more questions using auxiliary verbs and tag questions. Try to give some answers without using *Yes* or *No*.

D Further study

Choose two sets of question words from the list below and make two Part 2 type questions. Then, add three responses (one correct, two incorrect) to test your partner, in the next lesson.

Are you ...?	Could you ...?	Is she ...?	... , aren't you?
Did he ...?	Does this ...?	Do you ...?	... , isn't she?

Go to word list and quiz page 175.

10 Listening Test Part 3 Conversations

A

Focus: Being aware of same word distractors

In this part of the test, the recording can often use words that are the same or have the same meaning as words in the answer choices. This may cause you to choose an incorrect answer. Be careful not to choose an answer simply because you heard something similar in the listening.

Test tip

Part 3 sometimes uses the same words in the recording and answer choices, but with a different meaning

If you hear the same words in a conversation answer choice, be careful. It may not mean that this is correct.

1 Test tactic: Be aware of same word distractors

A Quickly skim Question 1 below and underline the key words. The question and 1A have been done for you.

1. Why didn't George attend the meeting?

(A) He was in the Human Resources section.

(B) He doesn't get along with Mr. Stubbs.

(C) He had to go to Anaheim.

(D) He was in New York.

B Now quickly skim the tapescript below to find sentences with the key words. For each one decide if it answers the question or not. Cross out the wrong answer choices. When you think you have found the answer, circle the correct answer choice. Compare your answer with a partner.

Tapescript

Man A: *Hey, Taylor. How did the Human Resources meeting go? I couldn't make it because I was on a visit to the Anaheim office.*

Man B: *Oh, hi George. You're lucky you missed it. There was a disagreement between Mr. Stubbs and the New York team over employee numbers.*

Man A: *Really? What was the problem?*

Man B: *Mr. Stubbs wants to drastically cut back on the sales staff on the East Coast. Jameson and the New York team were strongly in favor of increasing staff to increase sales.*

C Continue as above, with the remaining two questions.

2. What was the meeting about?

(A) A recent disagreement with employees

(B) A proposed trip to the East Coast

(C) Natural resources in the area

(D) Changes in the number of workers

3. What happened during the meeting?

(A) An increase in the number of bargain sales was reported.

(B) A disagreement between staff members took place.

(C) An increase in the sales figures was discussed.

(D) A winning number was drawn.

Test tip

Answers to Part 3 questions often use different words from the recording

The correct answer choice sometimes uses different words to say the same thing as the recording.

D Underline the key words in the following questions and answer choices. Then listen to one short conversation for each question and cross out the answer choices with similar word distractors.

1. What is the first woman looking for?
   (A) The stove
   (B) The coffee maker
   (C) The CD player
   (D) The kitchen
2. What is the woman's problem?
   (A) She has received a parking ticket.
   (B) She wants to sell her tickets.
   (C) The show is sold out.
   (D) The performance is canceled.
3. What is the woman complaining about?
   (A) She dislikes filing documents.
   (B) She was given directions to the wrong place.
   (C) Her work is always the same.
   (D) A coworker was careless.

Follow up: Listen again and choose the correct answer. Compare your answers with your partner.

1	Ⓐ	Ⓑ	Ⓒ	Ⓓ
2	Ⓐ	Ⓑ	Ⓒ	Ⓓ
3	Ⓐ	Ⓑ	Ⓒ	Ⓓ

unit 10

Test tip

Listen to who says what

Often the answer choice will have key words used by one of the speakers, but it may not be the speaker specified in the question. Noticing this can help you spot distractors.

2 Test tactic: Listen for who says what

A Quickly skim Question 1 below and underline the key words.

1. What is the man planning to do?

(A) Work in Chicago	☐ Woman	☐ Man
(B) Get a new job	☐ Woman	☐ Man
(C) Move away from his family	☐ Woman	☐ Man
(D) Move closer to ~~his~~ her father	☐ Woman	☐ Man

B Listen to the sample conversation and mark who says each of the key words (the man or the woman). Because the question is asking about the man's plans, the words the woman says can be ignored. Choose the best answer from the things the man says. Check your answer with your partner.

C Continue as above, with the question below. This time it's important what the woman says.

2. What does the woman want?

(A) A red sweater	☐ Woman	☐ Man
(B) A discount	☐ Woman	☐ Man
(C) Free shipping	☐ Woman	☐ Man
(D) A green sweater	☐ Woman	☐ Man

Tactics checklist

☑ Be careful if you hear the same words in the conversation as in the answer choices.

☑ Listen to who says what.

unit 10

Understanding natural English

In natural spoken English, sounds are sometimes changed, combined and dropped. Listen to these sentences spoken naturally and write in the missing words.

.... take a couple of years.

.... us there in five minutes.

3 Tactic practice

Use the tactics you have practiced for the next six questions. Before each passage begins use the time to a) predict the context and b) think of other ways to say the answer choices with your partner.

1. What is the woman unhappy about?
   (A) She made a mistake at work.
   (B) The people she works with are inexperienced.
   (C) She does not like her new boss.
   (D) She dislikes working in the advertising field.
2. What does the man suggest?
   (A) Talking to her boss
   (B) Changing to a job in advertising
   (C) Looking for another job
   (D) Talking with her coworkers
3. Why does she suspect she got the job?
   (A) The supervisor liked her.
   (B) She has a lot of experience.
   (C) Her company has high employee turnover.
   (D) She had worked there a year previously.
4. What does the woman request?
   (A) A refund
   (B) A receipt
   (C) A new coffee machine
   (D) A discount
5. What does she say is the problem?
   (A) The machine is broken.
   (B) The cups are too small.
   (C) She comes from a very large family.
   (D) The unit does not make enough coffee.
6. What does the man say?
   (A) The woman can have a refund.
   (B) She can choose a different model.
   (C) He needs to see the receipt.
   (D) Replacing the product will take a week.

1	Ⓐ	Ⓑ	Ⓒ	Ⓓ	4	Ⓐ	Ⓑ	Ⓒ	Ⓓ
2	Ⓐ	Ⓑ	Ⓒ	Ⓓ	5	Ⓐ	Ⓑ	Ⓒ	Ⓓ
3	Ⓐ	Ⓑ	Ⓒ	Ⓓ	6	Ⓐ	Ⓑ	Ⓒ	Ⓓ

Understanding natural English

B Mini-test

Now practice what you have learnt at the actual test speed with questions 1–12.

Use any time available to skim the questions and answer choices before the first listening starts. When you finish answering the questions about one conversation, immediately start previewing the questions for the next conversation.

1. How long has the man been at his current job?
   (A) One year
   (B) Two years
   (C) Six years
   (D) Seven years
2. What are the man's future plans?
   (A) To continue his education
   (B) To open his own business
   (C) To move to a new city
   (D) To change careers

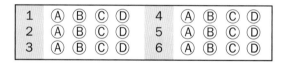

3. What does the man say about the company?
   (A) He has learned a lot while working there.
   (B) He plans to continue working there.
   (C) He wants to work for the company in a different city.
   (D) He hopes to become a manager in the company.

---

4. Where are the speakers?
   (A) At a bus stop
   (B) At an auto repair shop
   (C) At a taxi stand
   (D) At a parking garage
5. What is the man concerned about?
   (A) The way to get home
   (B) The traffic on the road
   (C) The cost of transportation
   (D) The time to fix the problem
6. What does the woman suggest?
   (A) Going to another shop
   (B) Using a taxi
   (C) Waiting a few hours
   (D) Buying a new car

---

7. What most likely is the man's job?
   (A) A police officer
   (B) An auto mechanic
   (C) A bus driver
   (D) A taxi driver

1	Ⓐ	Ⓑ	Ⓒ	Ⓓ	7	Ⓐ	Ⓑ	Ⓒ	Ⓓ
2	Ⓐ	Ⓑ	Ⓒ	Ⓓ	8	Ⓐ	Ⓑ	Ⓒ	Ⓓ
3	Ⓐ	Ⓑ	Ⓒ	Ⓓ	9	Ⓐ	Ⓑ	Ⓒ	Ⓓ
4	Ⓐ	Ⓑ	Ⓒ	Ⓓ	10	Ⓐ	Ⓑ	Ⓒ	Ⓓ
5	Ⓐ	Ⓑ	Ⓒ	Ⓓ	11	Ⓐ	Ⓑ	Ⓒ	Ⓓ
6	Ⓐ	Ⓑ	Ⓒ	Ⓓ	12	Ⓐ	Ⓑ	Ⓒ	Ⓓ

8. What is the problem?
   (A) The woman is in a hurry.
   (B) The woman is lost.
   (C) The woman is going the wrong way.
   (D) The woman has missed the game.
9. What will the man do next?
   (A) Buy baseball tickets
   (B) Drive to the stadium
   (C) Attend a meeting
   (D) Take a special route

---

10. What are the speakers discussing?
    (A) Watching sports
    (B) Driving long distances
    (C) Training for an event
    (D) Meeting relatives
11. When will the event take place?
    (A) May
    (B) June
    (C) July
    (D) August
12. What does the man say about his brother?
    (A) He visits often.
    (B) He lives a long way from his office.
    (C) He runs a business.
    (D) He eats healthy food.

C Learn by doing: Complaining

A Conversations complaining about goods and services or about other things sometimes appear in Part 3. Practice the following complaints with your partner. Then change the underlined words in the conversations using the phrases from the boxes.

Complaints about goods and services

Staff: Good afternoon. (1) May I help you?

Customer: Yes, I bought this (2) wallet, but (3) the zipper is broken. (4) Could you replace it?

Staff: Yes, that should be fine. (5) May I see your receipt?

Customer: (6) Here you are.

Staff: Thank you. Just one moment, please.

(1) Can I help you? How can I help?	(2) jacket rice cooker	(3) it's the wrong size it doesn't work properly
(4) I'd like a refund. Could I exchange it?	(5) Can I see ... Could I have ...	(6) Here you go. Here it is.

Complaints about other things

A: How (1) is your work these days?

B: (2) I'm afraid I'm not very happy.

A: Why, what's the matter?

B: Well, (3) my manager is very demanding. He's never satisfied.

A: What are you going to do?

B: I think I may (4) try to find a new job.

(1) ... is/new apartment? ... are/classes?	(2) Not great, I'm afraid. Not very well.	(3) ... the rent/high. I can't afford it. ... my teacher/ tough. He gives so much homework.	(4) ... look for a new place. ... have to work harder!

B Now make another conversation using your own ideas.

Follow up: Write three Part 3 type questions (no answer choices) for your conversation to test other students.

Culture note

When making a complaint, it is important to state what the problem is and how you would like it resolved, in a polite way.

D Further study

Think of something you were unhappy with recently, and write a conversation complaining about it. Write three questions (no answer choices) to test your classmates in the next lesson.

Go to word list and quiz page 176.

11 Listening Test Part 4 — Talks

A

Focus: Becoming familiar with different kinds of "what" questions

"What" questions are very common in the TOEIC test. Sometimes they ask for an overview or the main idea of the talk. Other times they ask for specific information. This unit will help you to deal with both types.

Test tip

Some "what" questions in Part 4 require you to understand the main idea of the talk

Listen for words that tell you information about the speaker, the location and the topic.

Test tip

Other "what" questions require you to listen for specific information

Always skim the questions and answer choices before listening. Identify key words, and listen carefully for these.

Test tip

Answers in Part 4 usually appear in the order in which they appear in the talks

Listen for answers in order.

1 Language building: Vocabulary for overview questions

A Use the words on the right to complete the overview questions.

1. What is the ...... of the presentation?	being described
2. What is this report .... ?	addressing
3. What is the speaker's reason for .... the group?	about
4. What product is .... ?	topic

B Look at the key words listed for four of the types of questions found in talks. Circle the most likely topic from the list below.

1. sales figures, increase, report, final quarter
   (A) A financial report (B) A sales demonstration (C) A school report
2. closure, bankrupt, debt, failure
   (A) It is very successful. (B) It is doing badly. (C) It hasn't changed.
3. customers, sale, ladies' fashion, department
   (A) Restaurants (B) Immigration (C) Shopping
4. ink, paper, documents, high quality, photographs
   (A) A desk (B) A printer (C) An office chair

Follow up: Discuss your answers with your partner and explain why you selected them.

2 Test tactic: Listen for answers in order

A Underline the key words in the following questions and answer choices. Then skim the tapescript and underline the words that tell you the answers.

1. Who will probably be interested in this advertisement?
   (A) Students
   (B) Retired people
   (C) Businessmen
   (D) Young families
2. What is offered free of charge?
   (A) A tour
   (B) A meal
   (C) A room
   (D) A flight

Tapescript

Alto-Pacific offers a special discount rate for seniors, so summer never has to end for travelers aged over 60. We offer discounts starting at 10% off regular rates, as well as room upgrade deals for early bookers. Not only do we offer cheaper than standard prices, but also special tour rates, complimentary breakfasts and a guaranteed quiet room. Whether you are looking to relax in a world-class resort surrounded by the blue waters of Micronesia, or enjoy a round of golf at one of our Hawaiian resorts, or perhaps explore the historical castles of Japan, we have something to cater for every taste.

unit 11

Test tip

Mark answers as you listen

If you hear an answer that is definitely correct, mark it as you listen. Answer all questions as quickly as possible.

B Listen to the three parts of a talk in turn. You have 30 seconds to skim the questions and answer choices. Then, listen and mark the answers as correct, maybe correct, or wrong. Note how the answers appear in order.

1. What kind of people might listen to this announcement?
   - (A) Politicians — (A) ☐ Correct ☐ Maybe Correct ☐ Wrong
   - (B) Venture capitalists — (B) ☐ Correct ☐ Maybe Correct ☐ Wrong
   - (C) Shareholders — (C) ☐ Correct ☐ Maybe Correct ☐ Wrong
2. What has changed in the European market in the last year?
   - (A) It has become twice as big. — (A) ☐ Correct ☐ Maybe Correct ☐ Wrong
   - (B) It has increased by one quarter. — (B) ☐ Correct ☐ Maybe Correct ☐ Wrong
   - (C) It has decreased by 50%. — (C) ☐ Correct ☐ Maybe Correct ☐ Wrong
3. What does the speaker say about the company's finances this year?
   - (A) The North American market was strong. — (A) ☐ Correct ☐ Maybe Correct ☐ Wrong
   - (B) There were good and bad results. — (B) ☐ Correct ☐ Maybe Correct ☐ Wrong
   - (C) The European market was disappointing. — (C) ☐ Correct ☐ Maybe Correct ☐ Wrong

Tactics checklist

- ☑ Identify any overview questions.
- ☑ Skim the questions and answer choices before listening to identify key words.
- ☑ Listen for answers in order.
- ☑ Answer any specific information questions as you listen.

3 Tactic Practice

Use the tactics you have practiced for the next two talks. You will have one minute before you listen to a) skim the questions and identify key words, and b) identify any main idea questions.

1. What does the speaker say about the house?
   - (A) It is old but well maintained.
   - (B) It was built 40 years ago.
   - (C) It has not been renovated.
   - (D) There are two bedrooms.
2. What is mentioned about the living room?
   - (A) It is a little dark.
   - (B) There is a bright lamp.
   - (C) It was renovated six months ago.
   - (D) It has a lot of space.
3. What will the speaker do next?
   - (A) Show the visitors the kitchen
   - (B) Take the visitors to the second floor
   - (C) Leave the house
   - (D) Talk about the price
4. What is the aim of this announcement?
   - (A) To describe Daniel Kanemoto
   - (B) To advertise a club
   - (C) To boast about achievements
   - (D) To improve people's fitness
5. What is the minimum age for members?
   - (A) 2
   - (B) 6
   - (C) 10
   - (D) 66
6. What is special about the head instructor?
   - (A) He is 66 years old.
   - (B) He is a junior regional champion.
   - (C) He won a title twice.
   - (D) He knows some basic self-defense.

1	Ⓐ	Ⓑ	Ⓒ	Ⓓ
2	Ⓐ	Ⓑ	Ⓒ	Ⓓ
3	Ⓐ	Ⓑ	Ⓒ	Ⓓ
4	Ⓐ	Ⓑ	Ⓒ	Ⓓ
5	Ⓐ	Ⓑ	Ⓒ	Ⓓ
6	Ⓐ	Ⓑ	Ⓒ	Ⓓ

Understanding natural English

In natural spoken English, sounds are sometimes changed, combined and dropped.

Listen to these sentences and write in the missing words.

As you .... see, it is in remarkably good condition.

You .... store your entire photo collection safely.

B Mini-test

Now practice what you have learnt at the actual test speed with questions 1–12.

> Use any time available to skim the questions and answer choices before the first listening starts. When you finish answering the questions about one talk, immediately start previewing the questions for the next talk.

1. When did Orgola Valley experience strong winds?
   (A) Last week
   (B) Yesterday
   (C) Last night
   (D) Today

2. What will happen tomorrow?
   (A) Temperatures will drop.
   (B) There will be heavy rain.
   (C) There will be strong winds.
   (D) Snow will fall.

3. According to the report, how could a listener get more weather information?
   (A) By calling a special telephone number
   (B) By going to a Web site
   (C) By listening to the weather channel
   (D) By reading the weather reports in the newspaper

---

4. What is the purpose of the talk?
   (A) To address customers' problems
   (B) To introduce a training session
   (C) To explain the company benefits
   (D) To describe a new product

5. Who mostly likely is the speaker addressing?
   (A) Job seekers
   (B) Company customers
   (C) New employees
   (D) Department heads

6. In which department does George Stevens work?
   (A) Human resources
   (B) Sales
   (C) Customer service
   (D) Marketing

---

7. What product is being described?
   (A) A cordless telephone
   (B) An all-in-one printer
   (C) A laptop computer
   (D) A digital camera

8. According to the advertisement, what is a special feature of the product?
   (A) The quality of the color photographs
   (B) The operating speed
   (C) The capacity to print photos from memory
   (D) The ease of operation

9. When will the sale end?
   (A) Friday
   (B) Saturday
   (C) Sunday
   (D) Monday

---

10. What is Chuck Adams responsible for?
    (A) Repairing computers
    (B) Ordering supplies
    (C) Maintaining the building
    (D) Delivering the mail

11. When is Chuck Adams leaving?
    (A) At the end of this week
    (B) At the end of next week
    (C) At the end of the month
    (D) At the end of the year

12. What is the purpose of this announcement?
    (A) To ask for donations for a gift
    (B) To present an award
    (C) To introduce a new staff member
    (D) To explain a new office procedure

1	Ⓐ	Ⓑ	Ⓒ	Ⓓ
2	Ⓐ	Ⓑ	Ⓒ	Ⓓ
3	Ⓐ	Ⓑ	Ⓒ	Ⓓ
4	Ⓐ	Ⓑ	Ⓒ	Ⓓ
5	Ⓐ	Ⓑ	Ⓒ	Ⓓ
6	Ⓐ	Ⓑ	Ⓒ	Ⓓ
7	Ⓐ	Ⓑ	Ⓒ	Ⓓ
8	Ⓐ	Ⓑ	Ⓒ	Ⓓ
9	Ⓐ	Ⓑ	Ⓒ	Ⓓ
10	Ⓐ	Ⓑ	Ⓒ	Ⓓ
11	Ⓐ	Ⓑ	Ⓒ	Ⓓ
12	Ⓐ	Ⓑ	Ⓒ	Ⓓ

unit 11

C Learn by doing: Tonight's news

A With a partner read the questions about two news reports below and make sure you understand all the words. Try to guess what the reports are about.

Business news report

1. What did FHL Electronics announce?
2. What caused the closure of the factories?
3. What did the president say about labor costs in Asia?
4. What did the president promise?
5. What is the best newspaper headline for this report?
   - Drop in Asian Labor Costs
   - FHL Announces Record Losses
   - President Introduces New Product

Local news report

1. What will open next week?
2. What is the first performance?
3. What will Tom Mason do?
4. What happened one month ago?
5. What is the best newspaper headline for this report?
   - Milltown Theater Opens Tuesday
   - Events in our Town
   - Famous Actor Spotted

B **Student A:** Look at Activity file 11a on page 163. Read the business news report to your partner. Student B will answer the questions about it above. Then listen to Student B's local news report and answer the questions about it.
Student B: Listen to your partner's business news report and answer the questions. When you are finished, switch roles. Look at Activity file 11b on page 165. Read your local news report to your partner. Student A will answer the questions about it above.

unit 11

D Further study

Write four or five sentences about your company, school or family, and write three "what" questions. Test your classmates in the next lesson.

Go to word list and quiz page 177.

12 Reading Test Part 5 Incomplete Sentences

A

Focus: Choosing gerunds and infinitives correctly
Improving your knowledge of phrasal verbs

Being familiar with the correct use of gerunds and infinitives and understanding phrasal verbs is helpful for many parts of the TOEIC test. This unit will make you more aware of how they are used, especially in Part 5.

unit 12

Test tip

Look at the verbs in gerund/infinitive questions

If the answer choices include both gerunds and infinitives, look at the verb in the question to help you decide which is correct.

Test tip

Learn to recognize gerunds and infinitives

Familiarize yourself with common phrases that include gerunds and infinitives. As you take the test, say the phrases silently to yourself, and try to hear which ones sound wrong. Avoid these choices.

1 Language building: Gerunds and infinitives

Gerunds are verbs in their base form + *-ing*, e.g. *doing*. Infinitives are verbs in their base form + *to*, e.g. *to do*.

Verbs commonly followed by a gerund

All the verbs below can be followed by gerunds, but some do not fit into the sentences. Choose the verbs from each list that do NOT fit the sentence. The first one is done for you.

1. I cannot .... meeting him before. ☐ recall ☒ admit ☐ remember
2. He .... smoking after his doctor warned him of the dangers. ☐ contemplated ☐ gave up ☐ quit
3. Increased sales indicate that customers .... getting the larger discount. ☐ appreciate ☐ value ☐ avoid
4. It starts at 5 A.M. but I .... getting up early. ☐ can't help ☐ don't mind ☐ am used to
5. The report .... reviewing the security systems in the new building. ☐ recommends ☐ advises ☐ risks

Follow up: Now write one sentence about yourself using a verb followed by a gerund and compare with a partner.

Verbs commonly followed by infinitives

All the verbs below can be followed by infinitives, but some do not fit the meaning of the sentences. Choose the verbs from each list that do NOT fit the sentence. The first one is done for you.

6. Although it was a reasonable offer, we .... them to increase it by 10%. ☒ pretended ☐ persuaded ☐ forced
7. Did you .... to meet Mr. Yamamoto when you were in Tokyo? ☐ intend ☐ expect ☐ hesitate
8. It was a successful sales meeting as they .... to purchase fifty units. ☐ decided ☐ threatened ☐ agreed
9. Because he had a lot of experience, he .... to be promoted. ☐ expected ☐ prepared ☐ deserved
10. Although he wasn't very fit, he still .... to complete a full marathon. ☐ managed ☐ decided ☐ reserved

Follow up: Now write one sentence about yourself using a verb followed by an infinitive and compare with your partner.

unit 12

Test tip

Learn as many phrasal verbs as possible

Phrasal verbs are sometimes tested in the TOEIC test. Familiarize yourself with as many common phrasal verbs as possible.

2 Test tactic: Familiarize yourself with phrasal verbs

The term *phrasal verb* refers to a verb + particle (i.e. adverb or preposition), which have a special meaning when used together.

A Choose the correct phrasal verb on the right to match the meaning given.

1.	to arrange (e.g. a meeting)	☐ set up	☐ call up
2.	to complete a blank area in a form	☐ fill out	☐ bring about
3.	to support (e.g. a colleague)	☐ fall through	☐ back up
4.	to review or check something	☐ go over	☐ take over
5.	to stop using something gradually	☐ buy out	☐ phase out
6.	to fail to stay on schedule	☐ fall behind	☐ back out (of)
7.	to investigate	☐ look into	☐ fill in for
8.	to continue	☐ keep on	☐ go through
9.	to delay or reschedule something	☐ shut off	☐ put off
10.	to consider carefully	☐ run out of	☐ think over

B Choose the correct phrasal verb to complete the following sentences.

1. Despite working overtime every day for two weeks, he still .... with his work.
   (A) went through
   (B) backed up
   (C) fell behind

2. The customer called three times this morning to .... a meeting.
   (A) set up
   (B) call up
   (C) take over

3. It was decided to .... buying the new equipment until next year.
   (A) put off
   (B) fill out
   (C) take over

4. The judge promised to .... any new evidence as soon as possible.
   (A) look out of
   (B) look into
   (C) look after

5. Visitors to the United States are required to .... an immigration questionnaire.
   (A) bring about
   (B) think over
   (C) fill out

6. The planned merger between the companies .... because they couldn't agree on the price.
   (A) took over
   (B) fell through
   (C) backed out of

7. When color televisions became popular, black and white sets were gradually ....
   (A) phased out
   (B) bought out
   (C) set up

8. A temporary worker was hired to .... Mary while she was on vacation.
   (A) take over
   (B) fill in for
   (C) fall behind

Tactics checklist

☑ Look at the verb in the question to help you decide whether a gerund or an infinitive is needed in the answer.

☑ Say phrases silently to yourself and try to hear if they sound wrong.

☑ Familiarize yourself with as many phrasal verbs as possible.

3 Tactic practice

Use the tactics you have practiced to answer the following questions.

1. Although I advised her to go by train, she decided .... instead.
   (A) drive
   (B) to drive
   (C) driving
   (D) drove

2. He was out when I called, but the receptionist kindly offered .... a message for me.
   (A) to take
   (B) taken
   (C) took
   (D) taking

3. It appears that our competitors are considering .... our takeover proposal.
   (A) to accept
   (B) accept
   (C) accepting
   (D) accepted

4. When buying a new car, it is advisable to .... the best deal you can find.
   (A) go through
   (B) look for
   (C) get into
   (D) fill out

5. We are .... on you to make a good impression at the conference next month.
   (A) taking
   (B) counting
   (C) putting
   (D) picking

6. After waiting for more than thirty minutes for my entrée to arrive, I asked .... to the manager.
   (A) speak
   (B) speaking
   (C) spoken
   (D) to speak

unit 12

B Mini-test

Now apply what you have learnt at the actual test speed with questions 1–12.

Recommended Time: 6 minutes (or less)
Try using the 2-pass method to help you make the most of the time available. Try to spend no more than about 30 seconds on each item. If you don't know the answer, guess and move on.

1. The president's limousine should be here soon, as we are expecting him .... by 7 P.M.
   (A) arrival
   (B) to arrive
   (C) arrive
   (D) arriving

2. The feeling .... the judges was that the submission had not been researched thoroughly enough.
   (A) along
   (B) among
   (C) after
   (D) around

GO ON TO THE NEXT PAGE

3. During the winter months many people enjoy .... a variety of indoor sports.
   (A) play
   (B) to play
   (C) to be playing
   (D) playing

4. Although I was pleased when I bought the camera, I later regretted not .... for a more advanced model.
   (A) waiting
   (B) wait
   (C) to wait
   (D) have waited

5. She was .... up by her grandparents from the age of seven.
   (A) brought
   (B) raised
   (C) taken
   (D) turned

6. Employees currently .... in overseas postings are eligible for an additional housing allowance.
   (A) work
   (B) worked
   (C) to work
   (D) working

7. The first applicant seemed to enjoy .... asked about his previous experience in the field.
   (A) to be
   (B) be
   (C) being
   (D) had been

8. Mr. Tan .... to see the presentation before he made the decision.
   (A) likes
   (B) would like
   (C) would have liked
   (D) had liked

9. The general manager has been .... making a decision on this issue for several months.
   (A) putting out
   (B) putting off
   (C) filling out
   (D) filling in for

10. Most workplace errors .... careless practices amongst employees.
   (A) stem from
   (B) leave out
   (C) start up
   (D) get into

11. .... visitors to the region visit the unique Al Hasqua mosque.
   (A) Almost
   (B) Each
   (C) Every
   (D) Most

12. Union leaders agreed to meet with management in order to talk .... an alternative proposal.
   (A) with
   (B) at
   (C) to
   (D) over

1	Ⓐ	Ⓑ	Ⓒ	Ⓓ	7	Ⓐ	Ⓑ	Ⓒ	Ⓓ
2	Ⓐ	Ⓑ	Ⓒ	Ⓓ	8	Ⓐ	Ⓑ	Ⓒ	Ⓓ
3	Ⓐ	Ⓑ	Ⓒ	Ⓓ	9	Ⓐ	Ⓑ	Ⓒ	Ⓓ
4	Ⓐ	Ⓑ	Ⓒ	Ⓓ	10	Ⓐ	Ⓑ	Ⓒ	Ⓓ
5	Ⓐ	Ⓑ	Ⓒ	Ⓓ	11	Ⓐ	Ⓑ	Ⓒ	Ⓓ
6	Ⓐ	Ⓑ	Ⓒ	Ⓓ	12	Ⓐ	Ⓑ	Ⓒ	Ⓓ

C Vocabulary practice

A Most phrasal verbs are made from very simple and common words. The articles below can be completed using phrasal verbs that start with *take* or *look*. Choose the correct particle to complete the phrasal verbs below. (More than one answer may be possible.)

Advertisement

If you are looking (1)..................... a relaxing vacation, then perhaps you should consider the Hotel du Rhône. Our highly-trained staff will take (2)..................... all your needs. We guarantee that you'll have wonderful memories that you'll look (3)..................... for years to come.

Company statement

As you know, we were in a three-way battle for ownership of Mediacom. We tried our best to take (4)..................... this company, but unfortunately our attempt was unsuccessful. However, it may not be all bad news, as we are currently looking (5)..................... some very interesting partnerships in Asia and our initial discussions have been very promising.

Phrasal verbs with *take* and *look*

Verb	Meaning
take over	assume control of (*The smaller firm was taken over by its larger competitor.*)
take in	learn (*There is so much to take in when starting a new job.*)
take up	start a new activity (*I decided to take up golf after joining the company.*)
take care of	be responsible for (*I'll take care of the arrangements for tomorrow's meeting.*)
take off	remove (*He took off his jacket when he came home from work.*)
take out	dispose of (*Take out the garbage when you leave, would you?*)
take back	retract (*I'm sorry I called you a fool. I take it back.*)

Verb	Meaning
look after	care for, nurture (*My mother looked after me when I was sick.*)
look for	search (*I've been looking for my car keys everywhere, but I can't seem to find them.*)
look up to	admire, respect (*I really look up to my father. He's achieved so much in his life.*)
look into	investigate (*I'll look into the best way of getting to the airport.*)
look back on	consider the past (*When he looked back on his life, he was glad he had done so many different things.*)
look forward to	Anticipate eagerly (*I am really looking forward to the holidays this year.*)

B Now write four sentences about your life using phrasal verbs with *take* and *look*. Tell them to your partner in the next lesson. Check a dictionary for other examples of phrasal verbs and note how they are used.

Go to word list and quiz page 178.

13

A

Reading Test
Part 6

Text Completion

Focus: Choosing the correct part of speech: adjectives and adverbs

Some questions in the TOEIC test will ask you to choose the correct part of speech. Learning to identify appropriate uses of adjectives and adverbs can help improve your score. This unit helps raise your awareness of how these words are formed and used.

Test tip

Learn suffixes to help you identify adjectives and adverbs

Some questions on the TOEIC test require you to select an appropriate adjective or adverb. Learning common suffixes will help you to identify these types of words.

Grammar note

Adjectives often follow the verb *to be* or other verbs related to senses (look, smell, etc.).

Examples

*The food is **terrible**.*
*It tastes **delicious**.*

1 Language building: Adjective and adverb endings

The sentences below use some common adjective and adverb endings found in the TOEIC test. Choose the correct adjective or adverb to complete each sentence.

1. We selected this hotel because the rooms are .... (comfort**able**/ comfortab**ly**)
2. We have .... problems in our Tokyo office. (seri**ous**/serious**ly**)
3. New recruits are expected to listen .... during training. (attent**ive**/attentive**ly**)
4. Our sales have been .... good in the last three months. (consist**ent**/consistent**ly**)
5. The response to the new commercial has been .... (wonder**ful**/wonderful**ly**)
6. The contract .... stated that delivery would be free. (specif**ic**/specific**ally**)

Follow up: With a partner think of two or three other words for each of the adjective and adverb endings below.

Adjectives	
-able (-ible)	
-ous	
-ive	
-ent (-ant)	
-ful	
-ic	
Adverbs	
-ly	

Now choose two of the words from the chart above and make sentences (either true or false) about someone or something in the room. Read your sentence to your partner and see if they agree or not.

Example

A: *Min Joon always studies English very carefully.*
B: *I don't really think so.*

Test tip

Understand the use of comparative and superlative forms of adjectives

Knowing how these are formed can help you choose the right answer.

2 Test tactic: Be aware of correct comparative and superlative forms

A Look at some examples of common comparative and superlative forms.

... ***as*** high ***as*** the market will support.
... ***more*** difficult ***than*** we first expected.
... fast***er than*** the competition.
... ***the*** cheap***est*** product.
... ***his/their/my*** great***est*** problem.
... ***the most*** important thing.

Use the examples above to help you choose the best word to complete the sentences.

1. The .... (good/better/best) thing about the offer is the price.
2. This system uses the .... (advanced/more advanced/most advanced) technology on the market.
3. This department may not be as .... (big/bigger/biggest) as some of the others, but its budget is much .... (large/larger/the largest).
4. They are our .... (important/more important/most important) customers by far.
5. The old distributor's delivery was much .... (fast/faster/fastest) than the new one.
6. Most attendees felt the first presenter was .... (informative/most informative/more informative) than the second one.

Follow up: Compare your answers with a partner. If you have any different answers, tell your partner why you chose your answer.

B With your partner, make comparative and superlative sentences about the means of transportation below.

Example
A train isn't as fast as an airplane.
Buses are cheaper than trains.

car train ship airplane motorcycle
(fast, cheap/expensive, convenient, etc.)

Tactics checklist

☑ Identity adjectives and adverbs by looking at their suffixes.

☑ Become familiar with how comparatives and superlatives are formed.

unit 13

3 Tactic practice

Use the tactics you have practiced to answer the following questions.

Questions 1–3 refer to the following article.

High among the many triumphs of man's courage and spirit is Walter Drake's and Olivier Vogel's .... climb to the summit of Mount Everest without

1. (A) amazement
(B) amazing
(C) amazingly
(D) amazed

oxygen tanks in 1967.

Although several attempts to climb Everest without additional oxygen had been made in the past, none had been successful. Drake and Vogel began moving cautiously up the south ridge towards the summit, which they reached after a grueling climb at 10:30. They lingered .... on the summit and then began

2. (A) highly
(B) shortly
(C) briefly
(D) quickly

the tiring climb down the mountain. They said it was the .... test of

3. (A) great
(B) greater
(C) greatest
(D) greatly

endurance they had ever experienced.

B Mini-test

Now apply the *Test tactics* at the actual test speed with questions 1–12.

> Recommended Time: 9 minutes (or less)
> Try using the 2-pass method to help you make the most of the time available. Try to spend no more than about 30–45 seconds on each item. If you don't know the answer, guess and move on.

Questions 1–3 refer to the following article.

Classic Film Archive Coming Soon

National Pictures has recently announced the re-release of some of the most famous films of the 1930s and 1940s, including Corsini's *Roma Viva Roma*, the original 1937 version of *The Angry Man*, and the classic *Drums Along The Zambezi*. These are some of the most respected and talked-about films of the .... days of talking pictures.

1. (A) early
(B) final
(C) happy
(D) long

National Pictures reported that the original prints have been re-mastered and .... restored to modern digital standards by experienced film

2. (A) care
(B) careful
(C) carefully
(D) caring

technicians to maintain the charm and flavor of the original prints. More information on these, and other films from National Pictures, can be found on their Web site, along with screen shots and ordering details. To access the complete .... of restored films, and order your own set, log on to

3. (A) costs
(B) sample
(C) movie
(D) catalog

www.nationalclassics.com today.

unit 13

GO ON TO THE NEXT PAGE

Questions 4–6 refer to the following letter.

Dear Mr. Phanom,

Thank you very much for your interest in becoming a dealer for our "Iron Duke" mountain bike. As you are probably aware, this is our latest model, and is by far the .... we have ever built.

4. (A) strong
(B) stronger
(C) strongest
(D) strongly

We believe it is this proven durability, along with its stylish design, that has allowed it to quickly gain such popularity .... the cycling community.

5. (A) within
(B) into
(C) about
(D) of

In answer to your question regarding how the Iron Duke has done in Asia, I can tell you that all of our retail partners there have reported that this year's sales of the model have been .... In fact, some of our dealers managed to sell their

6. (A) impressive
(B) worrying
(C) disappointing
(D) encouraged

entire stock in the first month after delivery.

I am including a full dealer reference package. Please don't hesitate to contact me if you have any further questions or would like to place an order.

Yours sincerely,

Wallace Minkly

Wallace Minkly
Asia Sales Representative
Avenger Cycle

unit 13

Questions 7–9 refer to the following letter.

Dear Oleg,

I am writing to let you know that on July 17 we are going be having a party to celebrate the launch of our new GX99 line of mobile phones. This .... held

7. (A) is
(B) had been
(C) was
(D) will be

in the Ambassador Room in the Dolton Grand hotel.

If you are free on this evening I would be very happy if you could join us. Your help in promoting the GX50 series was invaluable and we expect that with your input, the new line will be even .... successful than last year.

8. (A) extra
(B) very
(C) more
(D) most

I really hope you will be able to make the party as I expect that it will be an impressive one. In .... case, I will give you a call next week to set up

9. (A) no
(B) any
(C) every
(D) some

a meeting to finalize the designs for the January campaign.

Best regards and talk to you soon,

Miles

GO ON TO THE NEXT PAGE

Questions 10–12 refer to the following letter.

Dear Barnaby,

I have just returned from my visit to the Taiwan office and I must say I am impressed with the local marketing team. They are all very motivated and .... about the

10. (A) enthusiasm
(B) enthusiast
(C) enthusiastic
(D) enthusiastically

new line of evening wear from our Paris collection.

One issue did arise regarding the details of sales plan. I think we may want to move more .... on the introduction than we had originally planned.

11. (A) quick
(B) quickly
(C) quicker
(D) quickness

We have information that our largest competitor has also gone with a darker and more conservative pattern this year. I am worried that this will make both product lines seem very ....

12. (A) modern
(B) expensive
(C) innovative
(D) similar

We know they generally debut their line in May. As our image is based upon setting trends and being unique, I think we should push our release date up to March. Please consider this option and let's discuss it more fully when we meet on Monday.

Mikako

unit 13

C Grammar practice

Adjectives and adverbs

A Look at the gaps in the sentences below and decide whether they require an adjective or adverb. Then select the best word of the correct type from the list on the right.

1. John has .... had the best sales record for the last 5 years.
2. The print shop downstairs is quite expensive, but it is certainly ....
3. Swiss watches are famous for their .... timekeeping.
4. The manager .... displayed the trophy his branch had won for having the best sales record.
5. That company is famous for finding .... solutions to difficult problems.
6. All new staff are .... told not to make personal phone calls using the company line.

a specifically
b precise
c consistently
d proudly
e innovative
f convenient

unit 13

B Choose four adjectives or adverbs from the list in activity A and use them to write new sentences. Then test your classmates to see if they can choose the right words.

Comparative and Superlative forms

A Change the words to the correct form (if necessary) in order to complete the sentences.

1. Diamonds are much .... than rubies. (expensive)
2. Many countries would like to have the .... building in the world. (tall)
3. The new apartment wasn't as .... as the advertisement had claimed. (big)
4. The summit of Mt Everest is the .... place on earth. (high)
5. That company was .... for its low prices than for the quality of its products. (famous)
6. Many people believe that a pound of lead is .... than a pound of feathers. (heavy)

B Write four more sentences about yourself, your family, or your country. Compare your sentences with your classmates.

Go to word list and quiz page 179.

14 A

Reading Test Part 7 — Reading Comprehension

Focus: Using context to answer vocabulary questions
Using what you have learnt to help infer meaning

In Unit 7 we looked at answering specific information questions. In this unit we will look at the type of questions you should answer next – vocabulary, main idea and inference.

unit 14

Test tip

The context of the passage can give clues to vocabulary meaning

Read the sentences around the target word to try to guess the meaning.

Test tip

These questions sometimes use challenging vocabulary

If you don't know all of the words, ignore the ones you do know that don't answer the question. This will increase your chances of a successful guess.

1 Test tactic: Use context to answer vocabulary questions

A Look at vocabulary question 1 below. Find the word in the passage and cross it out. Brainstorm other words that might fit in the sentence and discuss your ideas with a partner.

1. The word "constitute" in paragraph 2, line 2, is closest in meaning to ...

> If there is a medical reason for the request, it must be received prior to the mid-point of the program. Refunds for sports and fitness programs will NOT be processed until ALL gym and pool passes have been returned.
> Please note that advising an instructor or not attending a program will not constitute a notice of withdrawal.
> Cash/check remittances will be refunded by check. Please allow our office 4 to 6 weeks to process your refund. Credit card refunds will go back on the original card.

B Look at the answer choices and choose the one that seems closest to your idea.

(A) begin
(B) signify
(C) remove
(D) understand

If you aren't familiar with some of the words and can't see an obvious answer, ignore any incorrect words you do know and make a guess with the remaining choices. Read the sentence (silently) with each remaining choice and choose the one that "sounds" the best.

C Do the same for the following question.
The word "process" in paragraph 3, line 2, is closest in meaning to

(A) examine
(B) replace
(C) handle
(D) maintain

Test tip

Answering the easier questions first gives you information

Answering the specific information and vocabulary questions first should help you to answer the main idea or inference questions. If not, skim the passage to confirm the most likely answer choice.

2 Test tactic: Use what you have learnt to infer meaning

A Underline the key words in the answer choices. Choice (A) is done for you.

2. What is this notice mainly about?
   - (A) The costs of summer college programs
   - (B) The way to obtain refunds for unattended courses
   - (C) Details of payment for summer programs
   - (D) Common reasons for withdrawal from college courses

Follow up: Compare your choices with a partner.

B Now answer the question above. You should already have enough understanding of the passage to make a choice (it is the same passage you used with specific information questions in Unit 7). If you still aren't sure, skim the passage and choose the one that seems closest to the overall meaning.

Summer program refund policy

The effective date of the withdrawal/cancelation is the date the withdrawal notice is received by the center, regardless of the date the participant stopped attending the class.

Withdrawal requests from all registered courses must be made before the second class is held. If the request is received 5 business days prior to the first class, the amount refunded will be the full amount, less the refund administration fee ($25.00). If the request is received after the first class, but before the second class, the amount refunded will be the full amount, less the cost of the first class and less the administration fee ($25.00). From the second lesson onwards, no refunds/credits will be issued.

If there is a medical reason for the request, a doctor's note must be received prior to the mid-point of the program. Refunds for sports and fitness programs will NOT be processed until ALL gym and pool passes have been returned. Please note that advising an instructor or not attending a program will not constitute a notice of withdrawal.

Cash/check remittances will be refunded by check. Please allow our office 4 to 6 weeks to process your refund. Credit card refunds will go back on the original card.

unit 14

Test tip

In inference questions the answers will not be stated directly in the passage

The correct option will relate to or paraphrase ideas from the text. Look for words or ideas in the passage related to the things noted in each answer choice.

C Write the letter of the answer choice in the appropriate column in the chart on page 76. Choice (A) is done for you.

3. Where might you see this notice?
   - (A) A student alumni magazine
   - (B) An insurance policy
   - (C) A medical journal
   - (D) A community services bulletin

			A
Things that are insured and things that aren't covered Monthly payments The insurance company name Policy number/date	Profile of a famous doctor Research on diseases Descriptions of new medical techniques Ads for health services	Upcoming courses, services, or events Details of costs and schedules for community services Available facilities	Profiles of famous ex-students Fund-raising information Information on student admission Upcoming special events at the university

unit 14

3 Tactic practice

Tactics checklist

☑ Use context to answer vocabulary questions.

☑ Use what you've learnt to answer main idea questions.

☑ In inference questions, look for words or ideas in the passage related to the things noted in each answer choice.

Use the tactics you have practiced to answer the following questions. Remember to start with the easiest questions and then go to the more difficult ones. Then answer them as quickly as you can.

1. What is the purpose of this letter?
   (A) To thank someone for a meeting held last week
   (B) To confirm the launch dates for a product line
   (C) To request information on future marketing strategies
   (D) To describe the ingredients in a skin care product
2. What can be inferred about the New Health product line?
   (A) It is aimed at women.
   (B) It will be expensive.
   (C) It will sell well.
   (D) It relates to skin care.
3. The word "anticipated" in paragraph 1, line 2 is closest in meaning to
   (A) expected
   (B) promised
   (C) required
   (D) awaited

Questions 1–3 refer to the following letter.

Roger,

It was a great pleasure to speak with you on the phone last week regarding our new product line that we will be introducing next year in Europe. Unfortunately, at that time, I was unable to confirm the anticipated launch date for the New Health line and the expected level of marketing support this product will receive.

I am now able to confirm that the launch date for our new range in our non-U.S. markets will be April 1. Prior to this date we will be launching a major marketing campaign for our new products which will include the placing of two-page spreads in leading health and fashion magazines, and TV advertisements. We are expecting to shortly confirm a well-known international model as the face for the campaign.

I will be coming to London early next month and I was wondering if we could meet to discuss our products and pricing strategies in more detail? I will be able to supply you with more information about not only the New Health line, but also the other facial and body moisturizing products that we offer.

I look forward to meeting you and discussing this sales opportunity with you further.

Regards,
Lewis

B Mini-test

Now apply what you have learnt at the actual test speed with questions 1–10.

> Recommended Time: 12 minutes (or less)
> Try to spend no more than about 60 seconds on each item; if you don't know the answer, guess and move on. If you have time at the end review any answers you weren't sure about.

Questions 1–2 refer to the following memo.

> **Memorandum**
>
> To: Sales Department Staff
> From: P.B. Anderson, Office Administrator
> Subject: Garbage disposal
>
> We received a complaint last Wednesday about improper garbage disposal by your department. Despite the recent guidelines, several bags of garbage were found in black plastic bags. We would therefore like to remind you of the following:
>
> - Transparent garbage bags should be used for all garbage.
> - Burnable and non-burnable items should be separated as previously advised.
> - All garbage must be taken out before 6 P.M. on Tuesday and Friday evenings. If garbage is not out by this time, the collection will be missed.
> - All glass and metal waste should be placed in the separate receptacle near the rear gate for pickup on Monday morning before noon.

1. What is the main purpose of this memo?
   (A) To describe how to dispose of metal and glass
   (B) To outline procedures for burnable waste
   (C) To reinforce waste disposal guidelines
   (D) To remind staff of the collection schedule

2. What have the sales staff failed to do?
   (A) Use specific garbage bags
   (B) Separate the garbage
   (C) Place metal waste in the correct receptacle
   (D) Take out the garbage at the correct time

GO ON TO THE NEXT PAGE

Questions 3–5 refer to the following advertisement.

> **New Muscles Gym opening in Collingwood**
>
> Muscles Gym is the place for serious fitness, with over 50 multi-purpose gyms nationwide. We are pleased to announce that a new Muscles Gym is set to open in January next to Main Street Station. This new Muscles Gym features a fully stocked workout gym including free weights, machines and a range of cardiovascular equipment. There is also an exercise studio, which will offer a comprehensive program of dance, aerobic and martial arts classes. Membership in the Main Street branch also allows full use of the pool and aquatics programs in either the Central or Lansdowne branches.
>
> We are now open for membership applications, so please visit us, take a tour of our wonderful facilities and see how we can truly add power to your dreams!
>
> - Monthly membership rates from as little as $60
> - Family packages available from $100
> - 20% discount for group membership (min. of 4 members)
> - Many other membership rates and packages
> - Sign up by December 31 and get a 10% discount and complimentary locker
>
> Membership inquiries:
> Reception open 12 – 6 P.M. weekdays, 9 A.M. – 6 P.M. Sat/Sun

3. What is the main purpose of this advertisement?
   (A) To announce the opening of a new gym
   (B) To give details of group membership rates
   (C) To notify the public of an equipment sale
   (D) To describe the available facilities in Lansdowne

4. What do people who join before the end of the year get?
   (A) A $60 membership rate
   (B) A 20% discount
   (C) A free locker
   (D) Special passes for family members

5. What is suggested in the advertisement?
   (A) People may sign up from 9–6 all week.
   (B) Joining will be more expensive after the new year.
   (C) Children are not able to use this gym.
   (D) The Main Street branch gym is convenient for swimmers.

Questions 6–9 refer to the following notice.

Notice to all guests of the Glenvale Inn

The management of the Glenvale Inn would like to apologize to all its guests for any inconvenience caused by our remodeling efforts. We assure you that the greatest efforts are being made to ensure all public spaces are kept immaculately clean, that all guests are provided with courteous professionalism, and that noise is kept to a minimum.

During the remodeling, we are also offering all guests 10% off their bill and 10% off their next stay as well, when the remodeling is complete.

Our new and improved facilities

- A 24-hour coffee bar in the lobby with a menu that will feature all your favorite specialty beverages as well as home-made baked goods.
- An expanded exercise room with spa and sauna will be available to melt away any chill you get on the slopes, plus personal trainers on hand for workouts or lessons in skiing or snowboarding.
- A massage salon will relieve any aches from your exercise in our gym or on the mountain.
- 20 log cabins, each complete with antique furnishings and bay windows overlooking the scenic valley and the main hotel building, will provide a little extra privacy but with all the amenities of one of our suites.

Once again, the management thanks you for your patronage and patience.

6. Why is the management apologizing?
   (A) There has been a lack of professionalism.
   (B) The exercise room is too small.
   (C) Some construction is underway.
   (D) Guests are being overbilled.

7. What is being offered to current guests because of the problem?
   (A) A discount on their stay
   (B) Personal training
   (C) Free coffee
   (D) A massage

8. The word "feature" in paragraph 3, line 1 is closest in meaning to
   (A) make
   (B) include
   (C) highlight
   (D) introduce

9. What is stated about the log cabins?
   (A) They have a good view of the area.
   (B) They have ultra-modern furniture.
   (C) They are not as well equipped as the suites.
   (D) They are connected to the main hotel.

GO ON TO THE NEXT PAGE

Questions 10–12 refer to the following job advertisement and letter.

Global Architecture Associates **Business Development Director**

The person filling this position will develop the company's development plan and oversee the expansion of the business. Candidates should be able to demonstrate a background in successful business planning.

JOB DESCRIPTION

Responsible for managing external contracts and relationships with local businesses and the local government offices. Responsible for tracking and evaluating the success of contracts and services.

QUALIFICATIONS, TRAINING and EXPERIENCE

A degree in business management. Minimum of five years relevant experience, preferably managing a multi-functional team. Excellent sales, negotiation and interpersonal skills are key requirements of the job. Strong numerical and analytical ability and a solid grasp of computer spreadsheet applications are essential. Personnel management required. Good communication skills are essential, both written and verbal. Must be willing to travel.

Send cover letter and résumé to:

Marko Cerise
Human Relations Manager
Global Architecture Associates

Dear Mr Cerise,

I read your job advertisement in *Professional Monthly* and believe that I am well suited to fill the position.

For the past 6 years I have been working as the regional promotions manager for a national chain of stationery stores. In this position, I was responsible for overseeing a team of six promotions and marketing staff. It was my responsibility to plan the sales events and promotional campaigns, and produce evaluation reports on the impact of each campaign. The position entailed regular visits to each of the nine branches in the area, so I am used to spending a significant part of my working week on the road.

A big part of the job was interacting with both senior management and individual store managers to ensure that new product lines were appropriately supported and within budget targets. I have found working in this position to be very rewarding but I feel I am ready for a change of horizons and look forward to facing new challenges.

In respect to my current position, I would be willing to start within one month of receiving a job offer.

For further employment and educational details please see the accompanying résumé.

Sincerely,

Jennifer Dankert

Jennifer Dankert

10. What kind of work is advertised?

(A) Human resources

(B) Architecture

(C) Management

(D) Marketing

11. In the letter, the word "impact" in paragraph 2, line 4, is closest in meaning to

(A) effect

(B) collision

(C) force

(D) problem

12. What requirement stated in the advertisement does Ms. Dankert NOT address?

(A) Budget management experience

(B) Experience with promotional events

(C) Knowledge of computer software

(D) Supervisory skills

C Reading in action

Role play

You bought a watch (a Seimex Accuron) a month ago. Yesterday, after swimming, you realized your watch wasn't working. You noticed there was some water inside the face. The watch is clearly labeled as "water-resistant" and is almost brand new!

Read the warranty below. Then answer the questions with a partner.

1. How long is the warranty good for?
2. What two things may the company do if it is broken?
3. What situations does the warranty not cover?
4. What should you do if you want to make a warranty claim?

SEIMEX INTERNATIONAL WARRANTY

Your SEIMEX watch is warranted against manufacturing defects by Seimex Corporation for a period of ONE YEAR from the original purchase date. Please note that Seimex may, at its option, repair your watch or replace it with an identical or similar model.

IMPORTANT – PLEASE NOTE THAT THIS WARRANTY DOES NOT COVER DEFECTS OR DAMAGE TO YOUR WATCH:

1) if the watch was not originally purchased from an authorized Seimex retailer.
2) from repair services not performed by Seimex.
3) from accidents, or use for purposes outside of those specified in the user's manual.

Report all warranty claims to your local authorized SEIMEX dealer for prompt service.

Task

With your partner, write a complaint letter (or complete the model on the next page) to the local Seimex dealer where you bought the watch. Include the following details:

- Tell them when you bought the watch (note the model).
- Explain what happened.
- Point out that
  - the watch hasn't been bumped or dropped
  - it is supposed to be water-resistant
  - there must be a problem with the watch
- Since it is still under warranty, find out how soon they can repair or replace the watch.

Culture note

When making complaints, try not to sound rude or personal, e.g. *You must fix the problem you caused ...*

It is better to say, *I really think this problem is covered by the guarantee, so it's only fair you should fix it.*

To whom it may concern,

I am writing to complain about a Seimex _________ watch I purchased

___________________ in your shop. I was quite happy with it until yesterday,

after a swim, ________________________________ and

_____________________________ inside the face.

During the time I have owned it, it hasn't been _____________ and since it is

clearly labeled as water-resistant there is obviously a ___________________

________________________.

Since it is still under warranty I would like to _________________________

____.

I look forward to hearing from you soon.

Yours sincerely,

unit 14

D Further study

Using your completed letter, write two Part 7 type questions (at least one should be a vocabulary, main idea or inference question) to test a partner in the next lesson.

Go to word list and quiz page 179.

15 Listening Test Part 1 Photographs

A

Focus: Listening carefully to every detail

Most incorrect choices in this part will use some correct subject, verb and object words and some wrong ones. This unit will help you to pick out and eliminate incorrect answer choices.

unit 15

Test tip

Listen for SVO words

Most TOEIC Part 1 questions follow a subject, verb or subject, verb, object pattern (SVO).

Listen carefully for SVO words and compare the words you hear to what is in the picture.

1 Language building: Listen for subject/verb/object words

A Look at the list of possible subjects/objects and verbs and make up sentences about each of the pictures with a partner.

1

2

Possible subjects/objects used			Possible verbs used		
man	train	suit	standing	sitting	reading
baker	newspaper	oven	making	baking	wearing
bread			putting		

B Listen to four correct sentences about these pictures. Listen carefully to the subjects/objects and verbs, and after each one pause the audio and tell your partner the words you heard. Decide together which picture you think the sentence matches.

Follow up: Write one new sentence for each picture. You may use different words. Test your partners to pick out the SVO words and choose the correct picture.

Test tip

Listen for wrong main subject, verb and object

Some distractors use correct key words, and incorrect ones. If you hear an incorrect one you can immediately ignore that answer choice.

2 Test tactic: Be careful of subject/verb/object problems

A For the following sentences underline the incorrect words and say how you could correct them.

1. The woman is carrying the baby.
2. The shopping cart is empty.
3. The man is carrying a drill.
4. The man is holding some gloves.

B Now write two correct sentences about each of the following pictures. Underline the subjects, verbs and objects.

Example: The man is sitting on the ground.

1

2

C You will hear four sentences about each picture. After each sentence, stop the audio and tell a partner the SVO words you heard, then mark below whether you think the sentence is Correct or Wrong.

1

(A) ☐ Correct ☐ Wrong
(B) ☐ Correct ☐ Wrong
(C) ☐ Correct ☐ Wrong
(D) ☐ Correct ☐ Wrong

2

(A) ☐ Correct ☐ Wrong
(B) ☐ Correct ☐ Wrong
(C) ☐ Correct ☐ Wrong
(D) ☐ Correct ☐ Wrong

Follow up: Compare with your partner the sentences you first made and the correct sentence.

3 Tactic practice

Use the tactics you have practiced for the next three photographs. You will have one minute to a) brainstorm vocabulary and b) predict possible statements with a partner. Then listen to and echo (silently) the answer choices, and after you hear each, mark whether you think it is correct, maybe correct, or wrong.

Tactics checklist

☑ Listen for SVO words.

☑ Listen for wrong subjects, verbs and objects.

1

(A) ☐ Correct ☐ Maybe correct ☐ Wrong
(B) ☐ Correct ☐ Maybe correct ☐ Wrong
(C) ☐ Correct ☐ Maybe correct ☐ Wrong
(D) ☐ Correct ☐ Maybe correct ☐ Wrong

2

(A) ☐ Correct ☐ Maybe correct ☐ Wrong
(B) ☐ Correct ☐ Maybe correct ☐ Wrong
(C) ☐ Correct ☐ Maybe correct ☐ Wrong
(D) ☐ Correct ☐ Maybe correct ☐ Wrong

unit 15

Understanding natural English

In natural spoken English, sounds are sometimes changed, combined and dropped. Listen to these sentences spoken naturally and write in the missing words.

A forest grows .... valley.

The man is standing .... wall.

3

(A)	☐ Correct	☐ Maybe correct	☐ Wrong
(B)	☐ Correct	☐ Maybe correct	☐ Wrong
(C)	☐ Correct	☐ Maybe correct	☐ Wrong
(D)	☐ Correct	☐ Maybe correct	☐ Wrong

Follow up: Now compare your answers with your partner, explaining your reasons, and what you remember hearing.

🎧 Understanding natural English

B Mini-test 🎧

Now practice what you have learnt at the actual test speed with questions 1–6.

Use any time available to skim the first pictures before the listening starts. After that you will have exactly 5 seconds between each question to mark your answer and focus on the next picture.

1

2

3

4

5

6

1	Ⓐ	Ⓑ	Ⓒ	Ⓓ
2	Ⓐ	Ⓑ	Ⓒ	Ⓓ
3	Ⓐ	Ⓑ	Ⓒ	Ⓓ
4	Ⓐ	Ⓑ	Ⓒ	Ⓓ
5	Ⓐ	Ⓑ	Ⓒ	Ⓓ
6	Ⓐ	Ⓑ	Ⓒ	Ⓓ

C Learn by doing: Three in a row game

To win this game you must make a line of three pictures in a row.

Choose a picture and say the number. Your partner will read a sentence and you must say if it is correct or wrong (and explain why). If you are right, you get the square. Take turns until you have a winner.

Student A: Look at Activity file 15a on page 164.

Student B: Look at Activity file 15b on page 167.

1

2

3

4

5

6

7

8

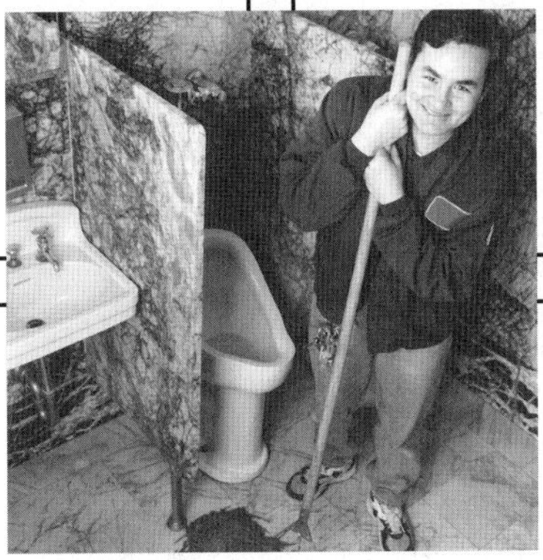

9

D Further study

Choose two pictures from C above, and write Part 1 type statements (one correct answer, three that are close but wrong) to test on your classmates in the next lesson. The incorrect answers should include some correct SVO words and at least one wrong one.

Go to word list and quiz page 180.

16

Listening Test Part 2 Question-Response

A

Focus: Becoming familiar with time and location structures

Questions about time and location are common in the TOEIC test. This unit will familiarize you with the types of questions and answer choices you will see in this part of the test.

Test tip

Answers to time and location questions often use common marker words

Being familiar with the prepositions and other words common to these answers will help you choose the correct answer.

1 Language building: Be familiar with time and location marker words

A The table below contains sentences that answer different time and location questions. Common marker words are shown in **bold**.

Match each answer to the correct question type. The first one is done for you.

	a We will be finished **in February**.
	b It's **at** Eastern State University, **on** the 3rd floor.
1 **Where/Directions?** b	c She's been working here **for** several months.
	d **Down** the hall, **turn left** and it's just **across** from the cafeteria.
2 **How long?**	e The package was delivered about **an hour ago**.
	f They've been in the meeting **since** 6:00.
	g **To** Florida, as usual.
3 **When?**	h I've had it **about** a month.
	i **On Tuesday July 7th, at** 1:00.
	j It's **in** the refrigerator, **behind** the vegetables.

Test tip

The correct answer may use very short or indefinite answers

Listen for these and decide what kind of question they could answer.

B Some questions do not have obvious time or location marker words. Write in the space whether the answer is for "Where/Directions", "How long", or "When" questions. The first one is done for you.

1 Where / Directions?	Berlin.
2	It could take all night.
3	Sorry, I'm not from around here.
4	Bermuda again. I can't wait!
5	It hasn't arrived yet.

Test tip

Learn to identify questions about location

Usually they involve the word *where*, but other words can also be used when asking for directions to a place.

C Now listen to four answer choices, and for each one mark whether it is a "Where/Directions", "When" or "How long" question. After the recording, compare your answers with a partner.

1. ☐ Where/Directions? ☐ When? ☐ How long?
2. ☐ Where/Directions? ☐ When? ☐ How long?
3. ☐ Where/Directions? ☐ When? ☐ How long?
4. ☐ Where/Directions? ☐ When? ☐ How long?

Test tip

"Where" questions can sometimes have a "Directions" answer

Listen carefully for this.

Test tip

Learn to identify "When" questions

Usually "When" questions involve the phrases *How long ...?*, or *When .../ What time ...?*

2 Test tactic: Identify and answer time and location questions

A For each question below, mark whether it is a "Where", "Directions", "When" or "How long" question. The first one is done for you.

1. Excuse me. Where are the stairs?
- ☑ Where?
- ☑ Directions?
- ☐ When?
- ☐ How long?

(A) Go out this door and walk around the corner.
(B) They're away on business.
(C) It's not polite to stare.

2. When did they cancel the order?
- ☐ Where?
- ☐ Directions?
- ☐ When?
- ☐ How long?

(A) Back in March, I think.
(B) Yes, they were ordered to do it.
(C) I really think we have to cancel it.

3. How long did you have to wait?
- ☐ Where?
- ☐ Directions?
- ☐ When?
- ☐ How long?

(A) Yes, it is very long.
(B) I was waiting for it on Tuesday.
(C) Not as long as I expected.

4. Do you know where my keys are?
- ☐ Where?
- ☐ Directions?
- ☐ When?
- ☐ How long?

(A) Yes, it's the wrong key.
(B) In the drawer, as usual.
(C) They went out.

5. Do you know of a good cleaner near here?
- ☐ Where?
- ☐ Directions?
- ☐ When?
- ☐ How long?

(A) I think it's not so clean.
(B) I prefer a different cleaner.
(C) There's one on Bank Street.

B Now listen and choose the best answers for each question. Be careful of the distractors noted in activity 1.

Follow up: Compare your answers with a partner.

Tactics checklist

☑ Listen for location questions, decide the type and listen for the appropriate answer.

☑ Listen for marker words in time questions.

3 Tactic practice

Use the tactics you have practiced for the next five questions.

1	Ⓐ	Ⓑ	Ⓒ
2	Ⓐ	Ⓑ	Ⓒ
3	Ⓐ	Ⓑ	Ⓒ
4	Ⓐ	Ⓑ	Ⓒ
5	Ⓐ	Ⓑ	Ⓒ

Follow up: Discuss with a partner which answers you chose and why.

Understanding natural English

Understanding natural English

In natural spoken English, sounds are sometimes changed, combined and dropped. Listen to these sentences spoken naturally and write in the missing words.

.... A4 paper kept?

.... taxi coming?

unit 16

B Mini-test

Now apply the *Test tactics* at the actual test speed with questions 1–12.

> You will have 5 seconds at the end of each item to make your choice. You must then be ready to listen to the next question.

1	Ⓐ	Ⓑ	Ⓒ	7	Ⓐ	Ⓑ	Ⓒ
2	Ⓐ	Ⓑ	Ⓒ	8	Ⓐ	Ⓑ	Ⓒ
3	Ⓐ	Ⓑ	Ⓒ	9	Ⓐ	Ⓑ	Ⓒ
4	Ⓐ	Ⓑ	Ⓒ	10	Ⓐ	Ⓑ	Ⓒ
5	Ⓐ	Ⓑ	Ⓒ	11	Ⓐ	Ⓑ	Ⓒ
6	Ⓐ	Ⓑ	Ⓒ	12	Ⓐ	Ⓑ	Ⓒ

unit 16

C Learn by doing: Time and location questions

A Look at the model conversation below. Use the words on the right to complete the conversation.

A: Where do you live, Ken?
B: Right now ....
A: Oh yeah? How long have you lived there?
B: Oh, ... I moved there ....
A: Really? Where did you live before?
B: ....

I lived in Georgetown with my family
just after university
I'm living in Hamilton
for about 5 years

B Now make a similar conversation with a partner, using the questionnaire below. Add some more questions of your own.

Interview your partner

Where do you live?
How long have you lived there?
Where did you live before?
How long does it take you to come to class?

Where do you think is the best place to eat around here?
If you could take a holiday anywhere in this country, where would you go?
How long would you like to stay there?
What time of year do you think would be best to go?
What other country would you most like to visit?

How long have you been studying for the TOEIC test?
When do you think you will be able to get the score you want?

D Further study

Think of a famous person and write two "Where", two "When", and two "How long" questions you could ask them. Then write the answers you think they would give. In the next class read the answers you wrote to see if your partner can guess the questions you asked and the famous person you chose.

Go to word list and quiz page 181.

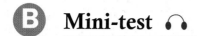

A

Focus: Using vocabulary clues to infer meaning

The answers for many of the questions in this part of the test are not stated directly. You will have to listen carefully and use your knowledge of related vocabulary and context to choose many of the answers.

Test tip

Sometimes the answers are not stated directly in the passage

Before the listening, think of other words related to the answer choices and listen to infer the general meaning.

1 Language building: Brainstorm vocabulary for locations, activities and occupations

A For each of the following, choose the words on the right that best relate to each answer choice, then add two more words for each answer choice. The first word is done for you.

1. Where is the man?

(A) At a hotel		~~rail~~ room
(B) At a car rental agency		track bed
(C) At a train station	rail	stadium fans
(D) At a sports event		car license

Follow up: Compare your list with a partner. Then think of another common place and brainstorm three related words. Say your words to your partner and see if they can guess the location.

2. What is the first man doing?

(A) Making a hotel reservation		table bride
(B) Getting married		room dinner
(C) Borrowing a book from the library		library card vacancies
(D) Making a restaurant reservation		novel dress

Follow up: Compare your list with your partner. Then think of another common activity and brainstorm three related words. Say your words to your partner and see if they can guess the activity.

3. What is the man's job?

(A) A delivery man		deposit truck
(B) A musician		discount concert
(C) A banker		withdrawal order
(D) A salesman		recording package

Follow up: Compare your list with your partner. Then think of another common job and brainstorm three related words. Say your words to your partner and see if they can guess the job.

B Now listen to the three conversations and choose the correct answer to each question. After each one, circle the word(s) on the lists in A that helped you find the answer.

1	Ⓐ	Ⓑ	Ⓒ	Ⓓ
2	Ⓐ	Ⓑ	Ⓒ	Ⓓ
3	Ⓐ	Ⓑ	Ⓒ	Ⓓ

2 Test tactic: Identify inference markers

Look at the three common inference questions in **bold**. Read the conversation below, choose the correct answer and underline the words in the tapescript that tell you it is correct.

unit 17

1. **What can be said** about the weather?
   (A) It is raining.
   (B) It is warmer than Arizona.
   (C) It has no effect on transportation.
   (D) It is sunny.
2. **Where most likely** are the speakers?
   (A) They are in a restaurant.
   (B) They are waiting at a bus stop.
   (C) They are at work.
   (D) They are in a taxi.
3. **What is implied** about the woman?
   (A) She often walks to work.
   (B) She used to live in another city.
   (C) She dislikes her job.
   (D) She is often late.

Test tip

Some questions clearly ask you to infer things about the situation

Look for common inference markers: *What can be said/implied/inferred ...?* and listen for related information in the recording.

Tapescript

M: *Hi, Brenda. It's really pouring today, isn't it? My bus was late because of the weather.*

W: *Oh no. I don't have an umbrella, and I have to walk across town to deliver some documents before lunch.*

M: *Well, you'd better take a taxi. It's supposed to stay like this all day.*

W: *It's not going to be easy to find one today. I really miss living in Arizona on days like this!*

Follow up: Compare the words that you have underlined with a partner and discuss your answers.

Tactics checklist

☑ Think of other words related to the answer choices before listening.

☑ Look for common inference markers and listen for related information.

Understanding natural English

In natural spoken English, sounds are sometimes changed, combined and dropped. Listen to these sentences spoken naturally and write in the missing words.

That's what we were .... expect.

You've always .... work overseas.

3 Tactic practice

Use the tactics you have practiced for the next six questions. Before each passage begins, use the time to a) predict the context and b) think of other ways to say the answer choices with a partner.

1. Where are the speakers?
   (A) In a library
   (B) In a book store
   (C) In a music store
   (D) In a gift shop
2. What is the woman doing?
   (A) Recording a CD
   (B) Looking for a present
   (C) Taking an order
   (D) Paying for something
3. What does the man imply?
   (A) The item is in stock.
   (B) The item will arrive very soon.
   (C) The item is extremely rare.
   (D) The item is popular.
4. What are the speakers doing?
   (A) Watching the news
   (B) Going overseas
   (C) Looking at a job ad
   (D) Planning a holiday
5. What can be inferred about the speakers' relationship?
   (A) They have known each other for a time.
   (B) They have just met.
   (C) They work together.
   (D) They live together.
6. What does the man imply?
   (A) He is desperate to work overseas.
   (B) He wants to go on holiday.
   (C) He has enough money to live for a while.
   (D) He would like to get a new place.

1	Ⓐ	Ⓑ	Ⓒ	Ⓓ	4	Ⓐ	Ⓑ	Ⓒ	Ⓓ
2	Ⓐ	Ⓑ	Ⓒ	Ⓓ	5	Ⓐ	Ⓑ	Ⓒ	Ⓓ
3	Ⓐ	Ⓑ	Ⓒ	Ⓓ	6	Ⓐ	Ⓑ	Ⓒ	Ⓓ

Understanding natural English

B Mini-test

Now practice what you have learnt at the actual test speed with questions 1–12.

Use any time available to skim the questions and answer choices before the first listening starts. When you finish answering the questions about one conversation, immediately start previewing the questions for the next conversation.

1. What has the man heard about Kingston?
   (A) It is an interesting place.
   (B) It is very sunny there.
   (C) It is usually crowded.
   (D) It has many festivals.
2. What does the woman say about her trip?
   (A) It was relaxing.
   (B) It was more expensive than she had anticipated.
   (C) It was exciting.
   (D) It was different from what she had expected.
3. Where was the woman's hotel located?
   (A) Next to the airport
   (B) In the carnival area
   (C) Outside of the town
   (D) Near the beach
4. Where does the conversation probably take place?
   (A) In a bank
   (B) In a department store
   (C) In a restaurant
   (D) In a doctor's office

1	Ⓐ	Ⓑ	Ⓒ	Ⓓ
2	Ⓐ	Ⓑ	Ⓒ	Ⓓ
3	Ⓐ	Ⓑ	Ⓒ	Ⓓ
4	Ⓐ	Ⓑ	Ⓒ	Ⓓ
5	Ⓐ	Ⓑ	Ⓒ	Ⓓ
6	Ⓐ	Ⓑ	Ⓒ	Ⓓ
7	Ⓐ	Ⓑ	Ⓒ	Ⓓ
8	Ⓐ	Ⓑ	Ⓒ	Ⓓ
9	Ⓐ	Ⓑ	Ⓒ	Ⓓ
10	Ⓐ	Ⓑ	Ⓒ	Ⓓ
11	Ⓐ	Ⓑ	Ⓒ	Ⓓ
12	Ⓐ	Ⓑ	Ⓒ	Ⓓ

5. What is the problem?
   (A) The man misunderstands a sign.
   (B) A bill has been calculated incorrectly.
   (C) The man cannot pay the bill.
   (D) The sale has not started yet.

6. Until what time was the offer available?
   (A) 1:15
   (B) 1:30
   (C) 2:00
   (D) 2:30

---

7. What are the speakers mainly discussing?
   (A) A sports team
   (B) A business meeting
   (C) A group project
   (D) A building design

8. What is scheduled to happen on Thursday?
   (A) A new project will begin.
   (B) An important game will be played.
   (C) A team will make a presentation.
   (D) A report will be sent out.

9. What is the man's concern?
   (A) His team will not finish on time.
   (B) He does not understand an assignment.
   (C) His team cannot work on other projects.
   (D) He disagrees with his team members.

---

10. Who most likely is the man?
    (A) A truck driver
    (B) A gardener
    (C) A repairperson
    (D) A car salesperson

11. How much time does the man probably need?
    (A) One hour
    (B) Two hours
    (C) Two and a half hours
    (D) More than three hours

12. Where are the speakers?
    (A) At a factory
    (B) At a garage
    (C) At a gardening store
    (D) At a home

C Learn by doing

Student A: Look at Activity file 17a on page 163.
Student B: Look at Activity file 17b on page 165.

Take turns to read one of the sentences from your file to your partner. They must say the job, location OR activity from the lists that best matches the sentence.

Jobs	Locations	Activities
office worker shoe salesman teacher train conductor	restaurant art museum supermarket sports club	buying clothes talking about a movie changing an appointment asking for directions

Follow up: Now choose a job, location or activity and make up your own sentences to test your partner.

D Further study

Think of a common job, location and an activity and write a short conversation. In the next class read your conversation and see if the other students can guess the job, location and activity you chose.

Go to word list and quiz page 182.

18 Listening Test Part 4 — Talks

A

Focus: Becoming familiar with re-statements
Being aware of questions involving numbers and quantities

Numbers and quantities are a commonly tested feature in the TOEIC test. The tactics in this section will help you to pick out the correct answers when dealing with Part 4 and other listening parts of the test.

> **Test tip**
> **The correct answer choice often uses different words from what you will hear**
> Be aware of this and listen for meaning, not just the key words.

> **Test tip**
> **Specific information questions sometimes appear in the same order they appear in the listening**
> Focus on the questions in order. When you hear the answer, mark it and move on immediately.

> **Test tip**
> **Be careful of questions involving number and quantity**
> Read the question and carefully note what it is asking, then quickly read the answer choices. When you hear one of the numbers in the listening decide whether it answers the question or not.

1 Language building: Re-statements of key vocabulary

A Look at the three questions with just the correct answer choice. Circle the words in the tapescript which repeat the same or a similar meaning to the words in the answer choice.

1. Where is the announcement made?
   (A) **At an annual convention**
2. Which of the following is NOT true about Dr. Abrahams?
   (B) **He has fewer than three qualifications.**
3. What will Dr. Abrahams do tomorrow?
   (C) **Take part in a seminar**

Tapescript

Our final speaker today was also our guest presenter at last year's conference. Dr. Harel Abrahams is perhaps best known for his best-selling work "Meeting Business Challenges", but his area of expertise extends far beyond the topics dealt with in that book.

A graduate of Yale University, with three graduate degrees to his name, he is the current chair of Economics at McGuire University, and we are delighted that he has agreed to speak to us once more. As well as today's lecture, Dr. Abrahams has kindly agreed to join tomorrow's round-table discussion, which I am sure you will all be keen to attend.

So, without further ado, to speak on "Small Companies and Macro Economics", let me present Dr. Harel Abrahams.

B Now listen to three sets of sentences and mark the answer choice that is closest in meaning.

1. Part of the shipment was damaged.	☐ A	☐ B	☐ C
2. They started the job a month ago.	☐ A	☐ B	☐ C
3. Mr. Holmes has been a huge help to the team.	☐ A	☐ B	☐ C

Follow up: Compare your answers with a partner.

2 Test tactic: Choosing the correct number/quantity answer

A Underline the key words in the question below, then quickly read the answer choices.

1. How many boats will join the event?
   (A) 14 (B) 17 (C) 35 (D) 70

Test tip

Be careful of sound distractors in numbers ending in *-teen* or *-ty*

Example: *13* sounds like *30*.

B Scan the following tapescript for the numbers in 1 A–D on page 95. When you find one, decide if it answers the question or not. Remember, the words in the question and the tapescript may be different even if the meaning is the same.

Tapescript

The Jamestown boat race starts Saturday afternoon at 14 hundred hours, that's 2 P.M., of course. With 70 racing boats competing this year for 3500 dollars in prizes, this is sure to be one of the sailing events of the season. Spectators should try ...

C Underline the key words in the question below. Now listen to the rest of the tapescript and choose the best answer.

2. How many salvaged items are on display?
   (A) 19
   (B) 90
   (C) 150
   (D) 200

Tactics checklist

unit 18

☑ Listen for words with the same meaning as the answer choices.

☑ Listen for numbers noted in the answer choices and decide if these answer the question or not.

☑ Be careful of similar-sounding number sound distractors, e.g. *13/30*.

☑ Expect information questions to come in the same order they appear in the answer choices.

3 Tactic practice

Use the tactics you have practiced for the next three questions. Before the start of each question a) predict the content and b) where possible, think of other ways to say the key words or phrases.

1. How many people are requested to attend the conference?
   (A) One
   (B) Two
   (C) Three
   (D) Four
2. How long does the conference last?
   (A) A couple of hours
   (B) One afternoon
   (C) All day Saturday
   (D) Two days
3. How much time off can volunteers expect?
   (A) About an hour
   (B) About four hours
   (C) A day
   (D) Two days

1	Ⓐ	Ⓑ	Ⓒ	Ⓓ
2	Ⓐ	Ⓑ	Ⓒ	Ⓓ
3	Ⓐ	Ⓑ	Ⓒ	Ⓓ

Understanding natural English

In natural spoken English, sounds are sometimes changed, combined and dropped. Listen to these sentences spoken naturally and write in the missing words.

I won't be able to make both .... conference.

She's .... top designers.

B Mini-test

Now practice what you have learnt at the actual test speed with questions 1–12.

Use any time available to skim the questions and answer choices before the first listening starts. When you finish answering the questions about one talk, immediately start previewing the questions for the next talk.

1. What type of movie is *Indigo Heart*?
(A) A romance
(B) A comedy
(C) A mystery
(D) A drama

2. Which movie features Deborah Legg?
(A) *Monterrey*
(B) *Long Vacation*
(C) *Phantom Knight*
(D) *Indigo Heart*

3. According to the announcement, how can someone reserve a ticket?
(A) By using an online service
(B) By calling the ticket office
(C) By stopping by the theater in advance
(D) By sending an e-mail

---

4. What does Elvira Kaur do?
(A) She is a fashion designer.
(B) She decorates houses.
(C) She is a student.
(D) She writes books.

5. What happened to Ms. Kaur in September?
(A) She graduated from college.
(B) She joined the company.
(C) She was promoted.
(D) She won an award.

6. What is the topic of Ms. Kaur's talk?
(A) Her fashion designs
(B) Next year's sales target
(C) Her academic background
(D) Plans for her group

---

7. Where is this announcement most likely taking place?
(A) In a university library
(B) At a department store counter
(C) In a company meeting room
(D) In a restaurant dining room

8. What comes in six colors?
(A) The spring catalog
(B) The Clam Case
(C) The Mini-Steamer
(D) The Kitchen Friend

9. What is stated about the Mini-Steamer?
(A) It is intended for travelers.
(B) It is waterproof.
(C) It is popular with students.
(D) It is useful in the kitchen.

---

10. What is being sold?
(A) Exercise equipment
(B) A training video
(C) A fitness club
(D) An exercise book

11. What is special about this product?
(A) It adjusts easily.
(B) It is expensive.
(C) It can be moved quickly.
(D) It fits in a small space.

12. What are customers offered if they place an order now?
(A) An instruction manual
(B) Free delivery
(C) A video
(D) A discount

1	(A)	(B)	(C)	(D)
2	(A)	(B)	(C)	(D)
3	(A)	(B)	(C)	(D)
4	(A)	(B)	(C)	(D)
5	(A)	(B)	(C)	(D)
6	(A)	(B)	(C)	(D)
7	(A)	(B)	(C)	(D)
8	(A)	(B)	(C)	(D)
9	(A)	(B)	(C)	(D)
10	(A)	(B)	(C)	(D)
11	(A)	(B)	(C)	(D)
12	(A)	(B)	(C)	(D)

C Learn by doing: Introducing people

A Look at the speech below describing Bill Gates. With a partner write down the questions you would need to ask to get the information that is underlined in the text.

Examples

Bill Gates – *May I have your name, please?*
famous for being the head of the computer company Microsoft – *What are you famous for?*

> *Today I would like to give you some background on Bill Gates. Although he is quite famous for being the head of the computer company Microsoft, that is not what I am going to talk about today.*
>
> *Born on Oct. 28, 1955, Bill grew up in Seattle, Washington with his two sisters. His father, William H. Gates II, was a Seattle attorney while his late mother, Mary Gates, was a schoolteacher.*
>
> *In 1973, Gates entered Harvard University, where he developed a computer operating system. This interest in computers continues to this day.*
>
> *Apart from computers Bill enjoys reading, and playing golf and bridge.*

B Interview your partner using the questions you wrote. Note their answers and make a similar speech, then write two or three questions about it.

Follow up: Test another group of students with your speech and questions.

unit 18

D Further study

Write a similar short biography about someone in your family or a famous person. Write two questions and answer choices to test your classmates in the next lesson.

Go to word list and quiz page 182.

A

Focus: Improving your knowledge of suffixes and prefixes

Knowledge of suffixes and prefixes can help you guess the meaning of unfamiliar words. This unit will familiarize you with some of the most common suffix and prefix forms.

Test tip

Learning common suffixes can help you to identify nouns and verbs

Questions that require you to select an appropriate noun or verb form are common in the TOEIC test. Learning to recognize noun and verb suffixes will help you to choose the right one.

1 Test tactic: Noun and verb suffixes

A The words below feature some of the most common suffixes used with nouns and verbs. For each word decide whether it is a noun or a verb.

cooperation	☐ N	☐ V	simplify	☐ N	☐ V	security	☐ N	☐ V
criticize	☐ N	☐ V	quickness	☐ N	☐ V	widen	☐ N	☐ V
partnership	☐ N	☐ V	activate	☐ N	☐ V	assistance	☐ N	☐ V
department	☐ N	☐ V	celebration	☐ N	☐ V	realize	☐ N	☐ V

B Now look at the list of suffixes and mark whether each is a noun or verb suffix.

-tion/-sion	☐ noun	☐ verb	-ise/-ize	☐ noun	☐ verb
-en	☐ noun	☐ verb	-ity	☐ noun	☐ verb
-ness	☐ noun	☐ verb	-ate	☐ noun	☐ verb
-(i)fy	☐ noun	☐ verb	-ment	☐ noun	☐ verb
-ship	☐ noun	☐ verb	-ance/-ence	☐ noun	☐ verb

C For each sentence below, first decide if it requires a noun or verb, then choose the best word of the correct type to fill in the blank.

investigation	identify	elevate	repetitiveness	criticize
document	internship	renovate	dependence	soften

1. The stockholders have called for a(n) ...... to find out where the money went.
2. Newspapers are starting to ...... the prime minister's actions.
3. Doing a(n) ...... is a good way for students to get work experience.
4. Miller Manufacturing's ...... on one supplier caused serious problems when that company went bankrupt.
5. A consultant was hired to ...... the company's main weaknesses and suggest solutions.
6. Bill realized he had forgotten to bring a key ...... to the meeting.
7. The company spent millions to ...... its main office in order to impress its customers.
8. The sculptor intended to ...... the statue by placing it on a pedestal so that people could see it more easily.
9. Many people dislike the ...... of working on a factory assembly line.
10. Cyclists often use special pads to ...... the seat for long-distance rides.

unit 19

Test tip

Being able to guess the meaning of unknown words is important for all parts of the test

Learning common prefixes can help you guess the meaning of words you don't know.

2 Test tactic: Use prefixes to help decide the best answer

A Look at the list of some of the most common prefixes below. Match the prefix to the meaning on the right. The first one is done for you.

1. dis- **un-** **non-** **im-/in-/ir-/il-**	discomfort (n), discontinue (v) unable (adj), unfasten (v) non-fiction (adj), non-political (adj) inconvenient (adj), illegal (adj)	
2. co-	co-founder (n), cooperate (v)	
3. sub-	submarine (n), subsection (n)	
4. inter-	interaction (n), international (adj)	
5. re-	re-organization (n), review (v/n)	
6. over-	overwork (v), overpriced (adj)	
7. mis-	mislead (v), misunderstanding (n)	

☐ **a** badly or wrongly
[1] **b** not
☐ **c** between
☐ **d** joint or together
☐ **e** again or back
☐ **f** below, under
☐ **g** too much

B Now use your understanding of prefixes to help you choose the best word to complete each sentence.

1. The company's bid was rejected because the quality of their work was ....
2. Jake Thomson and Phil Greene .... the project, each looking after one team.
3. There is a(n) .... in each room to allow all the staff to communicate easily, even between different floors.
4. A plumber was called to .... the blockage from the pipe.
5. After I returned from the shop, I realized I had .... for my new radio.
6. The woman thought she had .... the clerk when he told her the price of the room.
7. He didn't pay his phone bill so they came to .... his line.
8. The glass was so fragile that it broke even before we had a chance to .... it.
9. I often get very .... if there is heavy traffic when I am in a hurry.
10. Since the gift had been bought on sale it was ....

a misheard
b disconnect
c unwrap
d impatient
e co-supervise
f overpaid
g remove
h non-refundable
i intercom
j sub-standard

Tactics checklist

☑ Learning common prefixes can help you guess the meaning of words you don't know.

☑ Learning common suffixes can help you to identify nouns and verbs.

3 Tactic practice

Use the tactics you have practiced to answer the following questions.

1. The two presidents maintained a close .... despite their rival businesses.
   (A) friendly
   (B) friend
   (C) friendship
   (D) friends
2. Efforts were made to .... train track width across Europe in the late twentieth century.
   (A) standard
   (B) standards
   (C) standardization
   (D) standardize
3. The program seems easy to use, but the interface needs to be ....
   (A) simplified
   (B) simply
   (C) simplest
   (D) simplification
4. The machine could become dangerous if it is ....
   (A) circumscribed
   (B) restrung
   (C) dismantled
   (D) mishandled
5. He transferred from the parent company to one of its smaller ....
   (A) partnerships
   (B) subsidiaries
   (C) conglomerates
   (D) multinationals
6. To resolve their differences, they employed an .... to deal with the two sides.
   (A) investigation
   (B) intermediary
   (C) assistance
   (D) advice

B Mini-test

Now apply what you have learnt at the actual test speed with questions 1–12.

> Recommended Time: 6 minutes (or less)
> Try using the 2-pass method to help you make the most of the time available. Try to spend no more than about 30 seconds on each item. If you don't know the answer, guess and move on.

1. The addition of steel girders was designed to .... the roof support beams.
   (A) strong
   (B) strongly
   (C) strength
   (D) strengthen
2. Disagreements over the .... of the design eventually led to a court case.
   (A) own
   (B) ownership
   (C) owning
   (D) owned
3. It is essential to .... fully on the operation of the machinery in order to avoid accidents.
   (A) concentration
   (B) concentrating
   (C) concentrate
   (D) concentrates
4. He was known in the business for his .... attitude and astute business sense.
   (A) positive
   (B) internal
   (C) preventative
   (D) artificial

GO ON TO THE NEXT PAGE

unit 19

5. The public's .... to the advertising campaign was very encouraging.
   (A) reaction
   (B) suggestion
   (C) interjection
   (D) submission

6. Visitors to this part of the facilities must show proper ....
   (A) identity
   (B) identify
   (C) identification
   (D) identifying

7. Plans to .... the highway from four to six lanes were blocked by the local government.
   (A) wide
   (B) width
   (C) widely
   (D) widen

8. The meeting will have to be .... to a later date.
   (A) arranged
   (B) rescheduled
   (C) planned
   (D) prepared

9. Your free six-month .... to *Word Of The Day* includes online definitions and pronunciation clues.
   (A) prescription
   (B) subscription
   (C) designation
   (D) participation

10. Smart travelers research the prices of local hotels to ensure that they do not .... when traveling abroad.
   (A) pay
   (B) repay
   (C) underpay
   (D) overpay

11. Gift giving is considered standard amongst hosts, and guests should feel no .... to return the favor.
   (A) oblige
   (B) obliged
   (C) obliges
   (D) obligation

12. Tax .... is available for those earning less than the statutory minimum who have dependents.
   (A) refund
   (B) relief
   (C) identification
   (D) awareness

C Vocabulary practice

Use the following words to complete the crossword puzzle below. Two have been done for you.

devastate	interaction	overstocked	illiteracy
impatient	~~mislead~~	~~uncompromising~~	discontinue
criticize	obligation	renovate	intermediary

Across

1. Showing no willingness to reduce their demands or back down
3. Having too much of a product or item
6. An inability to read and write
7. Somebody who carries messages to try to bring about agreement
8. To seriously damage or destroy
9. Upset or annoyed at having to wait
10. To complain about something you think is wrong
11. To make something like new again

Down

2. To cause somebody to have a false opinion or belief
4. To stop doing something
5. Something that must be done because of legal or moral duty
6. Activity taking place between two or more people or things

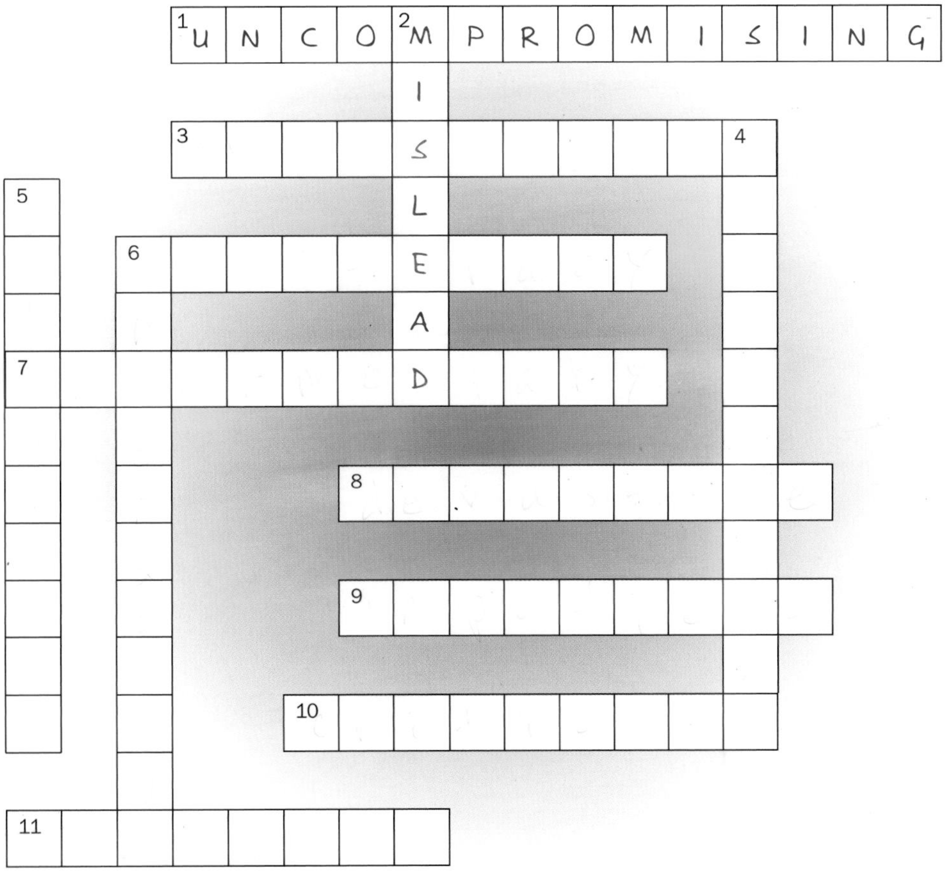

Go to word list and quiz page 183.

20 Reading Test Part 6 — Text Completion

A

Focus: Using clues in the question to help you choose the correct verb form: future, perfect

This unit will help you become familiar with the way that future and perfect forms are used and how they may appear in the TOEIC test.

Test tip

The sentence gives clues to the correct future form

Look for future time markers like *next*, *tomorrow*, *upcoming*, etc., to indicate that a future form may be required.

1 Language building: Ways of talking about the future

A Look at some common ways of talking about the future forms shown in the examples below.

will/be going to – plus base verb form

Examples

Are you going to work on Saturday?

They are going to buy the parts in Australia.

Do you think they will accept the offer?

They will not attend the presentation tomorrow.

Present continuous – *am/is/are* plus verb + *-ing*

Examples

I'm meeting the chairman at 3:00.

Mr. Bell is not coming to Paris next week.

Are they bringing the documents?

B Complete the sentences using the correct form of the verb.

1. Will they .... (send) us the agenda?
2. I am .... (discuss) the contract with them at the upcoming meeting.
3. I am going to .... (see) him at next May's sales meeting.
4. I promise that I will .... (send) the invoices to you by the end of the week.
5. He is not .... (take) the samples to the customer.
6. Why aren't they going to .... (meet) the schedule?

Follow up: Now write two sentences about yourself: one sentence using *will/going to* and one sentence using the present continuous. You could write about a job, studies, holidays, travel, or other plans. Compare your sentences with a partner.

Test tip

The sentence gives clues to the correct perfect form

Look for time markers like *how long, ever, since*, etc., to indicate that a perfect form may be required.

2 Test tactic: Look for clues to help you choose the correct perfect form

A Look at the forms shown in the examples below.

Perfect simple (present/past)
– *has/have/had* + past participle

Examples

Have you ever worked in Asia?

She hasn't seen the new outlines yet.

He had already solved the problem by the time I arrived.

Perfect continuous (present/past)
– *has/have/had been* + verb + *-ing*

Examples

They have been discussing the plans for more than three hours.

He had not been paying the sales staff for several months prior to the closure.

unit 20

B Choose the correct form of the verb to complete the sentences.

1. How long have you .... by your present company?
   (a) been employed
   (b) being employed
   (c) employed
   (d) be employed
2. Bill has been .... in Belgium since 1994.
   (a) worked
   (b) works
   (c) working
   (d) work
3. The interviewer had already been .... for an hour when she arrived.
   (a) wait
   (b) waits
   (c) waited
   (d) waiting
4. We had not .... a chance to meet the new director before the conference.
   (a) having
   (b) have
   (c) had
   (d) been having

Follow up: Now write two sentences about yourself: one sentence using the perfect simple and one sentence using the perfect continuous. Compare your sentences with a partner.

Tactics checklist

☑ Watch for word clues of future forms.

☑ Watch for word clues of perfect forms.

☑ Read the other sentences in the text to help you to find out when the action happens.

unit 20

3 Tactic practice

Use the tactics you have practiced to complete the following. For each answer underline the words that helped you and compare your answer with a partner.

Questions 1–3 refer to the following letter.

Dear Mr. Blackburn,

I am writing about the position in the accounting department that we spoke about last month. As you know I .... to work for a year before returning to school

1. (A) was planned
(B) had been planning
(C) will plan
(D) had been planned

to finish my masters course.

Since we spoke, my situation has changed. I am now .... to start my course

2. (A) intend
(B) intended
(C) have intended
(D) intending

this coming September, which means that unfortunately I will have to refuse your offer of a job for the coming year.

I hope this will not cause you any inconvenience. I would like to take this opportunity to thank you for your support in the past two years. Without your help I would not .... able to gain such valuable experience in accounting.

3. (A) be
(B) been
(C) have been
(D) being

Thank you again for your offer and all your help.

Sincerely,

Brad Jenkins

B Mini-test

Now apply what you have learnt at the actual test speed with questions 1–12.

> Recommended Time: 9 minutes (or less)
> Try using the 2-pass method to help you make the most of the time available. Try to spend no more than about 30–45 seconds on each item. If you don't know the answer, guess and move on.

Questions 1–3 refer to the following article.

Problems at Beeton Steel

Beeton Steel Company announced today that they will be .... their

1. (A) close
(B) closed
(C) have closed
(D) closing

Milltown plant at the end of this year. John Leighton, a spokesman for Beeton, reported that costs at the facility had been rising for some time and that attempts to increase profitability and reduce costs ....

2. (A) had failed
(B) will fail
(C) fails
(D) could have failed

Union officials have expressed concern for the workers employed at the facility. Up to 2,000 employees could lose their jobs .... the company changes

3. (A) after
(B) when
(C) unless
(D) if

its decision.

GO ON TO THE NEXT PAGE

Questions 4–6 refer to the following article.

The classical music event of the season!

Fans of classical music are in for a rare treat in December. The famed Dusseldorf Chamber Orchestra .... a one-night performance of Handel's *Xerxes* at

4. (A) has given
(B) gave
(C) will be giving
(D) gives

the Rondel Theatre.

The DCO is touring North America from October until the New Year, and we are very lucky that they .... a stop in our city.

5. (A) make
(B) to make
(C) have made
(D) will make

This is likely to be the last tour for famed conductor Vasily Krampfstein, as he has announced his retirement, ... be sure not to miss this

6. (A) but
(B) however
(C) as
(D) so

once-in-a-lifetime opportunity.

unit 20

Questions 7–9 refer to the following memo.

Memorandum

To: Pollville PAWS subscribers

From: Alice Dodds, PAWS President

Subject: PAWS Fundraiser

The Pollville Animal Welfare Society would like to inform you about an annual fundraising dinner in Pollville next month. For over 25 years PAWS .... , protected, and provided a home for thousands of animals

7. (A) had been rescuing
(B) rescues
(C) will rescue
(D) has rescued

in distress in Pollville and surrounding Duxham county.

Through this event we are hoping to raise $4500 to provide a new roof for .... new animal shelter and to build a new fence around the livestock yard.

8. (A) my
(B) our
(C) your
(D) her

The dinner .... held in the Pollville Community Hall.

9. (A) will be
(B) was
(C) has been
(D) had been

The tickets are $25 and may be purchased in all local stores from next Monday.

unit 20

GO ON TO THE NEXT PAGE

Questions 10–12 refer to the following memo.

Memorandum

2:30 P.M. Workshop on Elementary Bookkeeping

Due to unforeseen circumstances the presenter of this workshop is unable to attend the conference today. Therefore please note that the workshop ....

10. (A) rescheduled
(B) will reschedule
(C) has been rescheduled
(D) will have been rescheduled

Instead, it .... taking place on Wednesday morning at 10:45 in room G11.

11. (A) will be
(B) has been
(C) had
(D) was

This information will .... be posted on the notice boards in the foyer.

12. (A) then
(B) nevertheless
(C) however
(D) also

C Grammar practice

Match each sentence beginning on the left with the most appropriate ending on the right. The first one is done for you.

1. The annual conference has been ...
2. The famed musician announced that he is ...
3. The agricultural board announced that they will ...
4. Although Kenji had read the word before, he had ...
5. The shipment has been delayed but ...
6. I spoke to the shipping agent and he said he ...
7. The accountant's report shows that unless we reduce expenses ...
8. The wealthy businesswoman decided that she was ...

[3] ... ask for increased taxes on foreign livestock imports.

[5] ... we hope it will be delivered by Monday.

[6] ... will change the cargo invoices and send them to us next week.

[2] ... going to refuse the multi-million dollar recording contract.

[8] ... going to leave all her money to worthy charities.

[7] ... we will not be able to complete the project.

[1] ... canceled this year due to lack of funding.

[4] ... never heard it pronounced.

Follow up: Now make three true statements about your future to a partner.

Examples

After this lesson I am going to have lunch.

Next summer I'll fly to Florida for a vacation.

Further study

D

True or false

A Make three sentences about the most interesting things you have done. Two should be true, one should be false.

Examples

I have tried scuba diving.

I have ridden an elephant.

I have slept in the Sahara desert.

Tell a partner and see if they can guess which one is false!

B Now make three sentences (two true, one false) about things you plan to do in the future and play the same game.

Go to word list and quiz page 184.

21 Reading Test Part 7 — Reading Comprehension

A

Focus: Learning how to answer "NOT" questions, and questions with names, numbers, dates or times

Both "NOT" questions and questions that focus on names, numbers, dates, and times require you to first pick out the key words in the question, then skim the passage to find the correct answer. This unit familiarizes you with this type of question.

Test tip

Leave "NOT" questions to last

Answering the other questions may help you to answer "NOT" questions or to know where in the passage to find the answer.

unit 21

Test tip

For "NOT" questions, use what you've learnt doing the easier questions

Doing the other questions should help you to answer these questions. If not, skim the passage to confirm the most likely answer choice. To simulate this, task C uses a text that was also used in Units 7 and 14.

1 Test tactic: Pick out key ideas, eliminate incorrect answers in turn

A Underline the key words in the question and each answer choice. The question is done for you.

1. Which of the following is NOT true about the refund policy?
   (A) You must return your pool pass if you want a refund.
   (B) Cancelations will be accepted for medical reasons.
   (C) Credit card customers will not receive refund checks.
   (D) You must inform your instructor when leaving the course.

B If you know the answer (based upon the questions you answered about this text in Units 7 and 14), mark it and move on. If not, cross out the letter of any of the answer choices above that you feel are wrong.

C For each of the remaining answer choices, skim the text below to find words with the same meaning. Eliminate all these options and choose the remaining answer.

Summer program refund policy

The effective date of the withdrawal/cancelation is the date the withdrawal notice is received by the center, regardless of the date the participant stopped attending the class.

Withdrawal requests from all registered courses must be made before the second class is held. If the request is received 5 business days prior to the first class, the amount refunded will be the full amount, less the refund administration fee ($25.00). If the request is received after the first class, but before the second class, the amount refunded will be the full amount, less the cost of the first class and less the administration fee ($25.00). From the second lesson onwards, no refunds/credits will be issued.

If there is a medical reason for the request, a doctor's note must be received prior to the mid-point of the program. Refunds for sports and fitness programs will NOT be processed until ALL gym and pool passes have been returned.

Please note that advising an instructor or not attending a program will not constitute a notice of withdrawal.

Cash/check remittances will be refunded by check. Please allow our office 4 to 6 weeks to process your refund. Credit card refunds will go back on the original card.

Test tip

Eliminate incorrect answer choices and choose what's left

Ignore options with similar meanings in the passage (you need to find the one that is NOT true). The option you can't find is the correct answer.

D For each of the following, choose the option which does NOT have the same meaning as the original phrase.

1. Pets are not allowed in this establishment	a Animals prohibited from entry b No dogs or cats allowed c Owners are responsible for their pets' behavior
2. No refunds for opened goods	a Goods must be returned in a sealed condition b All products come with an unconditional money-back guarantee c Exchange only, on unopened products
3. Discounts for seniors	a Flat price all ages b Senior citizens get special rates c Reduced prices for older people

2 Test tactic: Name, number, date, and time questions

unit 21

A Underline the key words in the question.

1. At what time will Dr. Lee catch a plane?

(A) 11:30 A.M. (C) 8:30 P.M.
(B) 3:00 P.M. (D) 9:00 P.M.

B Scan the passage to find the first answer choice. Decide if it refers to the same event or a different one. Continue until you have found the correct answer.

From: mmcpeg@gltech.research.com
To: jholmes@gltech.com
Date: Feb 17
Subject: Dr. Lee's visit

John, here is the outline for Dr. Lee's visit.

You will meet Dr. Lee at the airport on Monday night at 8:30 and drive him to the hotel. The next day Tuesday, just after breakfast, we will bring him to the senior staff meeting, which is set for 11:30. We aim to have the conference call with the Zurich laboratories from 3:00, but we may have to reschedule it if the Swiss team are delayed.

Wednesday will be taken up with touring the plant and the research building. That should leave Dr. Lee enough time to interview the team leaders on Thursday before his flight back to Singapore at 9:00 on Friday evening.

Time is very tight on this visit and it is important that things go smoothly. Please ensure that all arrangements are made at your end.

Malcolm

C Use the same tactics for the question below.

2. When is Dr. Lee scheduled to have a conference call?

(A) On Monday night
(B) On Tuesday morning
(C) On Tuesday afternoon
(D) On Friday afternoon

Follow up: Confirm your answers with a partner.

Tactics checklist

☑ Leave "NOT" questions to last.

☑ Use what you've learnt doing the easier questions.

☑ Eliminate incorrect answers and choose what's left.

unit 21

3 Tactic practice: Name, number, date, time and "NOT" questions

Use the tactics you have practiced to answer questions 1–3.

Questions 1–3 refer to the following e-mail.

From: Alison Lockwood <ali_cat@inmail.com>
To: susan77@yourmail.com
Date: 29 May 20—, 3:30 P.M.
Subject: Julia's Party

Hi Susan,

Just a quick note to remind you we really need to organize Julia's party as soon as possible. Her birthday is on 10 June, but she's not working that day so I thought we could have it on her first day back, 11 June. This might be a good day to have it as everyone in the section is working an early shift that day. That means they will finish at 5 P.M. so there should be plenty of time to get to the restaurant for a 6:30 start … what do you think?

I've already spoken to the manager about it all. He says it's fine, but just needs to get the numbers by Friday so he can organize the food. I think we should book for around 12–15 people … is that OK?

Let me know what you think,

Ali

1. What is NOT true?
   (A) The party will be held in a restaurant.
   (B) Alison is writing to Susan about a party.
   (C) A party is being planned.
   (D) Between 10 and 15 people are expected.
2. At what time will the party start?
   (A) 12:15 P.M.
   (B) 3:31 P.M.
   (C) 5:00 P.M.
   (D) 6:30 P.M.
3. When will the party be held?
   (A) On May 29
   (B) On June 10
   (C) On June 11
   (D) On December 15

B Mini-test

Now apply what you have learnt at the actual test speed with questions 1–10.

> Recommended Time: 12 minutes (or less)
> Try to spend no more than about 60 seconds on each item; if you don't know the answer, guess and move on. If you have time at the end review any answers you weren't sure about.

Questions 1–3 refer to the following memo.

Memorandum

To: All staff
From: Dave Perrett
Re: Trip to Breakout Adventure Center

As promised, here's the revised schedule for next week's activities. I've spoken to the staff at the center and they've agreed that the changes can be made at no cost. See you all bright and early on Monday morning in the staff parking lot. (Please be there by 8:00 A.M. as the bus will depart promptly at 8:15.)

Date	Time	Activity	Place
Mon May 16	Noon	Arrival	Center
	7:00 P.M.	Barbecue	Beach
Tue May 17	All Day	Hiking	Holden Forest
Wed May 18	A.M.	Canoeing	Axe Lake
	P.M.	Surfing/Wind surfing	Axe Lake
Thu May 19	All Day	Mountain Biking	Center/Axe Valley
	9:00 P.M.	'Music Night'	Center
Fri May 20	All Day	Mountain Climbing	Center/Axe Valley
		OR	
		Paragliding*	Stratton Hill
	7:00 P.M.	Barbecue	Beach

* There is a maximum of 12 people for this activity, so sign up early.

1. What is NOT stated in the memo?
   (A) Canoeing will take place after hiking.
   (B) Water sports will be held at Axe Lake.
   (C) Both barbecues are at the beach.
   (D) Participants can go paragliding and mountain climbing.

2. What time is the bus scheduled to leave on Monday?
   (A) At 8:00 A.M.
   (B) At 8:15 A.M.
   (C) At 7:00 P.M.
   (D) At 8:30 P.M.

3. Where will the staff be on Monday evening?
   (A) In the parking lot
   (B) At the center
   (C) On the bus
   (D) At the beach

GO ON TO THE NEXT PAGE

Questions 4–6 refer to the following letter.

> S-Com Ltd.
> PO Box 10
> Western Avenue
> Aylesbury
>
> To whom it may concern:
>
> I am delighted to provide a letter of reference for Jason McCarthy, who worked as a graphic designer for this firm for eighteen months. I worked with Jason for twelve months, and was his project supervisor for eight months. Although Jason came to us straight out of college, his potential was quickly noticed and within six months he was transferred to the marketing department, where he produced work of a consistently high standard. In his time here he was able to make significant improvements in his computer skills and, although this is not his strongest point, he worked hard to develop in this area.
>
> During his time at S-Com, Jason maintained an exemplary attendance record and was always punctual, often arriving early for work in order to better prepare himself. He completed work on or ahead of schedule and was consistently a leader in group projects. We are very sorry to lose him here at S-Com, but I am more than confident that he will be able to adapt quickly to a new work environment.
>
> Please don't hesitate to contact me if you have any further questions.
>
> Yours faithfully,
>
> *Alan Knight*
>
> Alan Knight
> Marketing Manager
> S-Com Ltd.

4. Why did Alan Knight write this letter?
(A) To assist Jason McCarthy in applying to graduate school
(B) To justify giving Jason McCarthy a pay raise
(C) To assist Jason McCarthy in finding another job
(D) To encourage Jason McCarthy to improve his computer skills

5. How long did Jason work in the marketing department?
(A) For 6 months
(B) For 8 months
(C) For 12 months
(D) For 18 months

6. How is Jason described in the letter?
(A) Overconfident
(B) Reliable
(C) Uncooperative
(D) Experienced

Questions 7–9 refer to the following information.

Nagamori Department Store's Countdown to the Holidays!

Only 2 days to go
to place your order and get

SPECIAL FREE DELIVERY*

for delivery by June 24

It's almost your last chance to place your holiday gift orders and ensure free city-wide delivery* by June 24. Don't miss out on this great deal, and avoid leaving loved ones disappointed by submitting your order before 5 P.M. on Friday June 16.

Orders placed after this time and before 3 P.M. on Thursday June 22 will still be guaranteed to arrive by June 24 using our standard delivery option. This remains at our year-round low price of $7 per item (to anywhere in the city – regular rates apply outside of the Townsburg Metropolitan area).

Don't forget to wrap it: If you are short of time, go to our Gift Wrapping corner on this floor for a number of great options (at just $5.95 per item) and put a personalized message on your complimentary card.

* Free delivery applies to gifts delivered to addresses within the Metropolitan area only and to orders of $10 or more. For all other delivery rates (including international), please ask the staff at our Delivery Service on the ground floor of this store.

unit 21

7. Where does this information most likely appear?
(A) On a Web site
(B) In a newspaper
(C) In a store
(D) In an employee manual

8. How much does it cost to have an item gift wrapped?
(A) $3.00
(B) $5.95
(C) $7
(D) $10

9. What is NOT stated about the special free delivery?
(A) Orders must be placed before June 24.
(B) Delivery must be to locations within the city.
(C) Items must cost ten dollars or more.
(D) Items must be gift-wrapped within the store.

GO ON TO THE NEXT PAGE

Questions 10–12 refer to the following application form and letter.

Mountain Printers, Inc.

CHARITABLE CONTRIBUTION APPLICATION FORM

Instructions: Please complete the form and submit to Mountain Printers, Inc., Corporate Communications Dept, 159 N. Parkway, Mississauga, Ontario L5S 1N9 by mail, or fax to (905) 555-7234.

1. PROJECT TITLE: Center for Volunteers
2. LEGAL NAME OF ORGANIZATION: Southern Ontario City Helpers Group
3. TAX ID NUMBER: Under application
4. CONTACT: David Ison, Funding Coordinator
5. CONTRIBUTION REQUESTED: Office printer

Please answer the following questions.

A. What will be accomplished with the requested contribution(s)?
Use of a printer for our Peel County Office will allow us to print information handouts, maintain client records, and produce business correspondence to assist volunteer projects in the region.

B. Summarize the proposed activities. (Attach additional information as required.)
We organize an outreach program that solicits local community volunteers to assist a variety of local organizations.

C. How will the organization and the constituency you serve benefit from the contribution(s)?
We lack basic office supplies to maintain our records and correspondence with local companies and volunteers. A printer would allow us to minimize our costs.

Please attach the following information:

A brief summary of the organization: history, mission, major programs, other contributors, and highlights of your significant achievements. Please include financial information with explanations as required.

David Ison, Funding Coordinator
City Helpers Group
Georgetown, Ontario, CANADA
L7G 4S7

Dear Mr. Ison:

In response to your donation request, we at Mountain Printers are pleased to offer you a laser printer. This donation is part of our community service project in which we make donations to non-profit organizations in regions where we operate. It is our hope that this printer will assist City Helpers Group in continuing to organize volunteers and support for the community. Technical support may be obtained through our company Web site, www.mountain-printers.com/techsupport.

Before taking delivery of the printer, however, we would like you to send us the information from item number 3 on the application form. We require this information for our accounting records and will ship the printer immediately we receive your response.

Thank you for your work, and best wishes to your organization.

Beatrice Petrenko

Beatrice Petrenko

Public Relations Officer
Mountain Printers
Enclosures

unit 21

10. What does the City Helpers Group provide to the community?

(A) Printing services
(B) Package delivery
(C) Technical assistance
(D) Volunteer workers

11. What does Mountain Printers require from City Helpers before they will ship the printer?

(A) A tax ID number
(B) An application form
(C) Accounting records
(D) Client records

12. How should technical problems with the printer be addressed?

(A) In person
(B) Over the phone
(C) Through the Internet
(D) By mail

C Reading in action: Names, numbers, dates and times

The text below is a brochure for upcoming events in Bakerstown.

Student A look at the top three events (1 Jan–1 April)
Student B look at the bottom three events (3 April–10 June)

Choose:
Two names Two numbers Two times/dates

Then make questions for each to test your partner.
Examples
A: *Who should I call to get information on the Winter Carnival?*
B: *Sally Jameson.*

B: *What time is the Fiesta Days re-enactment?*
A: *It's at 2:30.*

A: *How much does the JazzFest cost?*
B: *It's free.*

Upcoming events in Bakerstown

- **Polar Bear Dip, 1 January:** The Bakerstown Polar Bear Club hosts this popular, annual splash-around in the icy York river from 9:00 A.M. Afterwards, everyone joins in the local New Year's Day tradition of warming up with home made bean and bacon soup, good music and beverages. Tickets $15 on the day. Call Burton Henderson at 555-8611.
- **Winter Carnival, 6–21 February:** One of the county's original festivals and parades, this year with 75 floats, as well as various contests and culinary festivals. Call Sally Jameson at 555-1234.
- **Festival on the Green, 31 March–1 April:** Festivities at this year's event will include a fine arts show and craft fair, dog show, musical performances, sporting events, over 25 local food vendors, a children's fair and more. FREE and open to the public. Open from 8:30 A.M.–10:00 A.M. Call Billy Madison at 555-3000.

- **Bakerstown JazzFest, 3–9 April:** Bakerstown historic Seville Square hosts this event filled with great jazz music performed by local and national talents. Over 16 hours of great music! Free admission. Call Monica Bell at 555-8382.
- **23rd Annual Bakerstown Salmon Toss, 28–30 April:** This is the twenty-third year in a row for the wacky annual tournament where participants compete in an actual (frozen) salmon toss. Open from 10 A.M. but fish tossing starts from 1:00 P.M. Live music, food, and drinks accompany this weekend. Admission (plus 1 fish) $35. Call 555-6838 and talk to Bob Plunkton.
- **Fiesta Days Celebration and Boat Parade, 1–10 June:** The 56th annual Fiesta Days Celebration starts with a light-hearted re-enactment of the founding of the city by English explorer Francis Baker, who first landed in Bakerstown in 1779. Immediately following is an evening of outdoor musical entertainment.
Re-enactment from 2:30 P.M., but the park is open all day. Free admission. Call Herman Frost at 555-6512.

D Further study

Write three more questions about things in the text, and for each one write three answer choices. One answer choice should be correct and two should be in the text but incorrect. Test your classmates in the next lesson.

Go to word list and quiz page 185.

22

Listening Test Part 1 | Photographs

A

Focus: Listening for the correct prepositions
Being aware of similar sounding words

Some questions in this section test your understanding of position and direction. Being familiar with the words used to describe where things are and where they are going will help you score well on this part of the test.

Test tip

Listen for prepositions

Many TOEIC test Part 1 statements talk about the position of people or objects in the picture.

Listen carefully for wrong prepositions in these pictures.

1 Language building: Listen for prepositions of position and motion

A Look at Pictures 1 and 2, then read the sentences below. Work with your partner and decide which picture is being described, and if the sentence is TRUE or FALSE.

1. The woman is on the counter.
2. The paper is next to the keyboard.
3. The computer is behind the woman.
4. The phone is in front of the woman.
5. The man is next to the board.
6. The keyboard is on the desk.

B Work with a partner and use the vocabulary below to make as many sentences as possible about the pictures.

1

2

3

4

Possible prepositions used		**Possible nouns used**	
on	next to	phone	computer
in front of	through	platform	board
behind	along	counter	woman/man
between		walkway	train

unit 22

C Look at the following two pictures and the four sentences below. Use prepositions from the box on page 121 to complete the sentences.

1

2

1. The couple are standing .... the house.
2. The young girl is riding .... her father.
3. The man is .... the woman.
4. They are riding .... the street.

Test tip

Be careful of similar sounds

If you hear a word that sounds similar to a word you can see or imagine in the picture, it may be a distractor.

2 Test tactic: Beware of similar sounding words

A Incorrect answers may include words that sound similar to key words you can see in the picture. Look at the two sentences below each picture (one correct and one incorrect) and underline any key words that sound similar.

1

The man is pointing at something.
The man is painting something.

2

The people are setting the table.
The people are sitting around the table.

3

The ship is in the harbor.
The sheep is near the water.

4

The woman is walking along the street.
The woman is working long hours.

B Look at the following two pictures and write two correct sentences about each one. Underline any prepositions you use.

Example: The woman is cycling <u>through</u> the city.

1

2

C Listen to four statements about each picture. After each statement, pause the audio and tell your partner (a) any prepositions you heard and (b) any words that sound similar to words you can see in the picture. Then tick if you think the sentence is correct or wrong.

(A)	☐ Correct	☐ Wrong	(A)	☐ Correct	☐ Wrong
(B)	☐ Correct	☐ Wrong	(B)	☐ Correct	☐ Wrong
(C)	☐ Correct	☐ Wrong	(C)	☐ Correct	☐ Wrong
(D)	☐ Correct	☐ Wrong	(D)	☐ Correct	☐ Wrong

Follow up: Compare the sentences you first made and the correct sentence with your partner.

Tactics checklist

☑ Listen for wrong prepositions.

☑ Be careful of similar sounds.

Understanding natural English

English has many words that sound similar. Note the similar words said in each pair below.

He .... for hours.

He .... for hours.

The .... is in the water.

The .... is near the water.

The man .... the food.

The man .... the food.

3 Tactic practice

Use the tactics you have practiced for the next three pictures. You will have one minute to (a) brainstorm vocabulary and (b) predict possible statements with a partner. Then listen to and echo (silently) the answer choices. After you hear each answer choice, mark whether you think it is correct, maybe correct, or wrong.

1

(A)	☐ Correct	☐ Maybe correct	☐ Wrong
(B)	☐ Correct	☐ Maybe correct	☐ Wrong
(C)	☐ Correct	☐ Maybe correct	☐ Wrong
(D)	☐ Correct	☐ Maybe correct	☐ Wrong

2

(A)	☐ Correct	☐ Maybe correct	☐ Wrong
(B)	☐ Correct	☐ Maybe correct	☐ Wrong
(C)	☐ Correct	☐ Maybe correct	☐ Wrong
(D)	☐ Correct	☐ Maybe correct	☐ Wrong

3

(A)	☐ Correct	☐ Maybe correct	☐ Wrong
(B)	☐ Correct	☐ Maybe correct	☐ Wrong
(C)	☐ Correct	☐ Maybe correct	☐ Wrong
(D)	☐ Correct	☐ Maybe correct	☐ Wrong

Follow up: Now compare your answers with your partner, explaining your reasons, and what you remember hearing.

Understanding natural English

unit 22

B Mini-test

Now apply the *Test tactics* at the actual test speed with questions 1–8.

> Use any time available to skim the first pictures before the listening starts. After that you will have exactly 5 seconds between each question to mark your answer and focus on the next picture.

1

2

3

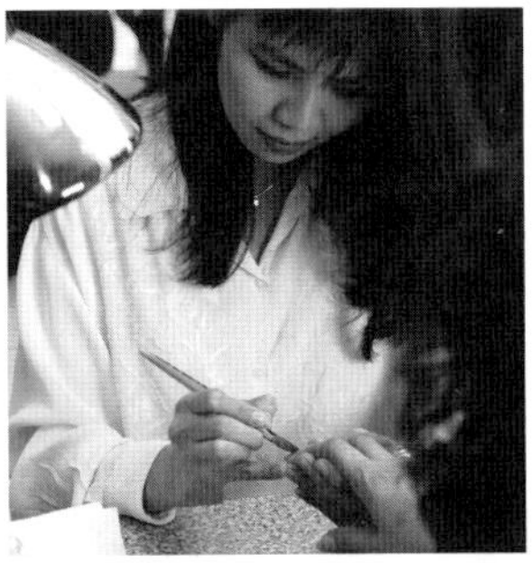

4

5

6

7

8

1	Ⓐ	Ⓑ	Ⓒ	Ⓓ	5	Ⓐ	Ⓑ	Ⓒ	Ⓓ
2	Ⓐ	Ⓑ	Ⓒ	Ⓓ	6	Ⓐ	Ⓑ	Ⓒ	Ⓓ
3	Ⓐ	Ⓑ	Ⓒ	Ⓓ	7	Ⓐ	Ⓑ	Ⓒ	Ⓓ
4	Ⓐ	Ⓑ	Ⓒ	Ⓓ	8	Ⓐ	Ⓑ	Ⓒ	Ⓓ

C Learn by doing: Right or wrong!

In this game you will take turns reading statements about the pictures below and on page 126.

Student A: Look at Activity file 22a on page 166. You will ask your partner questions about Set A.

Student B: Look at Activity file 22b on page 168. You will ask your partner questions about Set B.

Choose one picture from your set, tell your partner the number, then read one of the two statements about it.

For each picture, your partner has the chance to win up to three points:

One Point	if they can say if the statement is right or wrong
One Point	if they can say why the distractor is wrong (WRONG PREPOSITION or SIMILAR SOUND)
One Point	if they can spot (and say!) the wrong prepositions or similar sounds

The winner is the person with the most points at the end of the game.

Set A

1 

2 

3 

4 

5 

6 

7 

8 

9 

Set B

1

2

3

4

5

6

7

8

9

D Further study

Choose a word group from the list a–d. Look up any words you aren't sure of in a dictionary.

Write two sentences using at least two of the words, **plus one preposition**, then choose one of the sentences and make a simple drawing of it.

In your next lesson, show your partner the drawing, read your two sentences and see if they can identify the correct sentence!

a) bag/big/bug	b) tree/three/flea	c) boy/bay/toy	d) pig/peg/big

Example:
The bug is in the big bag.
The big bug is behind the bag.

Go to word list and quiz page 186.

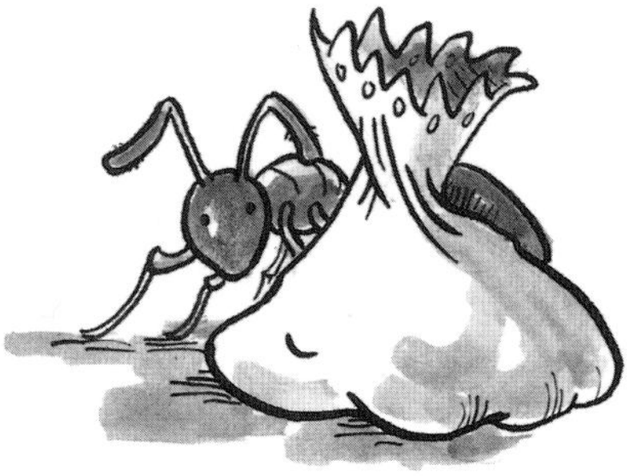

23 Listening Test Part 2 Question-Response

A

Focus: Becoming familiar with language used in offers, requests and opinions

Offers, requests and opinions are common in this part of the TOEIC test.
This unit will familiarize you with the types of questions and answers choices you will see in this section.

Test tip

Social interaction, including offers, requests and opinions, is a common feature of Part 2

Be aware of the language commonly used in these situations.

1 Language building: Become familiar with language for offers, requests and opinions

A Match each question on the left with the two best responses on the right. The first one is done for you. The words commonly used in each category are in **bold**.

Offers

1. **Would you like** some help with those? c, e	a **Actually**, it's **already** done.
	b **No, I've already** eaten.
	c **Yeah, could you** take this box?
2. **Do you need** (any) help with setting up the room?	d A cup of tea **would be lovely**.
	e **No, that's alright**. They aren't as heavy as they look.
3. **Can/May I** get you anything?	f **That would be great**. Let's start with the tables.

Requests

4. **Could/Can you** tell me how to use this machine?	g **Actually**, I'm a bit cold.
	h **I'm afraid** it's not mine.
	i **Certainly**, it's pretty easy.
5. **Would you mind if** I opened the window?	j **Sure**, give it back after class.
	k **I'm sorry**, I haven't been trained on it yet.
6. **May/Can/Could** I borrow your pen for a moment?	l No, **go ahead**.

Opinions

7. **How was** Mr. Smitt's presentation?	m **I don't think** we'll find a lower one.
	n **Frankly**, our sales staff isn't motivated.
8. **What's your opinion of** their price quote?	o **To tell the truth**, it seemed a bit long.
	p **I'd say** we need to lower our prices.
9. **What would you say is** our greatest weakness?	q **Good.** He really is an amusing speaker.
	r **It seems** a bit high to me.

B Now write one possible answer for each of the following questions.

1. Would you care for a slice of pie? ....
2. Can you tell Ms. Jackson that her parcel has arrived? ....
3. What do you think of your new boss? ....

unit 23

Test tip

Common distractors for this section include use of the same word/similar sounds or incorrect meaning

Noticing these types of wrong answer can help you to choose the correct one.

2 Test tactic: Identify correct/incorrect offer, request and opinion answers

For the question below, choose the correct answer. Tell your partner why the other choices were wrong: because they have the same/similar sounding word or because the meaning is incorrect.

1. Is there anything I can do to help with the project?
   - **a** Yes, they finished the project.
   - **b** No, that's fine. It's already taken care of.
   - **c** We could have done it last week.
2. Do you have a calculator I could borrow?
   - **a** Yes, I will call you later.
   - **b** I remember you borrowed it last week.
   - **c** Sorry, I left mine at home.
3. How was your test?
   - **a** You have to pass the test to get a license.
   - **b** On Wednesday.
   - **c** Harder than I expected.

Test tip

Repeat each question and answer choice silently after you hear it

This will help you to remember and compare the meanings.

Follow up: Now listen to two more questions followed by three answer choices. After each answer choice, pause the audio and repeat what you heard. If it is correct, circle the letter. If not, mark the distractor type(s).

1. (A) ☐ same word/similar sound ☐ incorrect meaning
   (B) ☐ same word/similar sound ☐ incorrect meaning
   (C) ☐ same word/similar sound ☐ incorrect meaning
2. (A) ☐ same word/similar sound ☐ incorrect meaning
   (B) ☐ same word/similar sound ☐ incorrect meaning
   (C) ☐ same word/similar sound ☐ incorrect meaning

Tactics checklist

☑ Listen for vocabulary common to offers, requests and opinions.

☑ Listen for and eliminate common types of distractors.

☑ Repeat each question and answer choice silently after you hear it.

3 Tactic practice

Use the tactics you have practiced for the next five questions. Pause the audio after each one to allow you to repeat each question and answer choice to your partner.

1	Ⓐ Ⓑ Ⓒ	4	Ⓐ Ⓑ Ⓒ
2	Ⓐ Ⓑ Ⓒ	5	Ⓐ Ⓑ Ⓒ
3	Ⓐ Ⓑ Ⓒ		

Follow up: After each question you will have one minute to discuss with your partner which answer you chose and why.

Understanding natural English

Understanding natural English

In natural spoken English, sounds are sometimes changed, combined and dropped. Listen to these sentences spoken naturally and write in the missing words.

.... carry these books for me?

.... mind showing Kim the supply room?

B Mini-test

Now practice what you have learnt at the actual test speed with questions 1–12.

> You will have 5 seconds at the end of each item to make your choice. You must then be ready to listen to the next question.

1	Ⓐ	Ⓑ	Ⓒ	7	Ⓐ	Ⓑ	Ⓒ
2	Ⓐ	Ⓑ	Ⓒ	8	Ⓐ	Ⓑ	Ⓒ
3	Ⓐ	Ⓑ	Ⓒ	9	Ⓐ	Ⓑ	Ⓒ
4	Ⓐ	Ⓑ	Ⓒ	10	Ⓐ	Ⓑ	Ⓒ
5	Ⓐ	Ⓑ	Ⓒ	11	Ⓐ	Ⓑ	Ⓒ
6	Ⓐ	Ⓑ	Ⓒ	12	Ⓐ	Ⓑ	Ⓒ

unit 23

C Learn by doing: Offers, requests and opinions

Look at the model conversations below. Practice them with a partner. Then make similar conversations by replacing the words in bold with the words below.

Offers	Requests	Opinions
A: Would you like me to **call you a taxi?** B: **No, It's not far. Thanks.**	C: Can **I reserve a table for 8:00?** D: **Sorry, we are fully booked for this evening.**	E: What do you think about **the changes to the retirement plan?** F: **I'm sure a lot of people will be upset.**
... open the door for you? ... help you with your homework? ... lend you some money?	... I borrow 10 dollars till pay day? ... you give me a hand with this table? ... you work late this Wednesday?	... the new sales manager? ... your new apartment? ... our chances of getting the contract?
No, thanks. That would be great. Yes, please. I'd appreciate it.	Yes, (of course). Sure. (I'd be glad to). I'm afraid/sorry, (I can't).	(He) seems (friendly). It's great. I'm really pleased. Frankly, I think we have an excellent chance./I don't think we will.

Follow up: Make more offer, request and opinion conversations, using your own ideas and words from the unit.

D Further study

Think of one offer, request and opinion you have used or heard recently and write them out in English. In the next lesson, say them to your partner, who should respond appropriately.

Go to word list and quiz page 186.

24 Listening Test Part 3 Conversations

A

Focus: Becoming familiar with polite ways of saying "no"
Listening carefully to the first exchange

Being familiar with the language and organization common to negative responses can help you to choose the correct answer. It is important to understand the first exchange, as this probably contains the answer to the first question.

Test tip

Conversations involving saying 'no' sometimes appear in the TOEIC test

Learn to identify denial and refusal phrases and listen carefully to the information that follows them. This information is often the focus of one of the questions.

unit 24

1 Language building: Become familiar with the vocabulary of denial and refusal

A Match each question on the left to the best response on the right. The common words and phrases used for denial and refusal are in **bold**. The first one is done for you.

1. Jane, would you like to join us for drinks tonight? e
2. Could you fix this radio for me?
3. We are going skiing this weekend. Can you and Mary come along?
4. Are we still having the sales meeting after lunch?
5. Is it OK to keep a cat in this building?
6. Do you accept personal checks?

a **We used to, but** we stopped doing it last year.

b **No, I'm sure they wouldn't** allow it. The building owner doesn't like animals.

c **We can, but** I would prefer to put it off till tomorrow. I have a lot of other work.

d **I'm afraid we can only** service Tri-sonic units, madam.

e **I'd love to, but** I'm afraid I have to pick up my sister.

f **I don't think we'll be able to** make it. My brother's family is coming on Saturday.

B Look at the questions and correct answer choices for the six dialogs above. Write the number of the question/response above that best matches each question and answer below. The first one is done for you.

1	Why won't the woman go out with her friends?	She has a previous commitment.
	What does the man suggest?	Postponing the meeting
	Why can't the woman get service?	Her radio is the wrong brand.
	What are the speakers discussing?	The store's payment policy
	How does the owner feel about pets?	He strongly dislikes them.
	What is the man planning for the weekend?	He is entertaining relatives.

C Now listen to three conversations and answer the following questions.

1. Why can't Eric do what the man asks?
   (A) He has to meet a client.
   (B) He needs to prepare some other papers.
   (C) He is leaving the office shortly.
   (D) He will be in a meeting until this evening.

2. How is the man planning on getting to the station?
   (A) He will take the train.
   (B) He will go by bicycle.
   (C) Daphne will drive him.
   (D) He will jog.

3. What does the woman say about the man's request?
   (A) The shirts cannot be cleaned and pressed on time.
   (B) The jacket can be repaired today.
   (C) The shirts will need to be repaired.
   (D) The jacket needs to be sent to another location.

Test tip

Most Part 3 conversations start with a question or request

Listen carefully to what the first speaker says, and to the response, as they may relate to the first question.

2 Test tactic: Understanding the first exchange

A Match the Part 3 question on the left to the first speaker's question/request on the right. The first one is done for you.

1. What advice does the man's friend give about trading in his car? b
2. What kind of summer vacation is the man considering?
3. What experience does the man have?
4. How does Mr. Green feel about his request?

a *"Mr. Green, I was wondering if it was OK if I took next Friday off."*

b *"Do you think I should get a new car? It seems to cost me more money in repairs each year."*

c *"I see you are applying for the sales clerk's job. Do you have any experience in sales?"*

d *"What are you doing for your vacation this year, Dario?"*

unit 24

B Now listen to the conversations from which the responses (a–d) above are taken. After each one, pause the audio and repeat as much as you can of the second speaker's response. Then choose the answer choice below that best matches the response you heard.

(A) The second speaker thinks the time is not good.
(B) The second speaker says the man may be able to save money over time.
(C) The second speaker says he has done some work in retail sales.
(D) The second speaker says he isn't sure yet.

Tactics checklist

☑ Listen for denial/refusal statements and the information that follows them.

3 Tactic practice

Before you listen to each conversation, take a few minutes to a) predict the context and b) think of other ways to say the answer choices.

1. What does the first man want to do?
   (A) Buy a house
   (B) Rent somewhere to live
   (C) Go to the beach
   (D) Decorate his bedroom

2. What is the problem?
   (A) The beach is too far away.
   (B) There are no suitable places left.
   (C) The price is too high.
   (D) The advertisement gave the wrong information.

3. What does the second man offer to do?
   (A) Show him the bedroom
   (B) Give him a discount
   (C) Show him a different place
   (D) Take him to the beach

4. What is Jim's problem?
   (A) He hardly knows Bob.
   (B) He only has a little money.
   (C) He wants to lend some money.
   (D) He does not have any money.

1	Ⓐ	Ⓑ	Ⓒ	Ⓓ
2	Ⓐ	Ⓑ	Ⓒ	Ⓓ
3	Ⓐ	Ⓑ	Ⓒ	Ⓓ
4	Ⓐ	Ⓑ	Ⓒ	Ⓓ
5	Ⓐ	Ⓑ	Ⓒ	Ⓓ
6	Ⓐ	Ⓑ	Ⓒ	Ⓓ

5. What does Bob do about the situation?
- (A) He will help Jim.
- (B) He suggests asking someone else.
- (C) He gives Jim a few dollars.
- (D) He offers to share his lunch.

6. What does Bob finally decide?
- (A) He will try to find the wallet.
- (B) He will have lunch at home.
- (C) He will not speak to Darryl.
- (D) He will pay for Jim's lunch.

Understanding natural English

In natural spoken English, sounds are sometimes changed, combined and dropped. Listen to these sentences spoken naturally and write in the missing words.

The meals were .... I've had in many restaurants.

We'll notify you .... we locate your suitcase.

B Mini-test

Now practice what you have learnt at the actual test speed with questions 1–12.

Use any time available to skim the questions and answer choices before the first listening starts. When you finish answering the questions about one conversation, immediately start previewing the questions for the next conversation.

1. What does the woman ask the man to do?
- (A) Meet with a customer
- (B) Give her a ride
- (C) Pick up a client
- (D) Help her move

2. At about what time does the woman need help?
- (A) At 8:30
- (B) At 9:00
- (C) At 10:00
- (D) At 11:00

3. What does the man plan to do tomorrow?
- (A) Meet a friend for breakfast
- (B) Drive to the airport
- (C) Keep an appointment
- (D) Arrive at work early

---

4. What does the woman want?
- (A) Transportation to the airport
- (B) An opinion of an airline
- (C) Accommodation in New York
- (D) A recommendation for a restaurant

5. What does the man say about his experience?
- (A) He was disappointed in the food.
- (B) He enjoyed the extra services.
- (C) The seating was uncomfortable.
- (D) The price was reasonable.

6. What did the man especially like?
- (A) The quick service
- (B) The clean room
- (C) The wide aisles
- (D) The tasty meals

---

7. Where does this conversation most probably take place?
- (A) At a clothing store
- (B) In an appliance store
- (C) At a dry cleaner's
- (D) In a repair shop

8. What is the problem?
- (A) The store does not allow exchanges.
- (B) Some merchandise does not work properly.
- (C) A customer cannot locate some merchandise.
- (D) The price of a product is not indicated.

1	Ⓐ	Ⓑ	Ⓒ	Ⓓ
2	Ⓐ	Ⓑ	Ⓒ	Ⓓ
3	Ⓐ	Ⓑ	Ⓒ	Ⓓ
4	Ⓐ	Ⓑ	Ⓒ	Ⓓ
5	Ⓐ	Ⓑ	Ⓒ	Ⓓ
6	Ⓐ	Ⓑ	Ⓒ	Ⓓ
7	Ⓐ	Ⓑ	Ⓒ	Ⓓ
8	Ⓐ	Ⓑ	Ⓒ	Ⓓ
9	Ⓐ	Ⓑ	Ⓒ	Ⓓ
10	Ⓐ	Ⓑ	Ⓒ	Ⓓ
11	Ⓐ	Ⓑ	Ⓒ	Ⓓ
12	Ⓐ	Ⓑ	Ⓒ	Ⓓ

9. What must the customer provide?
(A) The time and date a problem occurred
(B) A credit card number
(C) A receipt from a transaction
(D) A telephone number

10. Where does the conversation probably take place?
(A) In a travel agency
(B) At a hotel
(C) In a train station
(D) At an airport

11. What is the woman's problem?
(A) Her luggage has not arrived.
(B) She missed a connection.
(C) She cannot find her passport.
(D) Her purse is missing.

12. What does the man suggest?
(A) Calling her office
(B) Replacing some documents
(C) Notifying a sales representative
(D) Providing contact information

C Learn by doing: Refusing

Practice the following conversations involving a refusal. Then make new conversations by replacing the words in **bold** with the words in the boxes below.

A: A group of us are going **bowling** on **Tuesday night**. Would you care to join us?
B: I really would, but unfortunately I have **a tennis lesson**.
A: Oh, too bad. Maybe another time then?
B: Yes, for sure. Thanks for the offer.

C: Excuse me. Can I **park my car here?**
D: No, I'm afraid not. **This is a no parking zone**.
C: Oh, do you know of anywhere around here I can **park**?
D: Sorry, I'm afraid I don't.

for Greek food/Wednesday night/to pick up my sister from school	*cash a check in this shop/We don't accept checks/cash one*
to a movie/Sunday afternoon/to go to a wedding	*leave my bags here/We can't be responsible/leave them*
to have a barbecue/Saturday/to work	*use US dollars here/We only take local money/change money*

Follow up: Now make another conversation with a refusal using your own ideas.

D Further study

Choose two of the conversations with refusals you made in activity C, write out the dialogs, and write two questions to test your classmates in the next lesson.

Go to word list and quiz page 187.

25 Listening Test Part 4 Talks

A

Focus: Becoming familiar with re-statements involving "how" and "why" questions
Being aware of same word distractors

Brainstorming vocabulary related to the answer choices can help you identify information in the talk that restates the answer choices. Be careful of answer choices that use the same words as the recording, as these may be distractors.

Test tip

Brainstorming related words

Before you listen to the talk, try to look at the answer choices, and think of other ways the answer choice might be said.

1 Language building: Brainstorming related words

Underline the word from the list of related words on the right that does NOT match any of the words in the answer choices. The first one has been done for you.

1. How has the change affected business?

(A) It has decreased by 50%.	fallen, double, dropped, half, slumped
(B) The number of potential customers has gone up.	possible, clients, manager, increased
(C) There has been no change.	stable, increased, the same, constant

2. Why might guests need to dial 9?

(A) To contact the concierge	hotel staff, speak to, call, chef
(B) To arrange their flight transfers	pay, transit, sort out, organize
(C) To place a direct call	ring, telephone, luggage, make

Follow up: Now think of a word with a similar meaning for all the underlined words.
Example: double → 200%

Test tip

Listen for related words and restatements

The correct answer to a "how" or "why" question is sometimes a restatement of the wording in the recording. Listen for words with a similar meaning to one of the answer choices.

2 Test tactic: Listen for related words and restatements

A Underline the key words in the following questions and answer choices. Then read the tapescript on page 135 and choose the best answers.

1. Why must attendees wear their identification tags?
   (A) So that people can see their names
   (B) To get into the presentations
   (C) Because presentations are starting shortly
2. How can attendees find out about the presenters?
   (A) By looking at the schedule they were given earlier
   (B) By checking with the conference organizers
   (C) By checking the information on their telephones
3. Why do attendees have to use silent mode?
   (A) To ensure safety
   (B) To disturb the presentations
   (C) To avoid bothering the participants

Test tip

Be careful of same word distractors

If you see the same word in an answer choice as you heard in the recording, think carefully if it is related to the meaning of the question before making your choice.

Tapescript

The conference organizers would like to remind attendees that identification tags must be worn at all times, in order to gain entry to the lecture halls. The presentations will be starting shortly, but before that, there are a couple of other announcements to make. Firstly, I would like to remind all conference guests to read the presentation timetable, which includes the names of all the presenters. Secondly, I have to ask all guests to ensure their mobile telephones are on silent mode, so as not to disturb any presentations. OK. That's enough of me, I'll hand you over to your first presenter.

B Skim the questions and answer choices below and note key words. As you listen, circle any "same words" you hear, then decide if the answer is correct, maybe correct or wrong.

1. Why should customers choose Seymour suits?
   (A) They use high quality cloth but are reasonably priced.
   (B) They are expensive but good quality.
   (C) They are 25% warmer.

   (A) ☐ Correct ☐ Maybe Correct ☐ Wrong
   (B) ☐ Correct ☐ Maybe Correct ☐ Wrong
   (C) ☐ Correct ☐ Maybe Correct ☐ Wrong

2. How can customers tell if their suit is a genuine Seymour suit?
   (A) It is made of cheaper materials.
   (B) There is a special inner layer.
   (C) It will keep them warm in winter.

   (A) ☐ Correct ☐ Maybe Correct ☐ Wrong
   (B) ☐ Correct ☐ Maybe Correct ☐ Wrong
   (C) ☐ Correct ☐ Maybe Correct ☐ Wrong

3. Why should customers hurry to buy the suits?
   (A) It is winter.
   (B) The suits create a good first impression.
   (C) There are limited quantities.

   (A) ☐ Correct ☐ Maybe Correct ☐ Wrong
   (B) ☐ Correct ☐ Maybe Correct ☐ Wrong
   (C) ☐ Correct ☐ Maybe Correct ☐ Wrong

Follow up: Compare your answers with your partner, explaining your reasons, and what you remember hearing.

Tactics checklist

☑ Read the answer choices and brainstorm related words.

☑ Listen for related words.

☑ Be careful of answers containing words you hear in the recording.

3 Tactic practice

Use the tactics you have practiced for the next two talks. You will have one minute to a) skim the question and answer choices and identify key words and b) brainstorm related words. Then listen to the talks, and select the best answer choices.

1. Why should Mr. Heinrich go to the information counter?
   (A) To collect his unattended bag
   (B) To make an announcement
   (C) To retrieve an important travel document
   (D) To report an unattended package

2. Who is told to go to gate number 12?
   (A) Mr. G. Heinrich
   (B) Passengers traveling to Moscow
   (C) Passengers traveling to Berlin
   (D) Airport security

3. Why should passengers going to Moscow hurry?
   (A) Their flight will leave soon.
   (B) They must collect their packages.
   (C) The duty free shop is about to close.
   (D) They must collect their boarding passes.

4. How can guests purchase razors or toothbrushes?
   (A) By placing a call to the hotel front desk
   (B) By dialing 2
   (C) By visiting the housekeeper
   (D) By using a coin-operated machine

Understanding natural English

In natural spoken English, sounds are sometimes changed, combined and dropped. Listen to these sentences spoken naturally and write in the missing words.

The train was delayed by ....

They first charged only 10 ....

5. How can outside calls be made?
   (A) By dialing 1
   (B) By contacting the concierge
   (C) By dialing the number, followed by 9
   (D) By dialing 9 first, then the number

6. Why might guests visit the housekeeper on the first floor?
   (A) To get their clothes washed
   (B) To make an inquiry
   (C) To make an outside call
   (D) To purchase toiletries

1	Ⓐ	Ⓑ	Ⓒ	Ⓓ	4	Ⓐ	Ⓑ	Ⓒ	Ⓓ
2	Ⓐ	Ⓑ	Ⓒ	Ⓓ	5	Ⓐ	Ⓑ	Ⓒ	Ⓓ
3	Ⓐ	Ⓑ	Ⓒ	Ⓓ	6	Ⓐ	Ⓑ	Ⓒ	Ⓓ

Follow up: Now compare your answers with your partner, explaining your reasons, and what you remember hearing.

Understanding natural English

B Mini-test

Now apply what you have learnt at the actual test speed with questions 1–12.

Use any time available to skim the questions and answer choices before the first listening starts. When you finish answering the questions about one talk, immediately start previewing the questions for the next talk.

unit 25

1. Who is probably making this announcement?
   (A) A history teacher
   (B) A company executive
   (C) A tour guide
   (D) Samuel Weller

2. What is suggested about the candy?
   (A) It is named after a child.
   (B) It is a healthy dessert.
   (C) It is no longer available.
   (D) It is difficult to make.

3. What was the original price of a box of candy?
   (A) 10 cents
   (B) 25 cents
   (C) 10 dollars
   (D) 45 dollars

4. What change in weather is expected in the north?
   (A) It will get warmer.
   (B) It will become sunny.
   (C) It will begin to rain.
   (D) It will snow a little.

5. What temperature is predicted during the day?
   (A) 28 degrees
   (B) 33 degrees
   (C) 38 degrees
   (D) 40 degrees

6. Why should drivers be careful tonight?
   (A) The roads may be icy.
   (B) There will be heavy fog.
   (C) It will get dark early.
   (D) The roads will be very crowded.

7. Where is the announcement probably being made?
   (A) At an airport
   (B) At a bus stop
   (C) At a train station
   (D) At a travel agency

8. Why was there a delay?
   (A) There was a mechanical problem.
   (B) There was a power outage.
   (C) There was a great deal of traffic.
   (D) There was bad weather.

1	Ⓐ	Ⓑ	Ⓒ	Ⓓ
2	Ⓐ	Ⓑ	Ⓒ	Ⓓ
3	Ⓐ	Ⓑ	Ⓒ	Ⓓ
4	Ⓐ	Ⓑ	Ⓒ	Ⓓ
5	Ⓐ	Ⓑ	Ⓒ	Ⓓ
6	Ⓐ	Ⓑ	Ⓒ	Ⓓ
7	Ⓐ	Ⓑ	Ⓒ	Ⓓ
8	Ⓐ	Ⓑ	Ⓒ	Ⓓ
9	Ⓐ	Ⓑ	Ⓒ	Ⓓ
10	Ⓐ	Ⓑ	Ⓒ	Ⓓ
11	Ⓐ	Ⓑ	Ⓒ	Ⓓ
12	Ⓐ	Ⓑ	Ⓒ	Ⓓ

9. What does the speaker recommend?
- (A) Buying food and drink before departure
- (B) Finding a different mode of transportation
- (C) Reserving a seat
- (D) Delaying the trip

10. Why was the first presentation delayed?
- (A) The previous speaker took too much time.
- (B) There were technical difficulties.
- (C) There were announcements.
- (D) People had a lot of questions.

11. How might people know the next speaker?
- (A) He is a political leader in his country.
- (B) He is a well-known film producer.
- (C) He introduced a product to south-east Asia.
- (D) He attended the previous conference.

12. What is the topic of the next presentation?
- (A) The opening of a new factory
- (B) Political changes in Seoul
- (C) Developments in production technology
- (D) Competition among semi-conductor producers

C Learn by doing: Question my answer

Student A: Look at Activity file 25a "Why" questions on page 164.

Student B: Look at Activity file 25b "How" questions on page 167.

A With your partner check you understand the questions below. Then read out one of the answers for your Activity file. Your partner must read out the matching question to get one point. If they don't choose the correct question, you get a chance to steal the point by guessing the correct question. When all the answers are read out, the player with the highest score is the winner.

"Why" questions

1. Why is the manager concerned about sales?
2. Why are travelers advised to avoid the region?
3. Why is there a delay in releasing the new product?
4. Why did the visit have to be rearranged?
5. Why did the President miss the opening address?

"How" questions

6. How can guests arrange transport to the airport?
7. How is the new product different from the old model?
8. How will the weather be at the weekend?
9. How does the manager feel about the delay?
10. How can travelers find out about friends or family in the area?

B Think of a possible true answer for the following questions. Take turns to read out an answer. Your partner must guess the question.

Why are you taking this course?
How do you usually come to class?

How are you different from your father?
Why do you want to improve your English?

D Further study

Look at the "why" and "how" questions in activity C above. Write one more possible answer for each question.

Go to word list and quiz page 188.

26 Reading Test Part 5 — Incomplete Sentences

A

unit 26

Focus: Improving your knowledge of pronouns

Use of pronouns is tested in Part 5. Being aware of how they are used can help you improve your score.

Test tip

Decide whether the missing word is a subject or an object. Often the sentence in the test will feature both a subject and one or more objects. Decide whether the blank is replacing a subject or an object and choose the correct pronoun.

1 Language building: Subject/object personal pronouns

A For each of the following sentences decide whether the missing word is a subject (S) or object (O). The first one has been done for you.

1. Ms. Smithers will attend the function, but her sister will not be coming with .... [O]
2. The president gave a presentation while .... took extensive notes. [ ]
3. I bought my wife a watch but she told me .... didn't fit properly. [ ]
4. When Jack arrived at the meeting, the other members were already waiting for .... [ ]
5. The letter from Mr. Bildy's bank requested that .... verify some personal details. [ ]
6. The members were upset that dinner hadn't been arranged for .... [ ]

B Choose the best pronoun from the list below to complete each of the sentences above. The first one has been done for you.

Subject Pronouns		Object Pronouns	
[ ] I	[ ] he	[ ] me	[ ] him
[ ] you	[ ] she	[ ] you	[1] her
[ ] we	[ ] it	[ ] us	[ ] it
[ ] they		[ ] them	

Test tip

Often the answer choices will have both possessive adjectives (e.g. *my*) and pronouns (e.g. *mine*). Look at the sentence to decide whether the blank is modifying a noun (possessive adjective) or replacing it (possessive pronoun).

C For each of the following sentences decide whether the missing word is a possessive pronoun (P) or a possessive adjective (A). The first one has been done for you.

1. I would like to confirm that responsibility for the decision was .... alone. [P]
2. Ms. Evans was given a gift to commemorate .... years of service. [ ]
3. Once you sign the contract, the property will be .... to do with as you like. [ ]
4. The men have agreed to sell .... half of the business. [ ]
5. I believe your shop is responsible for the damage to .... car. [ ]
6. Tom Baxter started the program last year, so all the credit should be .... [ ]

D Choose the best pronoun from the list below to complete each of the sentences above. The first one has been done for you.

Possessive Pronouns		Possessive Adjectives	
[1] mine	[ ] his	[ ] my	[ ] his
[ ] yours	[ ] hers	[ ] your	[ ] her
[ ] ours	[ ] its (not common)	[ ] our	[ ] its
[ ] theirs		[ ] their	

Grammar note

Possessive adjectives are generally found next to the noun. Sometimes, though, there may be another adjective before the noun.

Follow up: Compare choices with your partner, then make one or two similar sentences with the pronouns/adjectives you didn't use.

2 Test tactic: Indefinite pronouns

Use the Test tip on this page to help you choose the answer choice that best matches each sentence below. The first one is done for you.

1. ...A... of the things that local people make would be in high demand on the open market.
2. .... told me that I had to submit the request three weeks in advance.

(A) Some
(B) Another
(C) Anybody
(D) Nobody

3. I can't think of .... else we could find a better location for the new branch.
4. John isn't riding his motorcycle because .... of its tires are flat.

(A) either
(B) somebody
(C) anywhere
(D) both

5. Please send .... of your receipts to the payroll section for speedy repayment.
6. The failed project has left us without .... working capital for the coming quarter.

(A) all
(B) every
(C) any
(D) many

3 Tactic practice

Use the tactics you have practiced to answer the following questions.

1. Please do not hesitate to contact us if there is .... else I can do to assist.
   (A) anything
   (B) anybody
   (C) anywhere
   (D) anyway
2. Ms. Bell has agreed to let us use the report .... prepared.
   (A) her
   (B) she
   (C) hers
   (D) herself
3. Our client is dissatisfied with the severance package offered to ....
   (A) he
   (B) himself
   (C) his
   (D) him
4. I'm afraid we do not have .... option but to complain to the union.
   (A) any
   (B) each
   (C) some
   (D) a lot
5. Jane and her new assistant attended the conference and .... were amazed at the huge turnout.
   (A) either
   (B) each
   (C) both
   (D) any
6. Unfortunately we cannot include .... in the list of presenters.
   (A) they
   (B) their
   (C) them
   (D) themselves

Test tip

Be aware of indefinite pronoun use tested in the TOEIC test

Below are some common indefinite pronoun uses tested in the TOEIC test.

Some(-one/-body/-where): used for sentences with a positive meaning

No(-one/-body/-where): used to give a negative meaning to a positive sentence

Any(-one/-body/-where): often used for questions and sentences with a negative meaning

All, any, both, few, many, more, other, several, some: used as plural

Every, each, either, -one: used as singular

Tactics checklist

☑ For personal pronouns decide whether the blank requires a subject or object pronoun.

☑ For possessives decide whether the blank is modifying a noun or replacing it.

☑ Watch for the common uses of indefinite pronouns.

unit 26

B Mini-test

Now apply what you have learnt at the actual test speed with questions 1–12.

> Recommended Time: 6 minutes (or less)
> Try using the 2-pass method to help you make the most of the time available. Try to spend no more than about 30 seconds on each item. If you don't know the answer, guess and move on.

1. Ms. Janus was not sure that there was .... we could have done to win the account.

(A) everyone
(B) everything
(C) anything
(D) anyone

2. The director was very .... to your ideas for revising our sales approach.

(A) receiving
(B) received
(C) reception
(D) receptive

3. In this situation I feel we must acknowledge .... shared responsibility.

(A) I
(B) my
(C) us
(D) our

4. The convention center is .... the office but on the other side of the river.

(A) between
(B) against
(C) along
(D) near

5. If your car is not fixed by the weekend you can borrow .... to pick up your mother.

(A) mine
(B) any
(C) some
(D) other

6. Bickertons has put in bids for several .... construction contracts as part of its urban renewal plan.

(A) valuably
(B) values
(C) value
(D) valuable

7. Our agents have informed us that .... of the containers were damaged in transit.

(A) one
(B) several
(C) any
(D) much

8. Our new line of women's fashions has proven .... to be a top seller.

(A) its
(B) hers
(C) herself
(D) itself

9. .... of the management staff realized the amount of time and effort that had gone into the job.

(A) Every
(B) Any
(C) Few
(D) Someone

10. In my opinion, ... of the candidates is particularly suitable for the position.

(A) neither
(B) both
(C) all
(D) either

11. No group meetings are .... unless special circumstances call for on-site evaluations of ongoing projects.

(A) necessitate
(B) necessarily
(C) necessity
(D) necessary

12. The results show that the decision to promote .... was entirely appropriate.

(A) you
(B) your
(C) yourself
(D) yours

C Grammar practice

A Pronouns allow us to talk without having to repeat the same words over and over again. Look at the story of Goldilocks and the three bears. Choose pronouns from the box below to replace the words in brackets to make the story sound better.

it	his	someone	they	she	my	her	their

The story of her (*Goldilocks*) and them (*the three bears*)

Once upon a time, there was a little girl named Goldilocks. One day (Goldilocks) (1) .... went for a walk in the forest. After a while (Goldilocks) (2) .... came upon a house. The door was open so (Goldilocks) (3) .... went in.

On the kitchen table, there were three bowls of porridge. Goldilocks was hungry, so (Goldilocks) (4) .... tasted the porridge from the first bowl.

"(This porridge) (5) ....'s too hot!" (Goldilocks) (6) .... exclaimed.

So, (Goldilocks) (7) .... tasted the porridge from the second bowl.

"(This porridge) (8) ....'s too cold," (Goldilocks) (9) .... said.

So, (Goldilocks) (10) .... tasted the last bowl of porridge.

"Ahhh, this porridge is just right," (Goldilocks) (11) .... said happily and ate (the porridge) (12) .... all up.

Goldilocks was very tired, so (Goldilocks) (13) .... went to the bedroom. (Goldilocks) (14) .... lay in the first bed, but (the bed) (15) .... was too hard. Then she lay in the second bed, but (the bed) (16) .... was too soft. Then (Goldilocks) (17) .... lay down in the third bed and (the bed) (18) .... was just right, so (Goldilocks) (19) .... fell asleep.

Soon the three bears came home.

"(An unknown person) (20) ....'s been eating (Papa bear's) (21) .... porridge," growled the Papa bear.

Then Mama bear saw that (an unknown person) (22) .... had been eating (Mama bear's) (23) .... porridge too.

Suddenly Baby bear noticed that (an unknown person) (24) .... had been eating (Baby bear's) (25) .... porridge too. "And (the unknown person or persons) (26) .... ate (Baby bear's porridge) (27) .... all up!"

(The bears) (28) .... decided to look around (the bear's) (29) .... house some more and when (the bears) (30) .... got upstairs to the bedroom, Papa bear growled,

"(An unknown person) (31) ....'s been sleeping in (Papa bear's) (32) .... bed."

"(An unknown person) (33) ....'s been sleeping in (Mama bear's) (34) .... bed, too" said the Mama bear.

"(An unknown person) (35) ....'s been sleeping in (Baby bear's) (36) .... bed and (a female person) (37) ....'s still there!" exclaimed Baby bear.

Just then, Goldilocks woke up and saw the three bears. (Goldilocks) (38) .... screamed, "Help!" and ...

B How do you think it ends? Finish the story, using pronouns correctly. In the next lesson share your story with your classmates. How was your ending different from theirs?

Go to word list and quiz page 188.

27 Reading Test Part 6 — Text Completion

A

Focus: Choosing the correct word: prepositions and conjunctions

Prepositions and conjunctions are common features of English writing. Understanding the ways they are used can help you choose the correct answer.

Test tip

Become familiar with how prepositions are used

Prepositions are tested in Parts 5 and 6. Familiarize yourself with the ways they are commonly used to help you eliminate wrong answers quickly.

unit 27

1 Language building: Understanding prepositions

English uses many prepositions to indicate time, location, movement/direction and place.

Time

A Choose the correct prepositions from the box on the right to complete the text. The first one has been done for you.

Mr. Sanchez will be arriving ...on... Monday the 25th (1) .... 5 o'clock. This will be his first visit here (2) .... April last year, so he hasn't seen our new factory (3) .... more than nine months. We are keen to show him the new production line, which opened (4) .... June, so we'll take him there (5) .... the 27th.

~~on~~
in
on
at
for
since

Follow up: Now discuss with your partner how to complete the following statements about time prepositions.

1. .... is used for times of the day.
2. .... is used for days and dates.
3. .... is used for months, years, and seasons.
4. .... is used for periods of time.
5. .... is used to refer to a point in time in the past.

Position

B Three common prepositions of place are *in*, *on* and *at*. Familiarize yourself with some common patterns of usage for these words.

in	**on**	**at**
She is in the living room. She is in her office. She works in Manhattan.	They are on the desk. They are on the bus. I found them on the floor.	He is at the bank. He is at work. Meet me at the corner of 11th and Broadway.

Follow up: Ask and answer the following "where" questions with your partner. Be careful which preposition you choose in your answer.

Where do you usually leave your keys?

Where do you usually meet your friends?

Where do you spend most of your time?

Where do you study English?

Direction

C Choose the correct prepositions from the box on the right to complete the text. The first one has been done for you.

I walk ..out of.. my house at 8 o'clock, get (1) .... my car, and drive (2) .... a parking lot, which is about five minutes on foot from my office. After parking, I walk (3) .... a short pedestrian street and then (4) .... the corner. From there I can see my office (5) .... the street. The traffic is always busy, but there is a tunnel that I generally walk (6) .... to get to the other side.	~~out of~~ along through around to into across

Follow up: Now describe your journey from your home/office to where you are now.

unit 27

Test tip

Compare two halves of a sentence

For questions testing conjunctions, compare the two halves of the sentence and consider their relationship. Use this information to help you choose the correct conjunction.

2 Test tactic: Understanding conjunctions

A Conjunctions are used to join two parts of a sentence together and express their relationship. If the answer choices are conjunctions, look at the two halves of the sentence before and after the conjunction to help you choose the correct word.

Choose the appropriate conjunction from the box below to complete the following sentences.

and	nor	but	or	because

1. We decided not to buy the parts .... the cost was too high.
2. He passed the first interview .... failed the second interview.
3. Workers can apply now .... wait until a position becomes available.
4. The restaurant is famous for its delicious food .... its friendly staff.
5. Neither the price .... the quality of service meet our requirements.

B Other conjunctions occur in natural pairs. Learn to recognize these patterns to help you identify the correct choices quickly. Study the list on the left for thirty seconds. Then answer the questions on the right as quickly as possible.

both ... and
not only ... but also
either ... or
neither ... nor
whether ... or

1. We have the service to suit you, ... you want to travel in luxury or are on a tight budget.
   (A) not only
   (B) whether
   (C) both
2. Entering the building requires not only a keycard, ... a fingerprint scan.
   (A) but also
   (B) or
   (C) and
3. We will .... have to take the bus or get a taxi in order to reach the office in time.
   (A) neither
   (B) both
   (C) either

Tactics checklist

☑ Eliminate wrong prepositions quickly.

☑ Compare the two parts of a sentence to choose conjunctions.

unit 27

3 Tactic practice

Use the tactics you have practiced to answer the following questions. Read the questions, and quickly eliminate any definitely wrong answers before choosing the correct answer choice.

Questions 1–3 refer to the following letter.

Dear Mr. Anderson,

I am writing in response to your letter, which was sent .... us on

1. (A) to
(B) with
(C) of
(D) from

September 17th, inquiring about the availability of replacement parts for the CX232 fan heater.

Unfortunately, our principal parts supplier, HX Industries, has been experiencing difficulties at one of their main manufacturing plants, ... this has caused a

2. (A) but
(B) and
(C) because
(D) whether

delay in the delivery of of replacement parts. This means that we will not have parts .... the 16th of this month.

3. (A) in
(B) across
(C) since
(D) until

The parts you require will be sent to you as soon as we receive them.

Thank you for your continued custom.

Yours sincerely,

Hamilton S. Williams

Hamilton S. Williams

CEO Fantech

B Mini-test

Now apply what you have learnt at the actual test speed with questions 1–12.

> Recommended Time: 9 minutes (or less)
> Try using the 2-pass method to help you make the most of the time available. Try to spend no more than about 30–45 seconds on each item. If you don't know the answer, guess and move on.

Questions 1–3 refer to the following article.

The Tei Kai region is famous for its towering mountains to the north, and its desert plains to the south. Long known as a dry and barren region, it has undergone a transformation .... the last fifty years.

1. (A) while
(B) since
(C) at
(D) in

During this time, visitors .... a major change in the landscape.

2. (A) will see
(B) have seen
(C) had seen
(D) see

The construction of the Wan Hei dam enabled engineers to channel the waters of the Gang River for agricultural purposes. The result has been a narrow but expanding corridor of greenery spreading .... the once barren land. There has also been

3. (A) through
(B) out
(C) between
(D) without

a subsequent rise in the population and wealth of the region.

GO ON TO THE NEXT PAGE

Questions 4–6 refer to the following message.

A major goal in the coming year is to maximize the effectiveness of our recruiting decisions. Managers should use the following guidelines .... they begin

4. (A) since
(B) during
(C) through
(D) before

the recruitment process. First, have a clear job description. This should form a checklist of requirements needed by the people we wish to bring ....

5. (A) for
(B) at
(C) into
(D) with

the company.

Second, consider all possible sources of recruits, including applicants for previous positions who were qualified, but not selected.

Use telephone interviews to make decisions on which applicants to consider further.

Lastly, following these simple guidelines can improve hiring procedures ....

6. (A) neither
(B) both
(C) also
(D) either

for us and for our potential employees.

Questions 7–9 refer to the following memo.

Dear Arnault,

I am writing to let you know about the agenda for your visit to QMG .... March 27.

7. (A) on
(B) at
(C) since
(D) by

We have arranged for you to be met .... the airport and taken to your hotel.

8. (A) into
(B) through
(C) at
(D) on

In the morning we plan to show you around the factory and the new production line. Jim Tavarey would like to have a meeting with you in the afternoon. We will arrange a time for this .... you leave.

9. (A) while
(B) since
(C) before
(D) after

I look forward to meeting you and hope you have a pleasant flight.

Hank

unit 27

GO ON TO THE NEXT PAGE

Questions 10–12 refer to the following letter.

Dear Mr. Lewis,

It was very nice to speak to you last week. As we discussed, I met with the other members of the team and we have agreed to set the date for the banquet for April 26. We .... the sunshine lounge in the

10. (A) rent
(B) will rent
(C) rented
(D) had rented

Grand Hotel.

.... is this venue very reasonable in cost, it is also one of the few

11. (A) Even
(B) Therefore
(C) While
(D) Not only

that is still likely to be available at this late date. I have asked one of our staff to call the hotel and make the booking as soon as possible.

I have also spoken with the senior members of our marketing group about your visit and was able to confirm that they will be available to meet .... you the day after the banquet.

12. (A) for
(B) to
(C) with
(D) by

Please let me know if you have any further requests for your visit.

Yours sincerely,

Eric Quinn

Eric Quinn
Eastern Region Manager.

unit 27

C Grammar practice

Read the following email and fill the gaps with either prepositions or conjunctions from the boxes on the left. Be careful – there are two extra words in each box. Compare your choices with a partner in the next lesson.

on	in
for	at
to	by
as	

at	about
outside	around
before	through

so	next to
or	around
because	before

From: Paul McCawley
To: Hernando Gonzales
Re: Your trip to Dallas
Sent: Monday, February 11

Dear Mr. Gonzales,

We are very much looking forward to meeting you next week. We are all excited to hear about your proposals (1) .... the solar electric generator at the developers' conference (2) .... the 25th. (3) .... I believe this is your first trip (4) .... Dallas, I will be sending my assistant, Colin, to meet you (5) .... the airport.

I understand your flight is due to arrive (6) .... around 4:30 P.M. It should take (7) .... 30 minutes to get (8) .... customs and immigration, so I have asked Colin to meet you (9) .... the arrivals gate by 5:00.

We have arranged your hotel and evening meal, (10) .... you can relax when you arrive. Don't feel that you need to bring a tuxedo (11) .... other formal wear. We'll take you to a restaurant (12) .... the corner from the office, where you can get a taste of the real Dallas.

If you have any questions (13) .... you leave, please do not hesitate to contact me.

Paul McCawley

Go to word list and quiz page 189.

28 Reading Test Part 7 — Reading Comprehension

A

Focus: Learning how to answer questions dealing with charts, tables, forms and double passages

Questions involving charts, tables and forms, and questions involving double passages, require a slightly different approach. This unit focuses on dealing with these question types.

Test tip

Understand parts of charts, tables and forms

This will help you quickly identify the parts of the passage/chart/table where the information you need can be found.

Test tip

Skim the questions and passage to find information quickly

This will help you identify which part of the text is referred to. Then compare the answer choices to that part of the chart, table or form.

1 Test tactic: Dealing with charts, tables and forms

A Below is a list of features which may be found in questions that contain charts, tables or forms. Match the features (A–F) with the section of the e-mail or the table (1–6) that it best describes. The first one (A) has been done for you.

A. Background information related to the chart/table/form or the people who use it
B. Details of how information in the chart/table/form is meant to be used
C. Information about who the text is from or intended for
D. Details/facts/numbers/dates/names
E. Extra details that indicate changes/differences to the information in the chart/table/form
F. The main focus of the chart/table/form

1. ☐
From: gordon_billings@effron.com
To: andrew_fisk@effron.com
Date: Feb 11
Subject: March visit

2. A
Dear Andrew,

During my visit next month, I would like to discuss some of the different approaches to improving sales that were discussed at last month's sales conference. I would appreciate if you would set aside the whole day on 3 March

3. ☐
so that I can meet with you and your sales staff. I am including the most recent sales figures for last year for you to review before my visit.

See you next month,

Gordon

4. ☐ Sales of Effron Vehicles 2005

5. ☐

	Jan – Mar	Apr – Jun	Jul – Aug	Sep – Dec	Total Sales
Excelsior	756	598	899	465*	2718
Avenger	1024	1245	995	1523	4787
Townstar	3484	4756	6498	3156	17894
Pucchino	4735	4986	6512	4720	20953

6. ☐ * model discontinued in November

Test tip

Be careful of the "small print"

Charts, tables and forms may include notes or extra information at the bottom. Check this before choosing an answer to avoid making unnecessary mistakes.

Test tip

Watch for connected information between texts

In each double passage there will be at least one question that will require you to look at both texts and connect the information.

Test tip

Double passage questions

For questions on double passages, it is important to read *both* passages before you answer.

B Now answer the following as quickly as you can.

1. What does the chart show?
   (A) The number of vehicles sold by one manufacturer
   (B) Sales figures for four years
2. Who sent this e-mail?
   (A) Andrew Fisk
   (B) Gordon Billings
3. Which model sold the greatest number overall?
   (A) Avenger
   (B) Pucchino
4. Which was the most successful period for sales of the Pucchino?
   (A) July–August
   (B) January–March
5. What happened in January?
   (A) There was a sales conference.
   (B) The Excelsior model was discontinued.
6. How many Excelsiors were sold in December?
   (A) 465
   (B) 0

Follow up: Compare your answers with your partner.

unit 28

2 Test tactic: Locate information in double text questions

A Look at the questions below and quickly identify (by checking the appropriate box) where on page 152 you should look to find the answer.

1. How did Kelvin Adams find out about the apartment?	☐ Ad	☐ E-mail	☐ Both
2. What feature probably attracted Kelvin to this apartment?	☐ Ad	☐ E-mail	☐ Both
3. How many rooms are there in the apartment?	☐ Ad	☐ E-mail	☐ Both
4. What does Kelvin request?	☐ Ad	☐ E-mail	☐ Both
5. Which of the following is likely to be a problem?	☐ Ad	☐ E-mail	☐ Both

1. Where did Kelvin Adams see the ad?
   (A) On the Internet
   (B) In the newspaper
   (C) In a shop
2. What feature probably attracted Kelvin to this apartment?
   (A) The central heating
   (B) The price
   (C) The location
3. How many rooms are there in the apartment?
   (A) 2
   (B) 5
   (C) 6
4. What does Kelvin request?
   (A) Directions to the apartment
   (B) Pictures of the apartment
   (C) An appointment in March
5. Which of the following is likely to be a problem?
   (A) The availability date
   (B) The policy on pets
   (C) The apartment size

Follow up: Compare your ideas with your partner.

B Now, look at the answer choices and choose the best answer.

Questions 1–5 on page 151 refer to the following advertisement and e-mail.

Apartment for rent

- Modern downtown studio apartment located 10 minutes from shops and public transportation
- 2 bedrooms, kitchen, living/dining room, bathroom, balcony
- Centrally heated (gas)
- Suit young couple or professional
- Part furnishing can be arranged
- Rent $985 per month plus utilities
- Deposit + 1 month's rent in advance
- No pets
- Available mid-March

Contact Karim Patel 555 2345

Email: karim98@s_mail.com

To: karim98@s_mail.com
Cc:
From: Kelvin Adams (kelheart2@s_mail.com)

Dear Mr. Patel

I saw your advertisement in the local newspaper. I'm very interested in the apartment for my family. We are currently living in Westside, but are looking to move closer to the town center, by the end of February so this apartment would be ideal. I was hoping to be able to arrange a visit sometime next week. Monday would be the best day for us, if this is convenient for you.

In the ad, you mentioned that the place could be part-furnished. We have a small amount of furniture ourselves, but probably not enough for a two-bedroom place. Could you possibly tell us what inventory is likely to be included with the apartment?

I would also really appreciate it if you could possibly send us a couple of pictures of the bedroom and living/dining room, as well as some directions as to how to get there. Thank you very much in advance.

Yours

Kelvin Adams

3 Tactic practice: Charts, tables, forms and double texts

Use the tactics you have learnt to answer the questions below. After each item, confirm with your partner the clues that told you the correct answer.

***Consumer's Friend* magazine**

We do the research, so you don't have to!

In our efforts to keep consumers informed, we continue to look hard at product and pricing trends throughout the region.

This month's report focuses on a year-long pricing study of the 4 largest supermarket chains in the Greater Altonville area. For this study we surveyed 2 main food staples, eggs and bread, in each chain over a full year. Surveys on individual products showed little quality difference between each of the four stores. The main difference was the price, as shown in our comparison chart below.

Questions 1–3 refer to the following chart.

Tactics checklist

- ☑ Check what different parts of the chart, table or form refer to.
- ☑ Skim questions to identify where to look for answers.
- ☑ Be careful of the "small print".
- ☑ Watch for connected information between texts.
- ☑ Read both passages before you answer.

Price comparisons of major supermarkets

April	Eggs (dozen)	Bread (sliced medium loaf)
Floor Mart	$1.25	$0.95
5-9 Stores	$1.29	$1.15
Leavinson's	$1.35	$1.35
VFG	$1.20	$0.90*

August	Eggs (dozen)	Bread (sliced medium loaf)
Floor Mart	$1.26	$1.05
5-9 Stores	$1.35	$1.15
Leavinson's	$1.39	$1.45
VFG	$1.25	$0.95

December	Eggs (dozen)	Bread (sliced medium loaf)
Floor Mart	$1.26	$1.10
5-9 Stores	$1.40	$1.20
Leavinson's	$1.45	$1.40
VFG	$1.30	$1.10

* This food item was introduced in October.

1. Who are the intended readers of this report?
(A) Reporters
(B) Store owners
(C) Researchers
(D) Shoppers

2. Which company sold the cheapest bread in the first four months?
(A) Floor Mart
(B) 5–9 Stores
(C) Leavinson's
(D) VFG

3. What happened to the price of eggs at Floor Mart throughout the year?
(A) It stayed largely unchanged.
(B) It dropped slightly.
(C) It rose dramatically.
(D) It matched their competitors.

Questions 4–8 refer to the following advertisement and letter.

Suntours Holidays

Experience the welcoming culture of the Greek islands. Suntours Holidays offers you a once-in-a-lifetime opportunity to visit the unspoiled island of Kefalonia. Stay at the recently renovated Casa Stanoupolos Hotel, just five minutes from the beautiful blue waters of the Aegean. Each room has a balcony with a view of the beach, and a private bathroom. The hotel has two pools and a jacuzzi, as well as its own highly-rated restaurant, where you can enjoy some of the island's more traditional meals. You can also visit one of the local villages, where life continues much as it has for the past few hundred years.

Holidays include all flights and transfers, as well as a choice of one of two exciting tours: either a two-hour boat trip to nearby Turkey, or a chance to snorkel in the pristine waters of the local undersea national park.
Call (415) 555 4873 for more information on this fascinating vacation opportunity.

unit 28

132B, West Bayside
San Francisco, CA 94105

24 August

Dear Sir,

I am writing to complain about a recent trip I took with Suntours. I originally signed up for a two week trip to the island of Kefalonia, as advertised in *Newsmonth* magazine, and was looking forward to enjoying the holiday. Unfortunately, I felt that a number of things spoiled the holiday for me. Firstly, I was led to believe that all rooms in the hotel had a balcony with a view of the beach. However, my room not only did not have a balcony, but it faced away from the sea. Secondly, only one of the hotel's pools was open, the other was still under construction, and the promised jacuzzi was not there at all. The hotel's restaurant was excellent, but it was closed two nights a week, meaning that my family had to walk about 30 minutes into the nearest town to eat, as there was no evening bus service. Finally, we took the tour to Turkey, but could not leave the boat, as nobody told us we had to arrange visas in advance. Had we known, we could have chosen the other option.

I feel very disappointed about the trip, and would appreciate some compensation.

Yours truly,

Dave Clayman

Dave Clayman

4. How far is the hotel from the beach?

(A) 5 minutes

(B) 30 minutes

(C) 1 hour

(D) 2 hours

5. What is advertised as part of the package?

(A) A suite of rooms

(B) A private beach

(C) A chance to visit a second country

(D) A chance to visit historic ruins

6. How does Mr. Clayman feel about the hotel?

(A) He is unhappy there was nowhere to swim.

(B) He is angry his balcony was too small.

(C) He did not like the size of the Jacuzzi.

(D) He feels the advertisement misrepresented the hotel.

7. What was Mr. Clayman NOT disappointed about?

(A) The view from his window

(B) The quality of the food

(C) The tour to Turkey

(D) The lack of a bus service

8. Which option does Mr. Clayman wish he had chosen?

(A) The visit to the local villages

(B) The trip to Turkey

(C) The snorkeling tour

(D) The visit to Kefalonia

B Mini-test

Now apply what you have learnt at the actual test speed with questions 1–12.

> Recommended Time: 12 minutes (or less)
> Try to spend no more than about 60 seconds on each item; if you don't know the answer, guess and move on. If you have time at the end review any answers you weren't sure about.

Questions 1–2 refer to the following bill.

La Traviata Restaurant

Cole Road,
Baton Rouge, LA

Spaghetti with Meat Sauce		$14.95
Seafood Spaghetti		$15.95
Pizza with Italian Sausage		$16.95
Pizza with Mushrooms and Pineapple		$18.95
Sparkling Mineral Water	2 @ $03.50 =	$07.00
Tropical Fruit Punch – house carafe	2 @ $12.85 =	$25.70
Desserts		
Ice Cream		$03.99
Cheesecake	2 @ $05.99 =	$11.98
Fruit Salad		$04.50
Coffee	4 @ $04.95 =	$19.80
Sub Total		$139.77
Tax @ 12.5%		$17.47
Total		$157.24

Service not included

1. What can be inferred from this bill?
   (A) Spaghetti is more expensive than pizza.
   (B) Three of the customers drank mineral water.
   (C) Four people ate a meal.
   (D) Only two of the guests had dessert.

2. What single menu item on the bill is the most expensive?
   (A) Spaghetti with Meat Sauce
   (B) Coffee
   (C) Tropical Fruit Punch
   (D) Pizza with Mushrooms and Pineapple

Questions 3–4 refer to the following form.

Holiday Booking Form

Mr/Mrs/Ms	Given name	Surname	Dep. Date	From	To	Class	Holiday insurance
Mr	Sam	Fletcher	April 25	London	Barbados	Economy	(Y)/ N
Mrs	Ana	Fletcher	April 25	London	Barbados	Economy	(Y)/ N
							Y / N
							Y / N
							Y / N

Hotel	Room type	No. of rooms	No. of nights	Meals (Full/Half/BnB)	Check in	Check out
Montego Bay	Twin	1	9	Full	April 26	May 5

Special Requests balcony, private bath		Contact details: Address: 3, Victor Louis Avenue, Lyon Tel: (+33 47) 555 1566 Email: sam_fletcher@apex.com
For office use only	Booking agent: Jim Ng	Package code: A 1 2 3 C

3. What kind of room do the guests wish to stay in?
   (A) A double room with a balcony
   (B) A twin room with a shared bathroom
   (C) A twin room with a balcony
   (D) A double room with a private bathroom

4. What is the name of the agent who booked the tour?
   (A) Sam Fletcher
   (B) Jim Ng
   (C) Ana Fletcher
   (D) Victor Louis

GO ON TO THE NEXT PAGE

Questions 5–7 refer to the following report and chart.

The results in the chart below show that, as predicted, the new interview procedure has shown a significant increase in the level of education of our new recruits, at no additional cost. As we refine the procedure it is expected that this positive trend will become even more pronounced over the coming years.

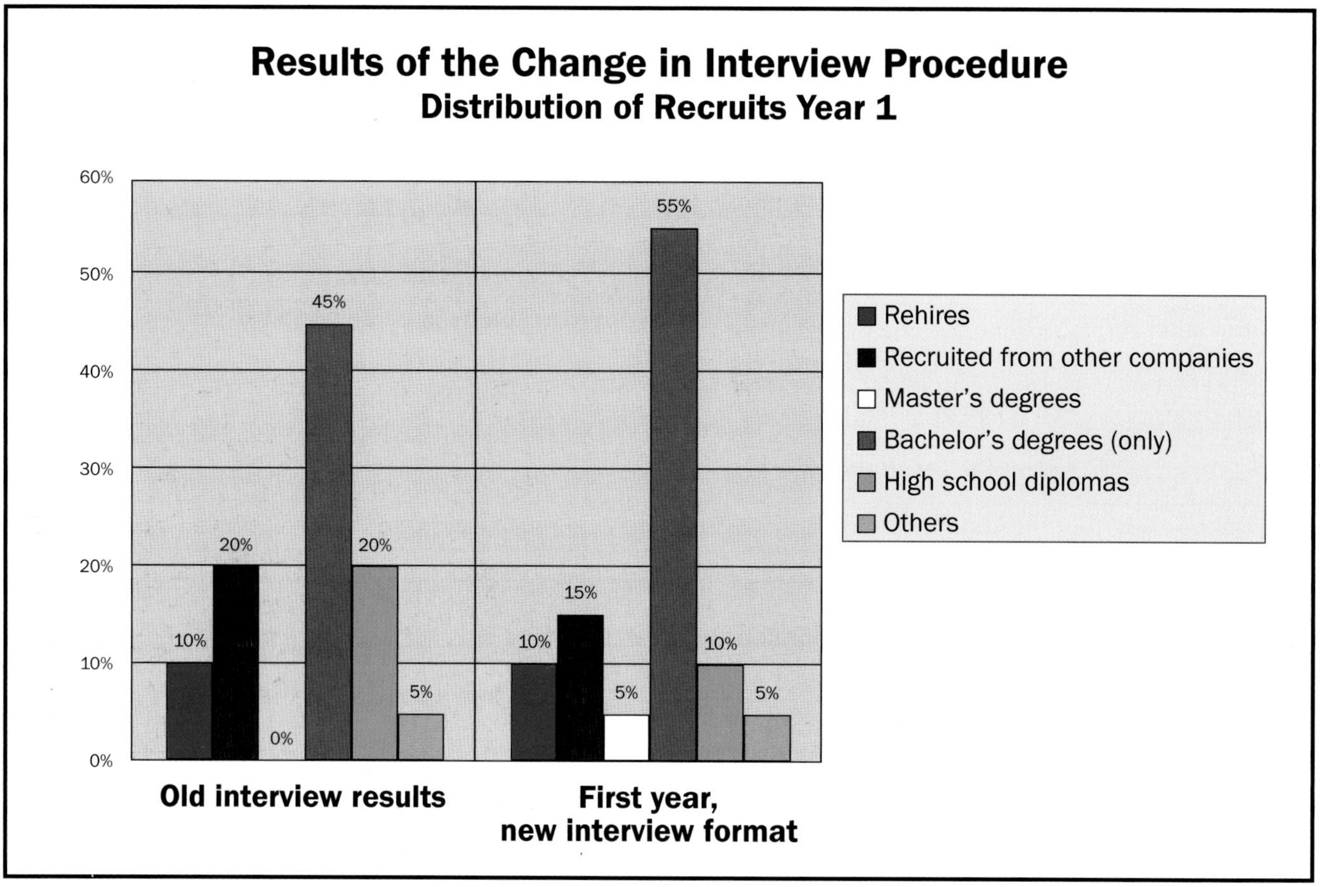

5. What does the writer note about the changes?
   (A) They need to be refined.
   (B) They will be expensive to implement.
   (C) They meet expectations.
   (D) They are insignificant.

6. Which group provided the fewest new employees over both years?
   (A) Candidates with Master's degrees
   (B) Recruits from other companies
   (C) Candidates who have only completed high school
   (D) Former employees

7. What is NOT indicated in the chart?
   (A) The percentage of university graduate recruits increased.
   (B) The percentage of rehires remained constant.
   (C) The percentage of recruits from other companies dropped.
   (D) In the old interview results most recruits were high school graduates.

Questions 8–12 refer to the following memo and e-mail.

MEMORANDUM

To: All members of the sales department
Re: Year-end party
From: Annette Derringer
Date: November 26

This is just a quick note to let you all know the arrangements for next week's year-end party. As you know, the party will be held at the Green Vale Country Club, which we have reserved between 7:30 P.M. and 10:00 P.M. on the evening of December 21st. I've received replies from almost all of you confirming attendance, but if you haven't let me know yet, please do so in the next day or two. Tickets for all employees have been covered by the company.

The Green Vale management have asked me to explain one or two things to those of you who have not been there before. Basically, there is sufficient parking space for only 100 vehicles, so they would like to ask those of you planning to drive, to try to car-pool as much as possible. Also, the number of lockers available is limited, so guests should try to keep belongings to a minimum.

Thanks in advance,

Annette

To: Annette Derringer aderringer@Belway.com
From: Kyle Berwick
Date: Nov 28
Subject: Year-end party

Annette,

This is to let you know that I will be able to attend the year-end party at the Green Vale Country Club on the 21st although I don't think I will be able to arrive before 8:30. I was wondering if it would also be possible to bring a couple of guests? I know it is a bit of a last minute request, but my brother and his wife are planning to visit us at that time, and I know they'd love to see the Green Vale. If it is not a problem, then can you let me know how much I should pay for their tickets? Also, assuming this is OK, I was planning to drive down in a single car, to reduce the need for parking and also to allow us to keep our belongings in the car.

I have a couple of days off before the party but I'll be in my office until the 17th, so could you get back to me before then?

Thanks a lot,

Kyle

8. What is the main purpose of the memorandum?
(A) To explain the arrangements for a special event
(B) To encourage people to travel by car
(C) To ask for help arranging a party
(D) To thank people for attending the party

9. Why does Kyle Berwick write to Annette Derringer?
(A) To ask the price of movie tickets
(B) To explain why he cannot come
(C) To request directions to a hotel
(D) To ask if he may bring guests to the party

10. Which of Kyle's points is NOT mentioned in the memo?
(A) Payment for extra guests
(B) Storage of personal items
(C) Parking restrictions
(D) Timing for the evening

11. What information does Kyle require?
(A) The date of the party
(B) The location of the Green Vale Country Club
(C) The price of additional tickets
(D) The name of the organizer

12. By when does Kyle ask Annette to contact him?
(A) By November 26
(B) By November 28
(C) By December 17
(D) By December 21

unit 28

C Reading in action

A Read the following advertisements, then discuss the questions below.

Position Available

High-level secretary required for firm located in central Los Angeles. Applicants should have good communication skills, reasonable computer skills and be able to type 80 words per minute.

Ability to speak French and Spanish an advantage.

3–5 years of experience with at least 2 years as secretary to top management a must.

Applicants should be prepared to work with high-level contacts while maintaining a calm and pleasant attitude.

Send résumé and cover letter together with two references to RTS International, Box 1244, Los Angeles, CA.

Secretarial position available in March

This job involves working for an independent film producer based in Los Angeles. You should be enthusiastic and knowledgeable about the movie business.

Minimum 2 years of experience required, secretarial skills, word processing, etc.

Send résumé and cover letter to Fanfilms, Box 1553, Los Angeles, CA

1. What kind of jobs are being advertised?
2. How much experience is required?
3. What special skills are needed?
4. What are the differences between the two jobs being offered?

B Now read the following reply to the first advertisement on page 160. Does this person fit the position?

RTS International
Box 1244
Los Angeles CA

Dear Mr. Williams:

I am writing in reply to your advertisement for a secretarial position, which I saw advertised in the *Gazette* on Monday.

After my graduation from secretarial school, I worked for a number of local companies for around four years, and developed my secretarial skills. I can type at 100 wpm, and I speak good Spanish, as well as basic French, which I am keen to improve. For the last two years I have been the personal assistant of the president of Shop-on, an Internet shopping company. I enjoy my work, but am looking for more of a challenge. I'm sure your company can provide me with that challenge.

I look forward to hearing from you.

Yours sincerely,

Miriam Masters

Miriam Masters

unit 28

C Complete the following cover letter for a person applying for the second job, using the words in the box below. Be careful: two of the expressions are not required.

secretarial duties	a secretary	would like to
have been responsible	good at word processing	my knowledge of
my enthusiasm for the job	very good typist	I am writing in reply
very excited to hear		

Fanfilms
Box 1553
Los Angeles CA

Dear Sir or Madam:

(1) .... to your advertisement in Movie Weekly. I was (2) .... about the position.

I have been working as (3) .... for the past three years, during which time I (4) .... for writing letters, answering the telephone and other (5) ....

I am (6) .... and have some experience with simple spreadsheets. I am also bilingual in English and Spanish.

I feel that (7) .... , coupled with (8) .... the movie industry, make me an ideal candidate for this job. I look forward to hearing from you.

Yours faithfully,

Consuela Peruzzi

Consuela Peruzzi

D Further study

Find a job ad or other advertisement in an English magazine or newspaper, and think of two or three questions to test your classmates. Write a response to the advertisement. Use your imagination.

Go to word list and quiz page 189.

Activity file 2

Student B

You are Barton Donovan, the Director of Seimex Watches America.
You just sent the following fax to your New York office.
You will get a call from Mr. Carson, as there are some parts of the fax he cannot read.

Task

- Read the fax now and confirm with your partner that you understand what it says.
- Then take Mr. Carson's call and answer any questions he may have.

Fax Message

Important

Re: August 14 meeting

Mr. Carson,

I am writing to let you know that I will be arriving on Tuesday August 13. I am flying with United Airlines and my plane is scheduled to land at 9:15 P.M. Could you arrange my hotel for me?

The main purpose of my visit is the problem with our Accuron Line of watches. We have had many complaints about water damage. We must discuss how we can deal with the problem. Please invite Paul Smith and Mary Davis also.

Barton Donovan

Activity file 8a

When your partner chooses a number, make a sentence to describe the picture. When it's your turn, choose a number and listen carefully to your partner. If they say one of the words on your bingo card you can mark it off. The first person to get all the words marked off is the winner.

Bingo card 1

B	I	N	G	O
holding	opening	sitting	wearing	shining

Activity file 8b

When your partner chooses a number, make a sentence to describe the picture. When it's your turn, choose a number and listen carefully to your partner. If they say one of the words on your bingo card you can mark it off. The first person to get all the words marked off is the winner.

Bingo card 1

B	I	N	G	O
standing	getting into	walking	enjoying	pushing

Activity file 11a

Read your partner the following business news report.

Your business news report
FHL Electronics announced its sales figures for the last financial year.
The president explained that the decrease in orders would lead to the closure of three factories.
The president blamed the disappointing results on increasing labor costs in Asia.
He apologized to his shareholders for the company's debts and promised that next year would be a much better one.

Activity file 17a

With your partner take turns reading one sentence at a time. They will try to guess the correct job, location or activity.

1. Sorry, I have to go to Boston on Tuesday. Could we make it for next Monday? (activities – **changing an appointment**)
2. Please open your books to page 20 and look at Unit 1. (jobs – **teacher**)
3. Would you like anything to drink with your meal? (locations – **restaurant**)
4. If you want to go to Bramston, you have to change at Union station to the central line. (jobs – **train conductor**)
5. This picture was painted by Samuel Evans just before his death in 1934. (locations – **art museum**)
6. Could you tell me how to get to the Miller building? (activities – **asking for directions**)

Activity file 15a

When your partner chooses a square read one of the questions from the same number square below. They must say whether it is "Correct" or "Wrong". If they are right, they get the square.

1.	2.	3.
A. The photographer is carrying the camera. **(Wrong)** B. They are filming a scene. **(Correct)**	A. The man is holding the dog. **(Wrong)** B. The dog is standing near the cowboy. **(Correct)**	A. The chef is cooking. **(Correct)** B. The woman is cleaning the kitchen. **(Wrong)**
4.	**5.**	**6.**
A. The machine is making a hole. **(Correct)** B. The worker is digging. **(Wrong)**	A. The boat is tied to the pier. **(Correct)** B. The ship is sailing across the bay. **(Wrong)**	A. The woman is making a bookshelf. **(Wrong)** B. She is reading. **(Correct)**
7.	**8.**	**9.**
A. The truck is plowing the road. **(Correct)** B. The road is clear of snow. **(Wrong)**	A. The man is using the restroom. **(Wrong)** B. The worker has stopped cleaning. **(Correct)**	A. The firemen are having a break. **(Correct)** B. The dog is standing near the truck. **(Wrong)**

Activity file 25a

Read out one of the following answers. Your partner must identify the question that best matches it. If they do, they score 1 point. If not, you have a chance to steal their point. Continue to take turns reading out all the answers.

Answers to "why" questions

(A) Governments are worried about their safety.

(B) They have decreased in the last few months.

(C) There was a clash with the annual general meeting.

(D) His plane took off late.

(E) The latest model is still under development.

Activity file 11b

Read your partner the following local news report.

Your local news report
The new Milltown Theater will officially open on Tuesday.
The first performance will be a modern version of *Romeo and Juliet*.
The famous actor, Tom Mason, plays the lead role.
Tickets went on sale one month ago and sold out almost immediately.

Activity file 17b

With your partner take turns reading one sentence at a time. They will try to guess the correct job, location or activity.

1. The acting was good but there wasn't much action. – (activities – **talking about a movie**)
2. What time does the pool close this evening? – (locations – **sports club**)
3. Yes, we have one with the same heel, but in brown leather. – (jobs – **shoe salesman**)
4. How much is a pound of tomatoes? – (locations – **supermarket**)
5. I'm not sure I like the color and the sleeves are a bit short. – (activities – **buying clothes**)
6. Can you help me copy these? I have a meeting in 15 minutes. – (jobs – **office worker**)

Activity file 22a

1. [PREPOSITION]
   A. The man is on top of the car.
   B. The man is leaning against the car.

2. [SIMILAR SOUND]
   A. The woman's hand is touching the box.
   B. The woman is turning the handle.

3. [SIMILAR SOUND]
   A. The flight attendant is wearing a red jacket.
   B. The door is very light.

4. [SIMILAR SOUND]
   A. The man is re-sitting the test.
   B. The man is sitting next to the control panel.

5. [PREPOSITION]
   A. The man is behind the computer.
   B. The keyboard is in front of the computer.

6. [SIMILAR SOUND]
   A. The man is cleaning the glass.
   B. The man is cutting the grass.

7. [PREPOSITION]
   A. The papers are on the desk.
   B. The papers are under the desk.

8. [PREPOSITION]
   A. The skiers are under the snow.
   B. People are on the chair lift.

9. [SIMILAR SOUND]
   A. The woman looks at the doors.
   B. There are locks on the doors.

Activity file 15b

When your partner chooses a square read one of the questions from the same number square below. They must say whether it is "Correct" or "Wrong". If they are right, they get the square.

1. A. Two men are standing near the camera. **(Correct)** B. They are watching a film. **(Wrong)**	**2.** A. The dog is running near the tires. **(Wrong)** B. The man is kneeling near the dog. **(Correct)**	**3.** A. The chef is working in the kitchen. **(Correct)** B. The kitchen is very dirty. **(Wrong)**
4. A. The worker is watching the digging. **(Correct)** B. The man is fixing the machine. **(Wrong)**	**5.** A. There is a lot of equipment on the pier. **(Correct)** B. The ship is leaving the water. **(Wrong)**	**6.** A. The woman is holding many books. **(Wrong)** B. She is standing near the shelf. **(Correct)**
7. A. The truck is pushing the snow. **(Correct)** B. It is snowing heavily. **(Wrong)**	**8.** A. The man is washing the sink. **(Wrong)** B. The worker is holding the mop. **(Correct)**	**9.** A. The firemen are sitting on the truck. **(Correct)** B. The dog is watching the men. **(Wrong)**

Activity file 25b

Your partner will read out one of the following answers. You must identify the question that best matches it. If you do, you score 1 point. If not, your partner has the chance to steal your point. Next it is your turn to read out an answer. (Check the key in the Tapescripts and Answer Key to make sure.) Continue to take turns reading out all the answers.

Answers to "how" questions

(F) By contacting the concierge.

(G) Much the same as today.

(H) There are a lot of innovations.

(I) By contacting the emergency number.

(J) It is a potential problem.

Activity file 22b

1. [SIMILAR SOUND]
   A. The plates are on the counter.
   B. The man is counting the plates.

2. [PREPOSITION]
   A. The student is leaning against the locker.
   B. The student is looking inside her locker.

3. [SIMILAR SOUND]
   A. The man is shipping some food.
   B. The customer is shopping for food.

4. [SIMILAR SOUND]
   A. The man tastes the food.
   B. The man tests the soil.

5. [SIMILAR SOUND]
   A. The people hide behind the building.
   B. The people hold umbrellas.

6. [SIMILAR SOUND]
   A. The diners sit around the table.
   B. Their dinner is on the table.

7. [PREPOSITION]
   A. The scientist is on the table.
   B. The student is in the laboratory.

8. [PREPOSITION]
   A. The people walk along the sidewalk.
   B. The commuters are between the buses.

9. [SIMILAR SOUND]
   A. The man is by a sign.
   B. The man is going to resign.

General glossary of terms

Terms used in instructions

brainstorm (v)	To think of many ideas on a topic quickly and creatively
focus (n)	The main or most important thing or things
key words (n)	The most important words in terms of meaning, usually nouns, verbs, adjectives and adverbs
paraphrase (v)	To restate something in other, usually simpler words
predict (v)	To say what is going to happen in the future. In the TOEIC test this usually means to guess what you are going to hear in the listening section
related (adj)	Connected in some way to an idea
scan (v)	To read quickly in order to pick out specific information (e.g. looking for a name in a phone book)
similar (adj)	Having some things in common but not completely identical (e.g. African elephants are very similar to Indian elephants)
skim (v)	To read quickly in order to get a general idea of the contents (e.g. quickly going over a movie review to see if it is worth watching)
tactic (n)	A method or technique used to achieve an immediate goal

Test-related terms

answer choices (n)	The four possible answers (A, B, C, D) you can choose from in the TOEIC test
context (n)	The background events or situation within which something belongs or takes place
denial (n)	A negative response to a request
distractor (n)	An incorrect option in a multiple-choice question
implied (v)	Something which can be understood or is suggested without being directly stated
infer (v)	To use context or related information to understand something that isn't directly stated
refusal (n)	A statement of an unwillingness to do something
response (n)	Something said or written in reply to a question or statement
similar sounds (n)	A common type of test distractor which uses a word or words which sounds similar to a possible correct answer

Grammar terms

noun (n)	A word which is used as the name of a person, place or thing (e.g. *John, Canada, pencil*)
verb (v)	A word that is used to show an action, or state (e.g. *run, is*)
adjective (adj)	A word that describes a noun or pronoun (e.g. *big, happy*), or gives extra information about them
adverb (adv)	A word that adds more information about place, time, manner, cause, or degree to a verb, an adjective, a phrase or another adverb (e.g. *look carefully, incredibly fast*)
subject (s)	A grammatical word describing the noun or noun phrase that performs the action in a sentence (e.g. ***Cats*** eat fish – "*Cats*" is the subject). Or in a passive sentence, the noun that is affected by the action of the verb (e.g. ***The tree*** *was blown over by the strong wind.*)
object (o)	A grammatical word describing the noun or noun phrase that is being acted upon or affected by the verb in a sentence (e.g. Cats eat ***fish*** – "*fish*" is the object)
preposition (prep)	A word which is used to indicate position, or movement in time or space (e.g. The ball is ***in*** the box, It finishes ***at*** 9:00, He is going ***into*** the store)
pronoun (pron)	A word that takes the place of a noun (e.g. *I, you, it*)
subject pronoun	A word that takes the place of a subject noun (e.g. *he, they*)
object pronoun	A word that takes the place of a noun (e.g. *him, us*)
indefinite pronoun	A pronoun that doesn't refer to any specific person or thing (e.g. *something, anything*)
suffix	A group of letters added at the end of a word that affects the meaning or use (e.g. "*-ed*" in "*amused*", "*-ly*" in "*slowly*")
prefix	A group of letters added at the beginning of a word that affects the meaning or use (e.g. "*bi-*" in "*bicycle*", "*pre-*" in "*predict*")

Word list and Quizzes

Unit 1

briefcase (n) a flat rectangular case for carrying papers, reports etc.
She had so many papers in her briefcase, it was difficult to close.

discuss (v) to talk about a subject with other people
The people are discussing something.
I would like to discuss our summer sales plans.

document (n) written paper which gives official information
They had all the necessary documents for the meeting.

keyboard (n) a set of keys used to type on a computer or word processor
His new computer came with a wireless keyboard.
While he was typing his essay, he accidentally spilled coffee on his keyboard.

pick up (v) to lift something from the ground or floor or another surface
The man and woman are picking up the wood.

presentation (n) a talk at which a new idea or information is given to an audience
The sales manager gave an excellent presentation of the new products.

wave (v) to move something back and forth
The man is waving his arms.

workshop (n) a place with tools and sometimes machinery where things are made
There are a lot of tools in the workshop.

Quiz 1

1 Complete the sentences with the following words.

briefcase discuss documents keyboard pick up presentation workshop waved

1 The computer is silver, but the .... is black.
2 My .... isn't big enough for all these papers.
3 He dropped his diary on the floor and quickly bent down to .... it ....
4 We need to .... a salary increase for our employees.
5 He had a little .... where he made some beautiful wooden furniture.
6 I .... at Jane, but she was on the other side of the road and didn't see me.
7 She made an excellent .... to the investors who agreed to back her idea.
8 I can't find those .... anywhere and I need them for the meeting this afternoon.

Unit 2

arrange (v) organize or make plans for something
Could you arrange my hotel for me?
My secretary will arrange the meeting time.

arrangement (n) a plan that has been made for an event
What are the arrangements for tomorrow?
We made the arrangement by telephone.

bother (v) to disturb or interrupt someone
I'm sorry to bother you Mr. Donovan, but I'm afraid we couldn't read your fax properly.

cheap (adj) low price, not expensive
Where can I buy a cheap air conditioner?
Airlines offer cheap prices to attract new customers.

complaint (n) a spoken or written statement expressing dissatisfaction with a product or service
The customer service department deals with all complaints.

customer (n) a person paying for goods or services
My customers live in Boston.
Why did the customer cancel his contract?

decide (v) to choose to do something after thinking about it carefully
I haven't decided yet.
I decided not to visit the conference this year.

(give someone a) lift (n) a ride in someone's car or other vehicle to a particular place
Mary gave me a lift.
I asked my father to give me a lift to the station.

goods (n) items that are produced by a company that are available for sale.
There's a range of goods.
We plan to expand our range of goods in the next two years.

notice (n) a sign displayed publicly giving information to a group of people
Have you seen the notice about the sheep?
The notice asked people not to smoke in the kitchen area.

parcel (n) a package, usually wrapped in paper, to be delivered by mail
What company did you use to ship the parcel?
The mailman delivered the parcel at 2 o'clock this afternoon.

profit (n) money made (usually by a business) above the money they spent
Has the sale improved profits?
The new product caused a profit rise of ten percent.

(be) receive(d) (v) the way people react to something
How were her findings received?
His presentation was very well received.

repairs (n) work done to fix something that was broken
How much are the repairs going to cost us?
The building needed a lot of repairs following the storm.

responsibility (n) an area of work you are in charge of
It's my responsibility to quality check the trainees' work.

terrible (adj) very bad, or shocking
Traffic can be terrible in this city.
The food at that restaurant is terrible.

Quiz 2

1 Choose the correct word.

1 I'm going to give Mr. Hargreaves a(n) .... to the airport.
(A) notice
(B) arrangement
(C) lift

2 The majority of customers have been satisfied with the way the company dealt with their ....
(A) customers
(B) complaints
(C) notices

3 I've already made a(n) .... to meet Howard tomorrow.
(A) bother
(B) lift
(C) arrangement

4 Please don't .... me again. I'm in a meeting.
(A) bother
(B) receive
(C) discuss

5 Helen's proposal was .... by most people at the conference.
(A) well received
(B) got along
(C) bothered

6 I applied for a new job because I wanted more ....
(A) hour
(B) presentation
(C) responsibility

2 Read the definitions and unscramble the words.

1 items produced by a company (*doogs*) g....................
2 a package (*epracl*) p....................
3 a person who buys things (*erctusom*) c....................
4 a sign (*entoci*) n....................
5 work done to fix something (*sparier*) r....................
6 low in price (*eaphc*) c....................
7 very bad (*ritrelbe*) t....................
8 choose to do something after thinking carefully about it (*eeidcd*) d....................
9 make plans to do something (*rrganae*) a....................

Unit 3

adapter (n) a device used to change the power from a socket to match the requirements of the appliance
You can run it with an AC adapter.
You'll need an international adapter to use your hairdryer overseas.

appointment (n) an arranged meeting, usually for some business purpose
He has to rush to an appointment.
I made an appointment to see the dentist next Thursday.

appreciate (v) to be thankful for something
I'd appreciate the company.
We appreciate your help.

assistance (n) help
She does not request assistance in moving her van.

block (v) to place an object or stand in a way that nothing can get past
You are blocking the emergency exit for the theater.
The boxes blocked access to the emergency exit.

branch (n) one of several offices or shops belonging to a larger group; part of a tree
She is at the wrong branch.
The bank has branches all over the country.
You should cut back the branches, they are hiding the sign.

company (n) having another person with you
I'd appreciate the company.
You can come with me to keep me company.

courier (n) a person, working for a delivery company, who is paid to take letters and packages from one place to another
The courier is going to pick them up in 15 minutes.
The fastest way to deliver items is to use a courier.

criticize (v) to say what you think is wrong with something
What did some trainees criticize?
His approach was criticized for being too aggressive.

feedback (n) information to let people know about their performance, usually at work
What kind of feedback did you get from the trainees?
The boss gives us encouraging feedback.

improvement (n) something that is better than a previous situation or version
It's an improvement on their previous one.
He has shown a steady improvement in the quality of his work.

included (adj) part of the contents of a package, not separate, not requiring additional purchase
The adapter isn't included.
Batteries are included.

label (n) a note attached to a product explaining some detail (e.g. the price)
The label is incorrect.
You can find the washing instructions on the label.

participant (n) a person taking part in an event
Comments from the participants...
3000 participants completed the marathon this year.

plug (it) into/in (v) to connect an electrical item to a socket
You can plug it into a socket.
Where can I plug my laptop in?

practical (adj) having a real and clear use
It doesn't have any practical value.
The training showed lots of practical ways to use the application.

purchase (v) to buy something
Purchase an adapter.
You can purchase tickets online.

replacement (adj) used in place of the original
...give a replacement part.
Since Tony left we haven't been sent a replacement worker.

request (v) ask for
She requested a vegetarian meal.
She requested assistance.

socket (n) the place you plug electronic items into the wall in order to provide them with power
You can plug it into a socket.
He plugged the television into the socket and switched it on.

stock (n) the number or amount of a product available to sell to customers
Check the part is in stock.
I'm afraid we don't have any of those in stock at the moment.

theoretical (adj) based on ideas rather than experience; opposite of practical
It was too theoretical.
The lecture was very theoretical, but seemed to make sense.

Quiz 3

1 Use the definitions to find the words to complete the puzzle.

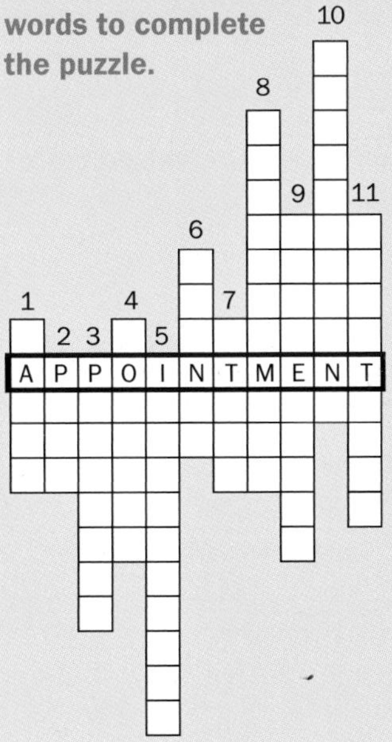

Clues

1 a note attached to something explaining its contents
2 to connect an electrical item to a socket
3 to buy something
4 a person who is paid to take letters and packages
5 something that is better than it was before
6 one of several offices or shops
7 the amount of goods available
8 something you use instead of something else
9 to feel thankful to someone
10 a person who takes part in an event
11 has a real and clear use

2 Complete the sentences with the following words.

adapter	assistance	block
company	criticized	feedback
included	requesting	socket
theoretical		

1 The cost of post and packing isn't .... in the price.
2 If your computer isn't working, check the .... Sometimes people forget to switch it on!
3 Please don't .... the entrance to the hospital.
4 I didn't get the job, but they didn't tell me why. I'm going to ask for some ....
5 I'd like some .... when I go to Singapore. I don't want to travel alone.
6 Don't forget to take your international .... to Japan. You'll need it for your laptop.
7 She asked for some .... in moving the boxes.
8 A lot of people have .... plans for a new supermarket in the area. They don't think it's needed.
9 The .... part of the exam requires a good knowledge of the highway code.
10 She received a wedding invitation .... her to attend.

Unit 4

apologize (v) to say sorry for an action
We apologize for any inconvenience.
He apologized for being late.

boost (v) to cause something to become better, larger or greater
We aim to boost our sales in this segment.
The good exchange rates have really boosted exports.

cancel (v) to request that an order or reservation be stopped
Service to Darby has been canceled for the foreseeable future.
I canceled my subscription to the newspaper as I didn't have enough time to read it.

complimentary (adj) offered without charge
We will shortly be serving complimentary tea.
The saunas are offered as a complimentary service to all guests.

deadline (n) the final date a piece of work has to be completed by
The deadline for the Q-com project has been moved forward by a week.
I need to ask for an extension to the deadline to allow me time to do more research.
getaway (n) a short holiday or place where you can make a holiday
A perfect spot for a tropical getaway.
We bought ourselves a little getaway in the Bahamas.
inconvenience (n) something that causes trouble or a problem for other people
We apologize for any inconvenience.
The road works caused a lot of inconvenience to commuters.
interrupt (v) to cause something to be stopped, to break into someone's conversation suddenly
Service has been interrupted due to the weather.
I'm sorry to interrupt your meeting, but there's an urgent call on line one.
isolate (v) to separate something from other things
Normally, our system would have isolated the virus.
The islanders were isolated from civilization for thousands of years.
neighborhood (n) district where people live
Help keep your neighborhood clean and attractive.
outline (v) to give a short general description of something
He outlined their business plans.
patience (n) an ability to wait without becoming frustrated or annoyed
Thank you for your attention to this matter and your patience.
His patience was rewarded.
pleasantly (adv) nicely, enjoyably
We were pleasantly surprised.
The evening passed pleasantly.
reduction (n) a change from a larger to a smaller number or amount
Sales showed a reduction in overall volume.
Workers had to accept a reduction in salaries due to poor sales figures.
refund (n) money paid back to a customer for an unsatisfactory product or service
We promise all our customers will be satisfied or we'll give you a full refund.
representative (n) a company's agent
Please contact our representative in your area, if you have any questions.
road conditions (n) the state of the road, usually due to weather or volume of traffic
Adjust your driving to road conditions.
secluded (adj) (of an area) hidden from sight, away from populated areas
It has miles of secluded beaches.
target (v) to aim at, to be intended for
The standard computer, targeted at the small business market, showed a reduction in sales.
tremendous (adj) very good, or a very large amount
It has a tremendous wealth of secluded beaches.
It was a tremendous effort to build the factory in such a short space of time.

Quiz 4

1 Choose the correct word.

1 The .... is Friday. Applications will not be considered after this date.
(A) getaway
(B) disposal
(C) deadline

2 Unfortunately, there has been a(n) .... in profits over the last few months.
(A) inconvenience
(B) reduction
(C) refund

3 The plane will be delayed by three hours. Thank you for your ....
(A) inconvenience
(B) patience
(C) notice

4 The train has been .... due to an earlier problem on the track.
(A) interrupted
(B) canceled
(C) refused

5 I'm sorry to .... your conversation, but the director would like to see you.
(A) apologize
(B) interrupt
(C) assist

6 The company is trying to .... its profits this year.
(A) boost
(B) include
(C) refund

7 The new manager has made a .... effort to be friendly.
(A) tremendous
(B) complimentary
(C) secluded

2 Read the definitions and write *true* or *false*.

1 *Inconvenience* means having an easy time.
2 If you get a *refund* you get your money back.
3 A *getaway* is a type of airplane.
4 *To apologize* means to be angry with someone.
5 *To assist* means to help.
6 If a beach is *secluded* it is very crowded.
7 If something is *complimentary* it's expensive.
8 If your house is *isolated* you don't live near other people.
9 Your *neighborhood* is where you live.
10 A *company respresentative* works for the government.
11 *Road conditions* are the state of the road.
12 If you *target* a group of people, you avoid them.
13 *Pleasantly* means horribly.

Unit 5

accommodation (n) a place to live or stay
The director was very happy with the quality of his accommodation.
I'm looking for new accommodation, as my current place is too small.
advantage (n) something that gives you a better chance than another person of success
Graduating from a famous university is an advantage for job hunting.
His ability to speak French gave him an advantage over the other applicants.
aid (v) to assist people in need of help, especially by giving money
The fund collects donations to aid local underprivileged citizens.
The government tries to aid health groups as much as possible.
(be) considered (v) thought by many people
Adam Antoniotti is considered to be one of the most impressive designers in the fashion industry today.
considerable (adj) significant
The rise in steel prices has resulted in a considerable increase in production costs.
convince (v) to persuade someone
He convinced me this was the right thing to do.
courier (n) a person, working for a delivery company, who is paid to take letters and packages from one place to another
The courier is going to pick them up in 15 minutes.
What time does the courier come in the evenings?
credit (n) money available to borrow from banks or other financial institutions
Careless use of credit can lead to trouble sooner than you expect.
Can I get this on credit?
distribution (n) the way goods are delivered from the factory to the shops
We can increase our sales margin by streamlining our distribution system.
The distribution of goods takes only a day or two.
donation (n) gift, often of money, to a charity
The hostel relies on donations from the public.
downturn (n) a change for the worse, usually of a country or company's economic situation
Small downturns in the US economy can have a global impact.
The financial situation took a bit of a downturn but it has now improved.
efficiently (adv) well, without wasting time and resources
They worked very efficiently as a team and completed the work in record time.
emergency (n) a sudden and serious situation
In an emergency, press the red alarm button.
Keep enough money to make a phone call in case of emergency.
immediate (adj) without hesitation, connected to now
...there was an immediate need to improve costs.
Is there any immediate action to be taken?

impact (n) the effect one thing has on another
Small downturns in the US economy can have a global impact.
The growth of the tourist industry has a tremendous impact on the environment.
improve (v) to make better
Customer service has improved considerably as a result of the new training programme.
influential (adj) having the ability to affect others
The news magazine published a list of the 100 most influential people in the world.
intently (adv) with great concentration
I listened intently to the directions he gave me because I didn't want to get lost.
optimistic (adj) having a positive feeling about something
They were optimistic about the outcome of the negotiations.
process (v) to deal with
It took the accounts department a couple of days to process the invoice.
reach (v) to communicate with someone by telephone
Please dial "9", then the number you wish to reach.
I've been trying to reach him all day.
recommendation (n) a suggestion, something thought to be a good idea
I don't think the consultant's recommendation will help the situation.
What is your recommendation for the main course?
retirement (n) time when you stop work because you have reached a certain age
She was pleased with her retirement present.
roughly (adv) approximately
You have to wait roughly 6 weeks for a refund.
select (v) to choose
Select a cell on the spreadsheet by clicking on it.
significant (adj) important, considerable
He noticed a significant change in his well-being once he started to eat healthily.
simplify (v) to make something less complicated
We can increase our sales profits by simplifying our distribution system.
We need to simplify our operations to reduce costs.
suggest (v) to put forward an idea, to propose
I suggest we take a break and come back to this tomorrow after a good night's sleep.
underprivileged (adj) poor and with less money and fewer opportunities than most people in society
The city welfare fund collects donations to aid local underprivileged citizens.
Charity should target the underprivileged.
welfare (n) money paid by the government to help those unable to help themselves
The city welfare fund collects donations to aid local underprivileged citizens.
Welfare payments account for 25% of all taxes.
work–life balance (n) situation when a person is happy with the amount of time they spend at work and not at work
A good work–life balance reduces stress.

Quiz 5

1 Complete the sentences with the following words.

accommodation advantage considered credit distribution downturn immediate impact recommendations retirement roughly

1 The latest project is .... to be our most ambitious.
2 Our company has a(n) .... fund that collects money for elderly people.
3 The use of .... when making purchases is convenient but should be used carefully.
4 We hope there won't be a(n) .... in the economy over the next few months.
5 The recent bad weather has had a(n) .... on the profits of many travel companies.
6 The director wants more people to receive our goods, so is planning to improve our .... service.
7 Mr. Green felt there was a(n) .... need to start a new project.
8 This .... isn't in a convenient location for our employees.
9 Simon has made several .... that the director has agreed with.
10 Speaking several languages is a(n) .... when working in the travel industry.
11 The application form takes .... one hour to complete.

2 Read the definitions and write *true* or *false*.

1 *Retirement* is an amount of money used to help workers with health costs.
2 An *attorney* is a businessman.
3 *Underprivileged* families have very little money.
4 If you *aid* somebody, you give them help.
5 To *simplify* means to make something simpler.
6 If you want to *reach* somebody, you want to get in touch with them.
7 A *courier* is a type of transport.
8 A company that is *optimistic* is worried about its future.
9 An *emergency* is a dangerous or very difficult situation.
10 *Considerable* means not very much.
11 If you *process* something, you don't understand it.
12 If you *select* something, you choose it.

3 Read the definitions and unscramble the words.

1 important, considerable (ficsigniant)
2 to propose something (guegsst)
3 to make better (rompive)
4 affecting others (alifinluent)
5 with great concentration (tyinlent)
6 to persuade someone (nonvcice)
7 gift, often of money, to a charity (nodation)
8 well, without wasting time and resources (yinefficetl)

Unit 6

audit (n) a financial review of a company, checking how much money or capital is present
Next week will be the annual expenses audit.
The audit discovered some financial irregularities.
complain (v) to express a feeling of dissatisfaction with something
I am writing to complain about the above noted large diesel generator.
We have to listen carefully when our customers complain.
confirm (v) to state that something is definitely correct
I am just writing to confirm...
I would like to confirm my attendance at next week's meeting.
consignment (n) a large amount of goods to be delivered
This vessel was carrying a consignment for our client.
We ordered a consignment of paper, but it has not yet arrived.
damage (v) to partially break
We found the camera lens was damaged.
fail (v) to not succeed
The ship failed to arrive as scheduled.
influential (adj) having a great effect on other people
He was one of the most influential scientists of the century.
His ideas were both brilliant and influential.
install (v) place something in the correct place, often used for computer software or hardware
The generator must be installed by the end of the week.
He installed a new hard drive to replace the broken one.
invention (n) a product or idea that nobody else has thought of before
His invention, the steam converter, was an important discovery.
His invention was patented and made him a millionaire.
licensing (n) getting permission to produce another company's design
We would like to discuss licensing of your design.
We are licensing our design to a Chinese company.
monument (n) a building constructed to remind people of a person or event
The city is building a monument to this great man.
The monument is in need of some repair work.
prompt (adj) done very quickly
A prompt reply would be appreciated.
He gave me a prompt response to my letter.
specification (n) how something is described, especially a technical product
The brackets were longer than our design specifications said.
We build all our products to the highest specifications.
tidy (adj) *clean and well organized*
He lived in a small, tidy house.
The desk is very tidy.
vital (adj) extremely important
It is vital that we receive these parts by Tuesday.
New capital is vital to our future success.

Quiz 6

1 Choose the correct word.

1 I'd like to .... about the poor service I received last week.
(A) evaluate
(B) complain
(C) confirm

2 Please would you .... that the parts will be available next Tuesday?
(A) install
(B) complain
(C) confirm

3 We were pleased to receive a .... reply from the company.
(A) prompt
(B) vital
(C) tidy

4 Ms. Lloyd is very .... She has changed the director's mind about many issues.
(A) influential
(B) tidy
(C) prompt

5 They are going to decide about .... our premises next week.
(A) licensing
(B) licensed
(C) license

6 A new air conditioning system is being .... today.
(A) reached
(B) installed
(C) carried

7 Mr. Rawson's desk is usually very .... , but today it's covered in papers.
(A) prompt
(B) vital
(C) tidy

8 It is .... that the generator is repaired immediately.
(A) prompt
(B) influential
(C) vital

9 When the goods arrived they were ....
(A) damaged
(B) damages
(C) damage

2 Match the words with the definitions.

audit consignment customer fail foreman invention monument specification

1 a formal examination of a company's accounts
2 if you don't succeed
3 a large amount of goods which are delivered to somebody else
4 a description of something especially something technical
5 a person that buys something
6 a new creation or discovery
7 something which is built in memory of somebody

Unit 7

administrative (adj) associated with the running of the company, especially organization of documents
He took an administrative position after graduation.
I'll show you your administrative duties after you have met everyone.

anticipate (v) to think about how something will happen
We anticipate complaints from our customers due to late delivery.
We couldn't have anticipated the demand for our products.

applicant (n) a person that sends their information to a company to try to get a job there
Due to the large number of highly qualified applicants, we have already filled the position.
Interested applicants should follow the procedure below to promptly receive their library cards.

assist (v) to give help with something
To assist customers, we offer a special 50% discount on Express costs.
The staff assisted us with our luggage problem.

barcode (n) a series of small black lines that, when read by a machine, give product details
Every product has a barcode to identify it.

benefit (v) to receive an advantage or help from something
Who will benefit from this?
Local residents will benefit from increased job opportunities.

certification (n) official documents
He provided certification to prove his qualification.

consignment (n) a large amount of goods to be delivered
...concerning the delay to your shipment, consignment number SD1278.
This vessel was carrying a consignment for our client.

enable (v) to give someone or something the ability to do something
You will receive a library number enabling you to place reservations.
The extra money enabled them to buy a new car.

facility (n) a building or piece of equipment used for a particular purpose
Follow the procedure below to make use of the full range of facilities.
The venue provides facilities for disabled visitors.

failure (n) lack of success
We are not responsible for failure to meet delivery schedules...
The failure to meet the deadline meant we had to change the schedule.

inquiry (n) a question or request asking for information
All general inquiries should be addressed to the Information Section.
The receptionist handles all basic inquiries.

intend (v) to plan or mean to do something
If your payment is intended for past-due charges...
How long do you intend to stay in Australia?

intended (adj) planned
Who is this shipment intended for?

intention (n) what someone plans or means to do
Please let us know as soon as possible about your intentions.
He did it with the best of intentions.

nominate (v) to make a decision and name it/them
Your card will be available at the branch library you have nominated.
He nominated Johnson as his successor.

non-payment (n) not paying for something
If your door has been tagged for non-payment, you must call 555-0874 to stop termination of water service.
Non-payment of bills will result in the telephone being disconnected.

potential (adj) possible
Who would not be a potential customer for this company?
It is a potential problem.

promptly (adv) quickly or as soon as possible
Follow the procedure below to receive your library card promptly.
He responded promptly.

reservation (n) an agreement that a hotel room, restaurant table, etc. is kept for the person who orders it
You will receive a library barcode number via e-mail (enabling you to place reservations)
Reservations can be canceled up to 24 hours in advance.

responsible (for) (adj) being a person's job or duty
I'm responsible for the overall running of the section.
Who is responsible for the maintenance of the company vehicles?

tag (v) to attach a label to something
If your door has been tagged for non-payment, you must call 555-0874
Tagged items should be taken to the cash register for removal of the devices.

termination (n) stopping something or bringing it to an end
If your door has been tagged for non-payment, you must call 555-0874 to stop termination of water service.
The termination date of the contract is April 30.

Quiz 7

1 Find nine words in the puzzle. Match them with their meanings.

R	E	S	E	R	V	A	T	I	O	N
C	R	U	O	S	B	D	I	F	N	T
E	Q	C	U	R	D	E	B	A	M	E
R	U	E	S	N	G	O	E	I	Y	R
T	D	A	E	E	G	D	I	L	N	M
I	A	T	C	U	O	E	N	U	E	I
F	N	I	E	C	B	S	A	R	L	N
I	E	N	R	A	O	E	R	E	T	A
C	I	A	A	N	E	S	U	I	E	T
A	B	C	N	A	K	S	R	E	N	I
T	I	N	Q	U	I	R	Y	A	B	O
I	E	F	A	C	I	L	I	T	Y	N
O	F	R	E	C	I	L	I	E	N	T
N	O	N	P	A	Y	M	E	N	T	M

1 something that is built or installed to serve a particular purpose
2 when something is ended
3 the opposite of success
4 the group of spaces, bars and numbers on something that are used to identify it
5 when something hasn't been paid
6 when something is kept back for somebody
7 giving something official recognition
8 request for information
9 to plan to do something

2 Complete the sentences with the following words.

administrative anticipate applicants assist benefit consignment enable intended intention nominate potential promptly responsible tag

1 Please .... somebody for *The employee of the year* award.
2 All .... for the post of manager should complete the following form.
3 My .... is to ask for a refund.
4 All employees will .... from the marketing course.
5 A credit card will .... you to buy things more freely.
6 We .... a rise in profits due to successful sales.
7 We can .... employees with their moving costs abroad.
8 I don't think I'm a(n) .... candidate for the job as I don't have enough experience.
9 The package didn't arrive at its .... destination. It went to Singapore instead.
10 The marketing director is .... for the problems we've had this year.
11 If we leave .... , we should arrive on time.
12 If your property has a .... on it, please take it to reception where it will be removed.
13 A new .... of goods arrived yesterday.
14 The order was placed twice due to .... errors.

Unit 8

collect (v) to gather things together and keep or bring them somewhere
The woman is collecting their cups.
He collects old swords and displays them in his living room.
customer (n) a person (or company) who buys goods or services
Marshall Steel is one of our largest customers.
guardrail (n) a rail acting as a safety barrier at the side of a road, or other dangerous area
The guardrail divides the highway.
His mother told him to hold tightly to the guardrail along the steep mountain path.
hang (v) to put something in a position so that the top part is fixed or supported and the lower part is free to move
They are hanging their jackets on a hook
harbor (n) a port surrounded by walls or land
The harbor was full of ships.
hold (v) to keep, carry or temporarily support something
The woman is holding a coffee cup.
Can you hold this light for me while I fix the engine?
lie (on something) (v) to be positioned on a flat horizontal surface
The snow lies deeply on the farmer's field.
I think I saw your hat lying on the bed.
monitor (n) a video device used to view data or images from a computer
The computer monitors cover the wall.
My new computer has a 19 inch flat screen monitor.
overpass (n) a road that crosses over another road
The overpass casts a shadow on the road.
The police car waits under the overpass to catch speeding cars.
passenger (n) someone traveling in a vehicle who is not the driver or a crew member
The passenger is getting out of the taxi.
The passengers of the boat were unhappy about the poor food.
revise (v) to study before an exam; also, to change something in order to correct, update, or improve it
The students met to revise their notes before the exam.
Her manager asked her to revise the report before the meeting.
shine (v) to be very bright or reflect light
The sun was shining over the lake.
The stars were shining so brightly we could walk without lights.
skyscraper (n) a building that is extremely tall.
The skyscrapers stand near the docks.
The bank built a 50-story skyscraper for its head offices.
tent (n) a portable fabric shelter used for camping
The tent sits on the beach.
tower over (v) to be much taller than something nearby
Skyscrapers tower over the harbor.
withdraw (v) to take money out of a bank account
The woman is withdrawing her money.
I would like to withdraw $20 from my savings account.

Quiz 8

1 Choose the correct word.

1 A(n) *overpass / freeway* is a road that passes over another road.
2 A *monitor / skyscraper* is a very tall building.
3 A *customer / passenger* is somebody who travels.
4 A *harbor / tent* is an area where there are boats.
5 To *hold / collect* means to gather things together.
6 To *revise / withdraw* means to study before an exam.

2 Complete the sentences with the following words.

customer guardrail holding lie monitor shining tent tower over withdraw

1 I need to .... some money for my holiday.
2 It's a dangerous road and should have a ....
3 I'm tired and I need to .... down.
4 The screen on my .... is dirty. I can't read the information properly.
5 I'm so tall, I .... my colleagues.
6 The .... asked for coffee, but the waiter brought him tea.
7 The sun was .... so we went for a walk.
8 The man was .... a bag and an umbrella.
9 I enjoyed sleeping in a .... when we were on holiday even though it was cold.

Unit 9

available (adj) free to do something (for people), or be used for some purpose (for objects)
Did she say when she would be available?
Are there any seats available on the flight?
briefcase (n) a kind of bag, usually made of leather and carried by business people to hold their documents
This is your briefcase, isn't it?
I left my briefcase on the train and had to go to the lost and found to claim it.
custom (n) a tradition or habit, usually associated with a country or region
Yes, it's an old custom.
The custom still continues in local areas.
depart (v) to leave a location, usually by some form of transportation
No, he's departing tomorrow.
My flight departs at 3 P.M. so I have to be at the airport by 1 P.M.
detailed (adj) including a lot of information
Yes, it was very detailed.
He gave me a detailed description of the product.
drive (v) to operate a motorized vehicle
Can you drive?
I learned to drive when I was 17 and I have never had an accident.
forget (v) to be unable to remember
No, I forgot to ask her.
I forgot to bring a pen, so can I borrow one from you?
handy (adj) convenient, or very useful
I thought it was very handy.
The cell phone is a handy tool for keeping in touch when on the move.
invite (v) to ask guests to attend a party or other function
Everyone has been invited.
I am going to invite some of my friends to dinner tomorrow night.
member (n) a person who has joined an organization or group
No, he's not a member.
I was a member of my school's soccer team.

mind (v) to feel strongly that something is not acceptable
Do you think they would mind if I came along?
I don't mind the heat, but I do mind the humidity.
prefer (v) to like one thing more than another
I prefer pop music.
Would you prefer to drink tea or coffee with breakfast?
prepare (v) to get something ready to be used
Could you help Laura to prepare the documents?
The men are preparing dinner in the kitchen.
probably (adv) likely to be true, also used to express an opinion in a more polite manner
You should probably call them first.
He'll probably arrive on the next train.
rearrange (v) to make an alteration to a plan or schedule
Could you rearrange the venue for me?
We can rearrange the meeting for next Tuesday, if that is convenient?
(read/go) through (adv) read or say something from beginning to end
You read through the notes, didn't you?
He went through the process to show us how it worked.
top (n) an item of clothing worn on the upper body
Yes, it's a new top.
Which top should I wear with my new skirt?
understand (v) to know the meaning of something and be able to follow it
Yes, but I couldn't understand them.
I understood the announcement.
unfortunately (adv) causing someone to feel regret, or express sadness or disappointment
Unfortunately, he can't join us because he's on holiday then.
We bought tickets, but unfortunately we didn't win anything.
upstairs (n) the floor above where the speaker currently is
I think he's upstairs.
The bathroom is upstairs, next to the master bedroom.
venue (n) the place where an event is to be held
Could you rearrange the venue for me?
The venue for this year's general meeting had to be changed at the last minute.

Quiz 9

1 Choose the correct word.

1 I've got a new, black, leather ....
(A) briefcase
(B) venue
(C) custom

2 I bought a .... to go with my new outfit.
(A) top
(B) venue
(C) briefcase

3 I need to .... a report for tomorrow's meeting.
(A) forget
(B) drive
(C) prepare

4 I don't .... doing overtime sometimes, but I don't like working every weekend.
(A) prefer
(B) mind
(C) understand

5 What kind of music do you ....?
(A) mind
(B) prefer
(C) rearrange

6 I .... to buy some milk. Could you get some on your way home?
(A) prepared
(B) minded
(C) forgot

7 Could we .... the meal? I'm busy this evening.
(A) prefer
(B) rearrange
(C) understand

8 I don't .... what you're saying. Could you repeat it?
(A) forget
(B) understand
(C) mind

9 .... the company hasn't done well this year.
(A) Through
(B) Unfortunately
(C) Neither

10 Let's .... the document together after work.
(A) go through
(B) do through
(C) be through

11 It's a .... in our office not to wear a tie on Fridays.
(A) briefcase
(B) custom
(C) top

2 Use the definitions to find the words to complete the puzzle.

Clues
1 leave
2 operate a vehicle
3 on a floor above
4 ask someone to a party
5 likely to be true
6 useful
7 a person belonging to a group
8 including a lot of information
9 a place where an event is held

Unit 10

argument (n) a disagreement that often involves people getting angry with each other
It turned into a major argument.
They haven't been able to settle their argument.
attend (v) to go to or be present at a function (usually formal)
Why didn't George attend the meeting?
I attended my sister's wedding.
carelessness (n) not taking care of what you should be doing
A worker's carelessness.
Carelessness in the factory causes accidents.
definitely (adv) certainly, surely, having no doubts
I definitely plan on staying with the company.
It's definitely not an easy test.
demanding (adj) for people, frequently asking for attention, usually unreasonably so; for jobs, very difficult
My boss is very demanding.
It is a demanding job.
disagreement (n) a difference of opinion between people (not as strong as an argument)
There was a disagreement between attendees.
There is still disagreement about what caused the dinosaurs to die out.
discount (n) a reduction in price
I would like a discount.
Can I get a discount if I pay by cash?
document (n) a piece of paper that contains important information
Who filed these documents?
I'll need those documents on my desk first thing tomorrow morning.
drastically (adv) change by a large amount, a sudden and marked difference
Stubbs wants to drastically cut back on the sales staff.
Sales of the product dropped drastically following the recall.
file (v) to place documents in their correct order in a cabinet
He hates filing documents.
We must finish filing these reports before we go home.
inexperienced (adj) new to a job or activity, not having much knowledge about it
The people she works with are inexperienced.
Inexperienced divers should be accompanied at all times.
mileage (n) the amount of gas used by a vehicle to operate
The gas mileage is very low.
Compact cars tend to get very good mileage.
pushy (adj) often making other people do what he/she wants them to do, usually unreasonably so
My new boss is very pushy.
I don't like pushy people telling me what to do.
receipt (n) a printed record of a cash transaction, used to prove purchase
He needs to see the receipt.
You'll need to provide the receipt in order to get a refund.
recent (adj) happening in the near past
To discuss a recent argument with employees.
The company has had several recent resignations.

refund (n) money paid back to a customer for an unsatisfactory product or service
The woman can have a refund.
We promise all our customers will be satisfied or we'll give you a full refund.
satisfied (adj) happy with a situation, reasonably content
I am not satisfied with it.
I was satisfied with our sales last year, but I think we can do even better this year.
seminar (n) a class or lesson where a group of people discuss a topic
It was a seminar on natural resources.
The management seminar will be held in room 202 this afternoon.
shipping (n) money paid for delivery of goods
Free shipping.
Shipping is not included in the price.
situation (n) what happens or happened to you
I was in the same situation with my dad.
We will try to avoid that situation if possible.
suggest (v) to offer your idea on how to do something
What does the woman suggest?
I suggest we wait until tomorrow before completing this project.
turnover (n) the amount of money made by a company; for people, the number of people leaving and replaced by the company
Her company has high employee turnover.
The company makes a turnover of $3 million.

Quiz 10

1 Read the definitions and write the words.

1 money you get back when you return an item (furedn) r....................
2 to be present at a function (ndtaet) a....................
3 to place documents in their correct order (efli) f....................
4 the kind of person who makes others do what he/she wants (usyhp) p....................
5 a reduction in price (cidsuont) d....................
6 a printed record of a transaction (ecirtpe) r....................

2 Find eight words in the puzzle which match the definitions in the next column.

D	I	S	A	G	R	E	E	M	E	N	T
E	S	S	T	H	U	S	W	U	L	E	I
T	H	E	U	E	T	Y	M	C	S	S	T
P	I	E	E	G	W	N	A	I	W	A	U
O	P	X	J	A	G	C	A	L	R	T	R
U	P	C	W	Q	Y	E	E	N	S	I	N
G	I	E	T	M	A	E	S	N	C	S	O
L	N	E	U	I	E	R	S	T	T	F	V
A	G	D	T	O	A	E	O	N	H	I	E
V	E	T	U	N	I	T	E	H	C	E	R
A	E	N	I	D	I	C	D	E	O	D	H
I	E	M	R	S	E	A	O	M	E	Q	P
U	E	W	E	R	B	U	T	I	P	U	I
S	D	O	C	U	M	E	N	T	E	B	D

1 a class or lesson where a group of people discuss a topic
2 a difference of opinion between people
3 money paid for delivery of goods
4 the amount of money made by a company
5 a piece of paper that contains company information
6 to offer an idea about something
7 happening not long ago
8 happy with a situation

3 Complete the sentences with the following words.

argument carelessness definitely demanding drastically inexperienced mileage situation

1 Our manager is in a very difficult .... because he agrees with the workers' complaints.
2 He knows a lot about the company, but he's very young and ....
3 There was a big .... at the union meeting last night.
4 .... is dangerous in a factory.
5 I'm .... going to apply for the job as foreman. I'm ready for a change.
6 The .... on our new car isn't very good, so we use a lot of gas.
7 Being a department manager is very .... sometimes.
8 They .... dropped the price for a quick sale.

Unit 11

bankrupt (adj) of companies or individuals, to not have enough money to pay expenses or debts
After years of bad sales, the company was bankrupt.
It is a bankrupt organization.
boast (v) to proudly talk about one's achievements; to be proud to possess
We are also proud to boast two junior regional champions.
He always boasts about his new car.
closure (n) the act of closing a factory, shop or other business
The closure of factories led to rising unemployment.
We will need to increase profits to avoid branch closures.
cordless (adj) not connected by any cables
It has a cordless telephone handset.
The cordless speakers work by using radio technology.
debt (n) money that is owed to another person or, often, a bank or other financial institution
He was unable to pay his debts.
The company accumulated large debts by unwisely expanding.
delighted (adj) very happy
I'm delighted to be able to report that sales are up.
He was delighted with his birthday gift.
double (v) to become twice as large
We almost doubled the number of customers.
The price has doubled since last year.
elderly (people) (adj) of people, old
There is a home for elderly people near my house.
Society has a responsibility to take care of the elderly.
expand (v) to increase in size
Last year we expanded our field of operations.
The number of Internet users expanded rapidly in the late twentieth century.
gesture (n) something done to express your feelings, often to express thanks
It would be a nice gesture to get him something for his birthday.
It was a generous gesture to donate your prize to charity.
mention (v) to tell someone a piece of news, often in casual conversation
Don't mention this to him.
John mentioned that he was thinking of moving to New York.
overall (adj) total, complete, related to the whole thing
It will improve your overall fitness.
politician (n) a government official, chosen by the people
The politicians will meet to discuss the new tax laws.
Our local politician will be visiting the hospital this week.
remarkable (adj) amazing, incredible, different to normal (generally used to express a positive feeling)
It was remarkable.
It is in remarkable condition.
renovate (v) to repair something to a condition as good as new
It was totally renovated just six months ago.
The house really needs to be renovated.
respond (v) to do something to meet another person's needs or request
You will need to be able to respond to customer needs.
I'd like you to respond to this inquiry.
responsible (for) (adj) being a person's job or duty
I'm responsible for the overall running of the section.
Who is responsible for completing the annual sales report?
shareholders (n) people that own stocks or shares of a company
Each shareholder receives a percentage of the company's profits.
There is a shareholders' meeting next week.
spacious (adj) large, wide, having lots of space
The kitchen is quite spacious.
There is a spacious office with a view of Manhattan.
unfavorable (adj) not to someone's advantage, bad
Sales were affected by unfavorable exchange rates.
We were unable to ski, due to unfavorable weather conditions.
venture capitalist (n) a person that invests in new businesses, expecting to make money in return
We approached some venture capitalists about support for developing our prototype.
Without venture capitalist money, the project would never have been successful.

Quiz 11

1 Choose the correct word.

1 I think it would be a nice .... to buy James a leaving present.
(A) closure
(B) gesture
(C) venture

2 The .... of the factory resulted in strikes.
(A) tremor
(B) debt
(C) closure

3 The company .... last year which means more people will be employed.
(A) renovated
(B) expanded
(C) struggled

4 I am proud to .... a huge increase in profits for the company.
(A) boast
(B) expand
(C) double

5 A good manager .... to the requests of his or her workers.
(A) boasts
(B) responds
(C) refunds

6 I need to .... the fact there will be some job losses next year.
(A) mention
(B) respond
(C) renovate

7 Our offices are small. We need something more ....
(A) delighted
(B) cordless
(C) spacious

8 There were a few problems, but the .... feeling was that the meeting went well.
(A) overall
(B) delighted
(C) remarkable

9 Simon is .... for the new project.
(A) depressing
(B) responsible
(C) overall

2 Read the definitions and write *true* or *false*.

1 If a price *doubles* it goes down by half.
2 A *politician* is a government official.
3 *Venture capitalists* are people that invest in new businesses.
4 *Shareholders* usually receive the whole of a company's profits.
5 A *debt* is money owed to somebody.
6 If a company is *bankrupt* it doesn't have enough money to continue.
7 To *renovate* means to improve the way somebody looks.
8 *Elderly* people are old.
9 If something is *unfavorable* it isn't to someone's advantage.
10 *Remarkable* means amazing.
11 If something is *cordless* it is connected by cables.
12 If you are *delighted* you are very happy.

Unit 12

advanced (adj) including recent technology
I wish I had bought a more advanced model.
The machines are the most advanced ones available.
advise (v) to tell someone what you think they should do
I advised her to invest in steel.
He advised me not to buy now.
alternative (adj) a further choice, or a different option
Union leaders agreed to discuss an alternative proposal.
We need to find an alternative route to the station.
applicant (n) a person that sends their information to a company to try to get a job there
There are at least fifty applicants for each job.
careless (adj) lacking in attention (Also see glossary Unit 10, **carelessness**)
Most workplace accidents are due to careless practices.
He was charged with careless driving by the police.
demand (v) to make a very clear request using direct language
I demanded to speak to the manager.
If it is not possible, then I demand to know why.
entrée (n) the main course of a meal in a restaurant
I waited more than thirty minutes for my entrée to arrive.
Would you like meat or fish for your entrée?
evidence (n) something used to connect a person with a crime
The judge promised to look into any new evidence as soon as possible.
gradually (adv) at a slow pace, not quickly
Black and white television sets were gradually replaced.
He is gradually recovering from his injuries.
impression (n) how something makes you feel, your initial feeling about it
You will make a good impression at the conference next month.
limousine (n) a long, luxury car, used to take (usually rich) passengers from one place to another
The President's limousine should be here soon.
We can send a limousine to meet you at the airport.
principal (adj) main, most important
It appears that our principal rivals are considering our proposal.
The principal reason is that customers traditionally stay at home on that day.
questionnaire (n) a series of written questions to determine a person's opinions, status or habits
Passengers must complete an immigration questionnaire.
Can I ask you to help me with this questionnaire?
regret (v) to feel bad about something you have done in the past; to wish something had been done differently
I regret not buying a more advanced camera.
Do you regret leaving your previous job?
rivals (n) competitors, those trying to achieve the same goal as an individual or company
Our business rivals strongly oppose our takeover proposal.
Following the takeover, there were no real rivals in their business.
takeover (n) when one company buys another company
Our principal rivals may be considering a takeover proposal.
We will resist any attempts at a takeover.
variety (n) choice, selection, many different things
During winter many people enjoy a variety of winter sports.
There was a wide variety of wines available.

Quiz 12

1 Choose the correct word.

1 I .... see the director immediately.
(A) demanded
(B) demanded to
(C) advised to

2 They .... not spending more money on advertising last year.
(A) demanded to
(B) regretted to
(C) regretted

3 The manager .... him to leave the company.
(A) advised
(B) resented
(C) demanded for

4 Everybody .... being at the meeting.
(A) resented to
(B) resented
(C) resented of

5 Unfortunately our .... applicant can't come for an interview today.
(A) principal
(B) advanced
(C) careless

6 Our company is planning a .... early next year.
(A) takeup
(B) takein
(C) takeover

7 The new model is more .... than our last one.
(A) advanced
(B) illegal
(C) careless

8 The accounts department made some .... mistakes.
(A) careless
(B) illegal
(C) principal

9 The workers aren't interested in the proposal, so the manager is going to discuss some .... ideas.
(A) prior
(B) principal
(C) alternative

2 Read the definitions and write *true* or *false*.

1 A *questionnaire* is an interview with somebody.
2 An *applicant* is a manager.
3 A *limousine* is a type of car.
4 Police need *evidence* to catch criminals.
5 People who do a *variety* of jobs have more than one responsibility.
6 Your *rivals* usually get along with you.
7 You would normally eat an *entrée* at the end of a meal.
8 If you make a good *impression*, people like you.
9 If something happens *gradually,* it happens very quickly.

Unit 13

attentively (adv) paying close attention to what someone is saying
The audience listened to the presentation attentively.

cautiously (adv) carefully, without taking any risks
...to begin cautiously moving up the south ridge.
Drive cautiously in bad weather.

comfortable (adj) pleasant or nice to the touch
Your new chair looks very comfortable.
Our suits are both comfortable and hard-wearing.

consistently (adv) without changing
Our sales have been consistently good in the last three months.
He has been consistently late since he started.

convenient (adj) easy, suiting someone's plans
It is more convenient to fly than to drive because of the volume of traffic.

endurance (n) the ability to survive extreme conditions or very hard work
It was one of the greatest tests of endurance they had experienced.
Marathon runners try to develop their endurance by a combination of training and diet.

grueling (adj) hard, taking a long time and requiring a lot of effort
They reached the summit after a grueling climb.
The Hawaii Iron-man is a grueling race.

highly (adv) very
All the candidates for the job seem highly intelligent.

input (n) contribution
Your input has been very helpful.

invaluable (adj) of great value
Your help has been invaluable.

restore (v) to repair something to its previous condition
The original prints have been restored to modern digital standards.
Painting damaged in the fire were restored by expert artists.

serious (adj) not to be taken lightly
We have serious problems in our Tokyo office.
The board had a serious discussion to decide the direction of the company.

triumph (n) a great achievement, a wonderful result
Their climb to the summit of Mount Everest was a triumph of courage and spirit.
England's triumph in the 1966 World Cup has never been forgotten by the English.

Quiz 13

1 Complete the sentences with the following words.

comfortable consistently convenient grueling highly invaluable restored serious

1 It's not .... for me to travel tomorrow. I have a lot of meetings.
2 Paul's .... motivated. He started work at 6 o'clock this morning.
3 We couldn't have done it without you. Your help has been ....
4 Rising prices are a .... problem at the moment.
5 The beds in the hotel are very ....
6 Ms. Howard's work performance has .... improved.
7 It was a .... three-day journey.
8 The damaged piano has finally been ....

2 Choose the correct word.

1 The difficult climb tested the men's ....
(A) triumph
(B) struggle
(C) endurance

2 The successful takeover was a .... for the company.
(A) harshness
(B) triumph
(C) comfortable

3 The manager thanked his team for their invaluable ....
(A) durability
(B) input
(C) rival

4 The project is difficult, so we'll continue ....
(A) cautiously
(B) highly
(C) eagerly

5 I listened .... to what my colleague said.
(A) attentively
(B) strictly
(C) wonderfully

Unit 14

alumnus (plural **alumni)** (n) previous student (usually of a university) that has graduated
A student alumni magazine
He is one of our more famous alumni.

anticipate (v) to think about how something will happen
We couldn't have anticipated the demand for our products.
I was unable to confirm the anticipated launch date.

application (n) a formal request, usually written, for something
We are now open for membership applications.
The university accepted applications from over one hundred different countries.

bulletin (n) a newsletter distributed freely, especially within a company
A community services bulletin.
This month's bulletin contains a lot of interesting articles.

campaign (n) carefully planned actions or a series of actions leading to a final goal
We are expecting to confirm a well-known model for the campaign shortly.
The President's campaign took him to each of the states.

cancelation (n) asking a reservation or order to be stopped
The effective date of the cancelation is the date the withdrawal notice is received by the center.
We must try to prevent the cancelation of contracts.

cardiovascular (adj) related to the heart and blood vessels
This new gym features a range of cardiovascular equipment.
You need to improve your cardiovascular system before attempting a marathon.

complaint (n) a spoken or written statement expressing dissatisfaction with a product
The customer service department deals with all complaints.
We received a complaint about improper garbage disposal.

comprehensive (adj) complete, without anything missing, very detailed
The exercise studio will offer a comprehensive program of dance...
The software comes with a comprehensive manual.

disposal (n) the throwing away of waste products or garbage
Improper disposal of waste materials can cause pollution.
We received a complaint about improper garbage disposal.

fail (v) to not succeed to do something
I failed my driving test three times.

feature (v) to be included
It's a great film and features the best Hollywood actors.
This new Muscles Gym features a fully stocked workout gym.

further (adv) additional, more
I look forward to discussing this sales opportunity with you further.
We walked further than last week.

improper (adj) not correct, not suitable, impolite
We received a complaint about improper garbage disposal.
He used improper language.
infer (v) how someone understands something based on their reasoning
What can be inferred about the New Health product line?
It can be inferred that the company was not performing well.
medical (adj) to do with medicine, doctors or treatment
If there is a medical reason for the request...
He requires urgent medical treatment.
memorandum (n) a written note or message without the formal address of a letter, usually distributed within a company
He left a memorandum on your desk.
Did you read the latest memorandum?
onwards (adv) continuing from
From the second lesson onwards,...
From that day onwards, his reputation was assured.
opportunity (n) a chance
This is a once-in-a-lifetime opportunity.
I look forward to meeting you and discussing this sales opportunity with you further.
participant (n) a person taking part in an event
The effective date of the withdrawal, regardless of the date the participant stopped attending the class.
3,000 participants completed the marathon.
refund (n) money paid back to a customer for an unsatisfactory product or service
Refunds for fitness programs will not be processed until...
The woman can have a refund.
regardless (adv) without consideration of something
The effective date is the date..., regardless of when the participant...
Anyone can do it, regardless of age or experience.
remittance (n) payments for goods or merchandise (a formal word)
Cash/Check remittances will be refunded by check.
All remittances must be made by the end of the month.
strategy (n) planning or way of doing something
I will be coming to London to discuss our pricing strategies in more detail.
His strategy is to wait for his opponent to attack, then counter quickly.
unattended (adj) not participating, not attending
The way to obtain refunds for unattended courses.
The gasoline pumps were unattended.
withdrawal (n) decision to stop taking part in some event
The effective date of the withdrawal is the date the withdrawal notice is received by the center.
His withdrawal from the race...

Quiz 14

1 Complete the sentences with the following words.

alumni applications bulletin campaign cancelation cardiovascular complaints memorandum participants refund remittance strategy withdrawal

1 There has been a long .... by the union to improve working conditions.
2 There have been three .... from the class and one person never attended.
3 There was a(n) ...., so I was able to get a seat on an earlier flight.
4 There were seven .... in the company football match.
5 There have been several .... this month from unhappy customers.
6 He got a small .... for his train ticket and other expenses.
7 There was a(n) .... reunion at the university.
8 The weekly .... gives information about staff benefits.
9 We have had six .... for the job of foreman.
10 I usually do .... exercise at the gym.
11 We hope our new marketing .... will improve sales.
12 Please could you confirm you have received my .... sent on 20 March?
13 I have been unable to download the software and so would like a ....

2 Read the definitions and write *true* or *false*.

1 If a meeting is *unattended* it means a lot of people were there.
2 If you *infer* something you say something clearly.
3 When you *anticipate* something, you expect it to happen.
4 To *feature* means to include.
5 *Medical* relates to doctors and hospitals.
6 If a program is *comprehensive*, it's incomplete.
7 If you *fail to do something*, you do not do it.
8 *Improper* means inappropriate.
9 If you do something *regardless* you aren't worried about any potential problems.
10 *Onwards* means in the past.
11 If you want to discuss something *further* you haven't finished talking.
12 An *opportunity* is a chance.
13 *Disposal* means getting rid of something.

Unit 15

backpack (n) a large sturdy bag, worn on the back by hikers and travelers
The backpack is being filled.
John's backpack was so heavy he could barely lift it.
brush (v) to clean with a brush
The man is brushing his jacket.
chef (n) a professional, usually trained cook
The chef is standing by the grill.
The restaurant was popular because of its famous chef.
discuss (v) to talk on a particular subject with two or more people
They are discussing the TV program.
I would like to discuss our sales figures for May.
draw (v) to make a picture with pens, pencils or anything other than paint
The children drew funny faces on their notebooks.
figurine (n) a small, often pottery or wood figure used for decoration
The wooden figurines are on sale.
He bought his mother a lovely figurine of a dancing girl.
fix (v) to repair something that is broken
They are fixing the boy's bicycle.
I sent the damaged radio back to the company to be fixed.
focused (adj) concentrated attentively on one thing
The man is focused on his work.
His goals were focused on completing the project by the target date.
forest (n) an area of land covered with trees
A forest grows in the valley.
I love to go hiking through the forest in the spring.
grill (n) a flat metal or barred plate used for cooking
The chef is standing by the grill.
The cook was cooking bacon and eggs on the grill.
hiker (n) someone who walks in the hills or countryside for recreation
The hiker is sitting on the ground.
The mountain trail was packed with hikers enjoying the nice weather.
pier (n) a long thin structure attached to the land that stands in the sea and that boats can be secured to
The boat is tied to the pier.
I used to fish off the end of the pier.
plow (v) to clear or cut a path through something
The truck is plowing the road.
The farmer plowed his fields every spring.
popular (adj) well known or liked by a large number of people
The seaside is popular today.
Barry Glimmer used to be a popular singer.
seaside (n) land on or close to the sea
The seaside is popular today.
The couple bought a small cottage near the seaside.
scene (n) a section of a movie or play
They are filming a scene.
I like the scene where the detective explains the crime.
stack (v) to arrange things into a pile
Logs are stacked in the yard.
Can you stack these cans in the display by the entrance?

steep (adj) with a sharply rising or falling slope
The mountain is steep.
The chart showed a steep drop in sales for the month.
studio (n) place where an artist works
The artist paints in his studio every day.
valley (n) an area of low land often between mountains
A forest grows in the valley.
The bottom of the valley featured a fast river.
wooden (adj) made of wood
The wooden figurines are on sale.
Wooden canoes are heavier than fiberglass ones.
yard (n) an area of ground used for a particular purpose
Logs are stacked in the yard.
He parked his truck in the storage yard next to the factory.

Quiz 15

1 Choose the correct word.

1 After dinner the children .... all the dishes in the kitchen.
(A) ruined
(B) fixed
(C) stacked

2 The path to the top of the mountain was too .... , so we were unable to reach the summit.
(A) steep
(B) valley
(C) popular

3 Please don't interrupt. I'm .... an important contract.
(A) discussing
(B) crying
(C) drawing

4 During exam week the students were .... their revision.
(A) focused on
(B) focused to
(C) focused with

5 Our day out to the .... was fantastic – we swam and walked along the beach.
(A) forest
(B) seaside
(C) valley

6 The .... enjoyed cooking on an open fire when they reached the campsite.
(A) applications
(B) figurines
(C) hikers

7 The Golden Temple is very .... ; more than half a million visitors go there every year.
(A) wooden
(B) bored
(C) popular

2 Choose the correct word to complete the definition.

1 A *chef / hiker* is a professionally trained cook.
2 A *valley / forest* is an area of low land between mountains.
3 A *grill / weight* is a flat metal plate that you can cook things on.
4 If you *draw / discuss* something you need a pencil and some paper.
5 A *studio / study* is usually full of paintings and brushes.
6 If you *brush / spill* something, you clean it.
7 To *plow / fix* something means to cut a path through it.

3 Complete the sentences with the following words.

backpack figurine fixed forest pier scene wooden yard

1 My grandfather made this old .... chair from a tree that fell down in the yard.
2 My watch is not working properly; I must get it ....
3 I'm going to get a new .... for my trip to the Rocky Mountains.
4 We have to move the old desks into the .... because new office furniture is arriving tomorrow.
5 Hikers are not allowed to light fires in the .... at any time of year.
6 They put the pottery .... on the shelf next to the other decorations.
7 Let's go down to the .... and watch the boats.
8 The film starts with a very dramatic ....

Unit 16

actually (adv) in fact, really, in truth
Actually, we don't have any plans.
I don't actually know.
bank (n) a place where customers can save and withdraw money, as well as getting help with other financial services
Could you tell me where a bank is?
I have to get some money from the bank before we go out tonight.
block (n) an area of town marked by streets on all sides
If you go across the street and turn left you should see a Chinese restaurant about a block down.
The bus stop is three blocks from here.
boardroom (n) a room in a company used to hold important meetings, especially those involving the president and top executives
How do I get to the boardroom?
The boardroom is not available this afternoon.
bored (adj) uninterested or having little to do
The man looks bored.
John soon became bored with life on the farm and moved back to the city.
cafeteria (n) a kind of restaurant where customers choose their food from a counter and bring it to the table themselves
Down the hall, turn left and it's just across from the cafeteria.
The food in the cafeteria is quite good.
deliver (v) to take something to give to someone
The package was delivered about an hour ago.
My paper wasn't delivered this morning.
drawer (n) part of a piece of furniture (e.g. a desk) that can be pulled open to reveal a box into which items can be placed
In the drawer, as usual.
The knives and forks go in the top drawer.
journey (n) a trip (usually long) from one place to another
How long did the journey take?
The journey takes twelve hours by plane.
(be) kept (v) be placed in a particular location
Where is the A4 paper kept?
The transport claim forms are kept in the bottom drawer.
(be) ordered (to do something) (v) be made to do something by another person
Yes, they were ordered to do it.
We were ordered to leave the building by the police.
package (n) an item, usually wrapped in paper or in a box, to be delivered by mail
When did the package arrive?
There is a package from head office on your desk.
polite (adj) displaying good manners
It's not polite to stare.
The waiter was not very polite to the customers.
refrigerator (n) a large kitchen appliance used to keep food chilled and fresh
It's in the refrigerator behind the vegetables.
There is no milk in the refrigerator.
several (adj) more than one or two
She's been working here for several months.
There are several ways to get to the airport.
stare (v) to look very directly at something or someone
It's not polite to stare.
She is staring at the goods on display.

Quiz 16

1 Complete the sentences with the following words.

actually bank blocks cafeteria drawer kept ordered polite several

1 Walk down three .... and turn right into 39th Street.
2 The holiday request forms are kept in the top .... of the filing cabinet.
3 You can use your credit card to withdraw foreign currency at the ....
4 Following the health inspection they were .... to close the kitchen immediately.
5 Let's have lunch in the .... ; it's quicker than going to a restaurant.
6 I can't find the key to storeroom. Do you know where it is .... ?

7 We have .... new products going on the market this season.
8 We live in the center of town, ... , not the suburbs.
9 It is .... to greet your neighbors when you see them.

2 Read the definitions and write *true* or *false*.

1 You keep food warm in a *refrigerator*.
2 You can send a *package* by mail.
3 The *boardroom* is where staff can enjoy cheap meals.
4 If you are *bored* by a presentation, the speaker has your attention.
5 To *deliver* something means to pick it up from the Post Office.
6 A *journey* is a kind of magazine.
7 To *stare* means to listen to someone very carefully.

Unit 17

available (adj) free to do something (for people), or be used for some purpose (for objects)
Did she say when she would be available?
The special is only available until 1:30 P.M.
celebration (n) special occasion
The Kingston carnival is an amazing celebration.
coach (adj) standard class on American trains
Coach class is fine.
We traveled coach class.
concern (n) worry
His main concern is that they won't finish on time.
crowded (adj) with too many people or things
The buses get very crowded in rush hour.
deposit (n) the act of placing money into a bank account (opposite of withdrawal)
Deposits can be made between 9 A.M. and 3 P.M.
I'd like to make a deposit, please.
desperate (adj) wanting, or needing to do something very much
He's desperate to work overseas.
The local people are desperate to leave the region.
(have) difficulty (doing something) (expression) find something hard to do
There was noise all night long. We had difficulty in sleeping.
disappointing (adj) not as good as expected
We had high hopes, but it was a bit disappointing.
heel (n) the bottom part of a shoe at the back which raises the foot
We have one with the same heel.
license (n) a document that allows the owner to do something otherwise restricted or controlled by law
You have to pass the test to get a license.
Could you show me your driving license?
package (n) an item, usually wrapped in paper or in a box, to be delivered by mail
When did the package arrive?
There is a package from head office on your desk.
rare (adj) uncommon, or limited in number
I think it's quite rare.
Pandas are now very rare in the wild.
reservation (n) an agreement that a hotel room, restaurant table, etc. is kept for the person who orders it
I'm sorry, but there is no record of your reservation.
right away (adv) immediately, without pause or hesitation
If you get started right away, it shouldn't be too much of a problem.
If we want to get there by six, we'll have to leave right away.
run out (v) to no longer have
We've run out of paper.
sleeves (n) the arms of a shirt, jacket or other upper body item of clothing
The sleeves are a bit short.
Is it possible to get the sleeves adjusted?
stadium (n) a large building, with seating all around it, where sporting events are held
The track finals will be held at the stadium later tomorrow.
The marathon runners finish their route at the Olympic stadium.
vacancies (n) empty rooms in a hotel, guest house or trip etc.
Do you have any vacancies for tonight?
We have only a few vacancies left on tomorrow's excursion.
withdrawal (n) the act of taking money out of a bank account (opposite of deposit)
The largest withdrawal that can be made in one day is $1000.
Can I make withdrawals from other companies' ATMs?

Quiz 17

1 Choose the correct word.

1 The museum section of the library has a special collection of .... books.
(A) available
(B) rare
(C) desperate

2 The hikers were .... to reach their destination; they didn't have enough food, water or medicine.
(A) remarkable
(B) rare
(C) desperate

3 I've booked two tickets .... class to New York.
(A) reservation
(B) available
(C) coach

4 The car hire company needs to see your driving .... and a form of ID.
(A) license
(B) vacancy
(C) reservation

5 I'd like to make a .... my savings account.
(A) deposit from
(B) deposit into
(C) deposit around

6 Special weekend rates are .... on all rooms – call today to make a reservation.
(A) available
(B) rare
(C) vacancies

7 I couldn't stay at the same hotel because they didn't have any ....
(A) vacancies
(B) calculations
(C) withdrawals

8 There is a .... for you in this morning's mail.
(A) package
(B) deposit
(C) reservation

9 She had .... finding a suitable jacket.
(A) difficulty
(B) concern
(C) desperate

10 The toner in the printer has ....
(A) run out
(B) gone
(C) lost

11 The jacket almost fits but the .... are a bit too long.
(A) heels
(B) sleeves
(C) concerns

2 Match the words with the definitions.

celebration concern disappointing heel reservation right away stadium withdrawal

1 a special occasion
2 part of a shoe
3 immediately
4 something you are worried about and think about a lot
5 large sporting events are held here
6 not as good as expected
7 taking money out of a bank account
8 a booking agreement; for example, for a hotel room, or a plane ticket

Unit 18

adjust (v) change the settings of how something works or appears
You can adjust the level of resistance.
If the picture is not clear, try to adjust the aerial.
ambitious (adj) something done on a large scale, usually confidently
It is our most ambitious yet.
We have ambitious plans for the European market.
apprentice (n) someone who works for a skilled person in order to learn a trade
She went from being an apprentice to head of our design team.
background (n) information about the past of a person, object or event
I would like to give you some background on Bill Gates.
We need some more background information.

condition (n) fitness
Are you trying to improve your overall condition?
delighted (adj) very happy
We are delighted that he has agreed to speak to us.
He was delighted with his birthday gift.
feature (v) to be included (usually in a movie, show or other production)
Indigo Heart, a new movie featuring Andy Vega.
It's a great movie that features some of the hottest new Hollywood talent.
imaginative (adj) creative
We are sure her imaginative creations will push sales beyond target.
latecomer (n) a person that arrives late for an event
The conference was held up for thirty minutes to allow latecomers to find their seats.
realize (v) to understand something (often suddenly)
I realize that this is a non-working day.
The staff realized the amount of time that had gone into the job.
salvage (v) to save or recover something, e.g. a ship or building, from destruction
The ship was recently salvaged from Jamestown harbor.
We can try to salvage this deal.
schedule (v) to arrange an event on a timetable
There are three plenary discussions scheduled for Saturday.
We should try to schedule a meeting next week.
spectator (n) a person watching an event
Spectators should try to get down to the Jamestown marina early.
Ten thousand spectators watched the finals.
support (v) to provide help or assistance to others
He did a lot of things to support the members of his group.
New employees can expect the support of their colleagues.
target (n) result to aim for, goal
It will push sales beyond target.
waterproof (adj) not letting water through
The waterproof case comes in a variety of sizes.
My watch isn't waterproof.

Quiz 18

1 Find six words in the puzzle. Match them to their definitions.

I	B	N	O	V	A	T	I	O	N
T	W	E	T	I	W	O	Y	E	M
D	E	L	I	G	H	T	E	D	G
E	T	H	A	I	P	K	O	I	E
R	Q	S	P	L	I	O	P	R	T
T	H	C	O	A	R	I	U	U	S
C	A	H	I	N	E	T	L	Y	A
S	P	E	C	T	A	T	O	R	L
A	T	D	U	E	L	U	M	T	V
I	P	U	F	U	I	Y	N	R	A
P	U	L	Y	Y	Z	T	B	E	G
E	F	E	T	T	E	F	G	S	E
O	T	I	M	I	S	T	I	C	A

1 a person watching an event
2 a timetable
3 very happy
4 to recover something that is badly damaged
5 to understand
6 to be included in a film

2 Complete the sentences with the following words.

adjust ambitious apprentice background condition imaginative latecomers support target waterproof

1 I'm training every day to try and improve my overall ....
2 He joined the company as an .... but was quickly promoted.
3 We have reached our sales .... for this quarter.
4 They are trained to be .... ; they all want top jobs.
5 Once the concert has begun, ... cannot enter the auditorium until the interval.
6 The engineering department provides technical .... and maintains all the machinery.
7 The film's storyline is very ....
8 If you want to .... the volume, simply press here.
9 Raincoats are made out of .... material.
10 Is there any .... information on this company? We're thinking of buying some shares.

Unit 19

bankrupt (adj) of companies or individuals, to not have enough money to pay expenses or debts
That company went bankrupt.
After paying the legal expenses he was bankrupt.
co-supervise (v) two or more people taking responsibility for a project or department
Jake Thomson and Phil Greene co-supervise the project.
I co-supervise the sales team.
criticize (v) to say what you think is wrong with something
The strategy was criticized for being too aggressive.
Jon's boss would often loudly criticize him.
dependence (n) reliance, needing something in order to survive
The company's dependence on a single supplier caused problems.
Our dependence on imported parts is costing us a lot of money.
disconnect (v) to detach something from its power source, to remove (especially a telephone) from the network
The phone company came to disconnect his line.
You should disconnect the printer before switching the power on.
document (n) a piece of paper that contains company information
He hates filing documents.
He realized he had left a key document on his desk at home.
elevate (v) to raise to a higher position
The sculptor intended to elevate the statue by placing it on a pedestal.
He was elevated to the post of Finance Director.
identify (v) to find and name someone or something
A consultant was hired to identify the company's main weaknesses.
I couldn't identify the man, as he was wearing a mask.
impatient (adj) to be annoyed or frustrated due to an inability to wait
I often get very impatient if there is heavy traffic when I am in a hurry.
I am impatient to hear the result of the election.
intercom (n) an electronic device used to communicate with people inside and outside of a room
There is an intercom in each room.
Call me on the intercom and I'll let you in.
internship (n) a period of work where students are given professional supervision
Doing an internship is a good way for students to get work experience.
Law students usually look for an internship during their final year at college.
investigation (n) an organized way to find out information about how something happened
The stockholders want an investigation to find the money.
The investigation will take at least a week.
mishear (v) to fail to hear something correctly
Sorry, I think I misheard you.
I misheard the announcement and went to the wrong gate.
non-refundable (adj) not possible to receive money back for something purchased
Since the gift was on sale it was non-refundable.
All sale items are non-refundable.
overpaid (adj) given too much money
After I returned from the shop, I realized I had overpaid.
I don't believe that miners are overpaid; they work very hard.

remove (v) to take away
A plumber was called to remove the blockage from the pipe.
renovate (v) to repair something to a condition as good as new
The house needs to be renovated.
The company spent millions to renovate its main office.
repetitiveness (n) the feeling of something being done the same way many times
Many people dislike the repetitiveness of working in a factory.
I didn't mind the repetitiveness of the work.
soften (v) to make something soft
Cyclists often use pads to soften the seat for long-distance rides.
Add extra water to soften the mixture.
unwrap (v) to remove the paper layer from a parcel or gift
The children couldn't wait to unwrap their presents.
Don't unwrap the parcel until Christmas.

Quiz 19

1 Match the words with the definitions.

bankrupt criticize dependence document impatient intercom internship investigation non-refundable repetitiveness

1 trying to find out the truth about something
2 doing the same thing again and again
3 a two-way communication system that uses a microphone and a loudspeaker
4 a file of some kind
5 a person or a company that has terrible financial difficulties that can't improve
6 easily annoyed or irritated
7 when you can't get your money back
8 a period of work done by a student that is supervised by professionals
9 relying on somebody or something to help you
10 the opposite of *praise*

2 Choose the correct word.

1 I'm sorry, but we've .... you. Could you return the money?
(A) unwrapped
(B) disconnected
(C) overpaid

2 We've .... the problem. It's bad management in the accounts department.
(A) criticized
(B) identified
(C) renovated

3 It's a beautiful old building, but it would cost a lot of money to .... it.
(A) devastate
(B) resurface
(C) renovate

4 The fallen tree was quickly .... from the road.
(A) removed
(B) placed
(C) disconnected

5 I must .... these new hiking boots. They hurt my feet.
(A) soften
(B) unwrap
(C) mishear

6 She was .... to head of department.
(A) overpaid
(B) identified
(C) elevated

7 The two managers are currently .... the takeover.
(A) disconnecting
(B) co-supervising
(C) mishearing

8 I must have .... John. I thought he said he was leaving the company, but he isn't.
(A) co-supervised
(B) misheard
(C) criticized

9 They .... our electricity because we forgot to pay the bill.
(A) identified
(B) criticized
(C) disconnected

10 The director is going to .... his leaving present. I wonder what they brought him.
(A) unwrap
(B) disconnect
(C) identify

Unit 20

chairperson (n) the head of a company or the leader of a meeting
I'm meeting the chairperson at 3:00.
The chairperson called for any questions.
charity (n) organization helping people in need
She is going to leave all her money to worthy charities.
employ (v) to give somebody a job, to pay somebody to do a job
How long have you been employed at your present company?
The company employs more than two thousand people.
facility (n) a building or piece of equipment used for a particular purpose
Costs at the facility had been rising for some time.
The laboratory has all the latest facilities.
famed (adj) famous, known by a lot of people
The famed orchestra will be giving a one night performance.
The town's famed clock tower is the first place tourists visit.
foreign (adj) from another country
The agricultural board will increase taxes on foreign imports.
We are looking to expand into foreign markets.
fundraising (n) trying to gather money for charitable purpose
The Animal Welfare Society is having its annual fundraising dinner.
The fundraising achieved its goal of ten thousand dollars.
intend (v) to plan
My plans have changed and I am now intending to start the course this September.
invoice (n) an official receipt of payments, usually given to a company
The shipping agent said he will change the cargo invoices.
We keep all our invoices for tax-calculation purposes.
lack (n) to be without something or to be in need of it
The annual conference has been canceled this year due to lack of money.
We lack experience in this area.
livestock (n) animals on a farm
This year they are hoping to repair the damage caused to the fence in the large livestock run...
Livestock arrives at the market every day.
opportunity (n) a chance
This is a once-in-a-lifetime opportunity.
We may not have many opportunities to do this later.
outline (n) a basic description without much detail
He hasn't seen the new outlines yet.
Have the design team drawn up an outline?
profitability (n)
Attempts to increase profitability and reduce costs failed.
raise (v) to collect money, usually for a charity
This year they are hoping to raise $4500 to repair the damage
The telethon raised more than three million last year.
rare (adj) uncommon, one of only a small number
Fans of classical music are in for a rare treat in December.
It was a rare sight to see him in the office on time.
refuse (v) to not agree to do something
I have to refuse your offer of a job for the coming year.
Our rivals refused our offer to merge.
report (v) to tell people, usually in an official manner
John Leighton reported that costs at the facility...
reschedule (v) to change a plan
The workshop will be rescheduled for next week.
rescue (v) to save something or move it from a dangerous situation
For over 25 years PAWS has rescued... thousands of animals...
retirement (n) the period of life after someone has stopped working, usually from around 60 years old
I am looking forward to my retirement.
Vasily Krampfstein has announced his retirement.
situation (n) what happens or happened to you
I'm afraid since we spoke, my situation has changed.
We will try to avoid that situation if possible.
surrounding (adj) in the area, close to a location
PAWS has provided a home for thousands of animals in distress in Pollville and the surrounding area.
There are plenty of shops and services in the surrounding area.

upcoming (adj) due to take place soon
I'm discussing the contract with them at the upcoming meeting.

Quiz 20

1 Read the definitions and write *true* or *false*.

1 A *chairperson* runs a meeting or a company.
2 *Outlines* are basic descriptions.
3 A *charity* is an organization which helps people or animals.
4 If you *raise* money you collect it.
5 If you *intend* to do something, you plan to do it.
6 A *facility* is a kind of university.
7 If you *reschedule* a meeting, you arrange it for a different time.
8 *Famed* means not very well-known.
9 When there is a *lack* of something, there's a lot of it.
10 *Fundraising* means increasing the profits of a company.
11 An *opportunity* is a chance to do something.
12 *Livestock* is farm animals.

2 Complete the sentences with the following words.

employed foreign invoice rare refuse report rescued retirement situation surrounding

1 I am looking forward to my .... when I will finally have time for myself.
2 Our .... has changed, so we aren't going ahead with the takeover.
3 We plan to expand into .... markets.
4 I've just e-mailed you my .... for last week's work.
5 The company .... twenty-five new people last year.
6 I .... to do overtime at the weekend. I've already made plans.
7 While the boss is away I have to .... that sales for this quarter are down.
8 It's .... that he's late.
9 Last week, the group .... three dogs from bad treatment.
10 I know the city and the .... area well.

Unit 21

beverage (n) a drink
...the local New Year's Day tradition of warming up with home made...bean and bacon soup, good music and beverages.

complimentary (adj) offered without charge
We will shortly be serving complimentary tea.
Put a personalized message on your complimentary card.

culinary (adj) associated with food and cooking
One of the county's original culinary festivals.
His culinary expertise is evident.

the elderly (n) old people
Reduced price for the elderly...

ensure (v) to make certain of something
To ensure safety...
Please ensure that all arrangements are made at your end.

explorer (n) a person who tries to go somewhere that others have not gone to before
The celebration starts with a light-hearted re-enactment of the founding of the city by English explorer Francis Baker in 1879.
The first explorers were amazed to find buildings larger than anything in the civilized world.

festivities (n) celebrations
Festivities at this year's event will include over 25 local food vendors, a children's fair and more.
All guests are welcome to join in the festivities.

founding (n) the starting of a town, company or nation
The celebration starts with a light-hearted re-enactment of the founding of the city by English explorer Francis Baker in 1879.
The founding of the city is believed to have happened before the Romans arrived.

guarantee (n) a promise to cover the quality of goods or services
All products come with an unconditional money-back guarantee.
There is an option to purchase a five-year guarantee.

hiking (n) taking long walks in the mountains or countryside
Hiking is very popular in my country.
The west coast is a great place to go hiking.

host (v) to welcome guests or visitors to an event that the person is organizing
The Bakerstown Polar Bear Club hosts this popular, annual...
The Giants host the Cougars in tonight's big game.

personalized (adj) made different to suit each individual
Put a personalized message on your complimentary card.

prohibit (v) to not allow or to stop something according to a rule
Animals prohibited from entry.
It is prohibited to take any dangerous items on board.

re-enactment (n) the recreation of a historical scene by modern actors or performers
The celebration starts with a light-hearted re-enactment of the founding of the city by English explorer Francis Baker in 1879.
The Sealed Knot are famous for their re-enactments of British Civil War battles.

revised (adj) done again, altered
As promised, here's the revised schedule for next week's activities.
The revised edition contains fewer errors than the original.

senior citizens (n) old people, a more polite way to describing the aged
Senior citizens get special rates.
The number of senior citizens taking up sports is on the increase.

tradition (n) a custom or habit usually associated with a particular country, region or group
...the local New Year's Day tradition of warming up with home made...bean and bacon soup, good music and beverages.

unconditional (adj) without any conditions
All products come with an unconditional money-back guarantee.
The unconditional surrender of arms was a key aspect of the peace process.

vendor (n) a person selling goods, often from temporary shops or stalls
Festivities at this year's event will include over 25 local food vendors, a children's fair and more.
Market vendors have a reputation for honesty.

Quiz 21

1 Choose the correct word.

1 Children under 12 are .... entry.
(A) prohibited from
(B) prohibited to
(C) prohibited

2 .... get a discount on their tickets.
(A) Explorers
(B) Vendors
(C) Senior citizens

3 I'd like to see the .... for tomorrow's course.
(A) tradition
(B) schedule
(C) beverages

4 This product still has a .... so I'd like my money back.
(A) vendor
(B) founding
(C) guarantee

5 There isn't going to be any food, but there will be ....
(A) traditions
(B) re-enactment
(C) beverages

6 The show will start with a(n) .... of the climbing of Everest.
(A) re-enactment
(B) hiking
(C) guarantee

7 The .... of the city was an important historical event.
(A) elderly
(B) founding
(C) re-enactment

8 The offer is .... so they do not need to get any licenses.
(A) personalized
(B) unconditional
(C) culinary

9 The food is expensive, but there's a .... drink with every meal.
(A) complimentary
(B) unconditional
(C) culinary

2 Find eleven words in the puzzle. Then match them with their definitions.

O	R	I	E	N	T	E	E	R	I	N	G	G
M	E	K	S	U	R	V	N	B	D	C	H	F
T	L	E	M	R	S	E	J	E	L	A	R	E
U	D	N	F	L	T	G	V	P	O	K	A	S
X	E	P	A	S	D	U	W	I	C	E	V	T
P	R	T	O	E	M	R	O	Z	S	H	I	I
L	L	H	E	N	S	U	R	E	X	E	J	V
O	Y	V	R	B	F	E	N	H	R	L	D	I
D	U	T	R	A	D	I	T	I	O	N	E	T
I	C	M	A	E	X	P	L	O	R	E	R	I
Z	E	P	C	Y	V	H	E	D	S	I	A	E
A	C	U	L	I	N	A	R	Y	O	F	R	S
P	E	R	S	O	N	A	L	I	Z	E	D	A
K	O	J	V	E	N	D	O	R	T	G	N	H

1 cooking
2 a person who sells things
3 make certain
4 fun events
5 customs and beliefs
6 somebody who discovers new places
7 racing across the countryside
8 old people
9 made for a particular person
10 changed
11 the person holding a party or an event

Unit 22

commuter (n) a person traveling to work
The commuters are between the buses.
The train is full of commuters this morning.
control panel (n) a part of a machine that allows the operator to use it, or that shows whether it is functioning correctly or not
The man is sitting next to the control panel.
The warning light on the control panel lit up.
counter (n) a flat, raised surface on which to place items, e.g. in a shop
The woman is at the counter.
You can leave your bags behind the counter.
customer (n) a person paying for goods or services
The customer is shopping for food.
The shop assistant is helping the customer.
cycle (v) to ride a bicycle
The woman is cycling through the city.
He used to cycle to work.
decorate (v) to make something beautiful by placing colorful items, flowers, etc. on or around it
The student decorates the cakes.
We decorated the hall for the farewell party.
deserted (adj) having no people present
The room is deserted.
The beach is usually deserted until 10 A.M.
display (n) an arrangement of goods in a shop designed to attract customers
The guitars are on display.
flight attendant (n) an airline employee that takes care of passengers on board an airplane
The flight attendant is wearing a red jacket.
Your flight attendant will demonstrate the safety procedures.
harbor (n) the place where boats are kept when not in use
The ship is in the harbor.
We can catch the ferry at the harbor.
hide (v) to place an item or yourself, so that it cannot easily be found
The woman is hiding some clothes.
The children are hiding from their parents.
keyboard (n) an input device for entering letters and numbers into a computer
The keyboard is on the desk.
Type your name using the attached keyboard.
lean (v) to stand at an angle
The man is leaning against the car.
The Tower of Pisa leans slightly to one side.
locker (n) a container for personal items that can be fastened with a key or other kind of lock
The student is looking inside her locker.
He lost the key to his locker.
outfit (n) a set of clothes, usually for a woman
The woman is looking at the outfit.
She wore her new outfit to the interview.
point (v) to indicate towards something usually using the index finger
The man is pointing at something.
Several signs point the way to the gate.
raise (v) to lift something
The couple raise their glasses.
The crane raises the crate high above the ship.
set (v) to place an item in a particular position
The people are setting the table.
He set the glass on the counter.
sweep (v) to clean the floor, using a broom or brush
The man is sweeping the street.
The woman uses the broom to sweep the kitchen.
walkway (n) a passage or path only used by pedestrians
A moving walkway connects the station to the shopping center.
Take the pedestrian walkway to get to the mall.

Quiz 22

1 Complete the sentences with the following words.

control panel counter cycling decorate deserted display harbor keyboard outfit pointed raise set

1 The .... is next to the computer.
2 I need a new .... for my cousin's wedding next month.
3 Please pay for your goods at the ....
4 Dinner is nearly ready – could you .... the table, please?
5 When the World Cup final was showing on television, the shops were ....
6 Children always get excited when they .... the classroom with pictures.
7 Let's go down to the .... , and we can watch all the boats come in.
8 .... is good exercise.
9 The art projects were put on .... in the main hall.
10 If there's a problem, the .... lights up and shows you what's wrong.
11 Do you think they will ever .... the *Titanic* from the sea bed?
12 The teacher .... to the capital cities on the map.

2 Choose the correct word to complete the definition.

1 A *customer / commuter* travels to work everyday.
2 A *flight attendant / control panel* works on board a plane.
3 To *decorate / sweep* means to clean the floor with a broom.
4 You can keep your personal items in a *locker / counter*.
5 A person paying for goods is a *customer / counter*.
6 A *walkway / harbor* is used by pedestrians.
7 When you are *pointing / hiding* no-one can see you.
8 To *lean / loan* means to stand at an angle.

Unit 23

amusing (adj) funny, likely to make people laugh
He really is an amusing speaker.
I saw an amusing program on the television last night.
appreciate (v) to feel grateful to somebody because of what they have done for you
Yes, I really appreciated all your help yesterday.
I would appreciate it if you could turn the volume down.
book (v) to arrange to have something for a particular time. Similar to reserve
Sorry, we are fully booked for this evening.
Can I book a table for three for nine o'clock?
borrow (v) to take something with permission, and then return it later
Can I borrow your pen for a moment?
My sister borrowed the car for the weekend.
calculator (n) an electronic device used for mathematical functions
Do you have a calculator I could borrow?
We'll need a calculator to work out the bill.
deliver (v) to take something to give to someone
The package was delivered to the wrong address.
My paper wasn't delivered this morning.
expect (v) to imagine something, to believe that something will happen
Harder than I expected.
I was expecting to be met at the airport.
fill out (v) to write in all the details of a form or questionnaire
Can you show me how to fill out this card?
All passengers have to fill out an immigration form.
frankly (adv) honestly, truthfully
Frankly, our sales staff isn't motivated.
He spoke frankly and told us exactly what he felt.

license (n) a document that allows the owner to do something otherwise restricted or controlled by law
You have to pass the test to get a license.

maintenance (n) work done to keep something in good working condition
Call maintenance staff to fix it.
The machines need regular maintenance.

make sense (v) be easy to understand
I don't think it makes much sense.
The instruction manual made perfect sense to me.

motivate (v) to make others want to try harder to do something
Frankly, our sales staff isn't motivated.
The management try hard to motivate their workers.

opinion (n) a person's beliefs or feelings about a subject
What's your opinion of the price quote?
I don't have a strong opinion about the issue.

policy (n) an idea or set of ideas used to make decisions, usually decided by politics or business management
What is your opinion of the new policy?
That goes against company policy.

quote (n) the price someone says they will charge to do a job
What's your opinion of the price quote?
We chose the company that gave us the lowest quote.

reserve (v) to arrange to keep something (e.g. a room at a hotel) for yourself and nobody else
Can I reserve a table for 8:00?
I reserved the room two months ago.

retirement (n) the period of life after someone has stopped working, usually from around 60 years old
What do you think about the changes to the retirement plan?
I am looking forward to my retirement.

terrific (adj) very good
Terrific! It was really well done.
That was a terrific speech you gave last night.

upset (adj) to feel unhappy or angry about something
I'm sure a lot of people will be upset.
What are you upset about?

Quiz 23

1 Choose the correct word.

1 I'd like to .... a table for four at 8.00 P.M.
(A) borrow
(B) quote
(C) reserve

2 We're .... the shipment to arrive on Friday.
(A) delivering
(B) expecting
(C) motivating

3 They were very .... when they heard the bad news.
(A) amusing
(B) terrific
(C) upset

4 First you need to .... this form and attach a photograph.
(A) fill
(B) fill out
(C) fill up

5 He spent more time with his grandchildren after his ....
(A) license
(B) maintenance
(C) retirement

6 I've changed my .... about the new manager; he's not as efficient as I thought.
(A) opinion
(B) policy
(C) quote

7 Please send this by courier and have it .... by hand.
(A) booked
(B) chaired
(C) delivered

8 Students are not allowed to use a .... in the math exam.
(A) calculator
(B) committee
(C) license

9 Who calculated these figures? They really don't .... to me.
(A) borrow
(B) make sense
(C) expect

2 Find eleven words in the puzzle. Then match them with their definitions.

R	T	F	R	A	N	K	L	Y	L	R
A	W	E	R	T	Y	M	G	D	I	E
M	A	I	N	T	E	N	A	N	C	E
U	P	A	S	I	D	F	G	H	E	P
S	P	E	T	T	O	H	A	I	N	O
I	R	O	Q	U	O	T	E	K	S	L
N	E	I	A	D	K	Q	U	I	E	I
G	C	U	T	E	R	R	I	F	I	C
R	I	Y	T	B	D	S	E	R	T	Y
O	A	T	B	O	R	R	O	W	Y	U
A	T	G	M	O	T	I	V	A	T	E
T	E	B	U	K	I	O	P	S	E	T

1 a proposed price
2 to reserve a room or a table
3 a set of ideas used to make a decision
4 a document that allows you to do something
5 funny
6 honestly
7 to feel grateful
8 to take something and return it later
9 to make people want to try harder
10 very good
11 work done to keep something in good condition

Unit 24

aisle (n) passage between rows of seats in a plane
The aisles were very narrow.

allow (v) give permission for somebody to do a particular thing
I'm sure they wouldn't allow it.
We are not allowed to smoke anywhere inside the building.

appliance (n) equipment for a particular purpose
They sell kitchen appliances.

awkward (adj) feeling uncomfortable or embarrassed
I'd feel a little awkward asking him to borrow money.
It is an awkward situation.

favor (n) a helpful action
Could you do me a favor and photocopy this report?

locate (v) to find
The airline will contact you when they have located your missing luggage.

notify (v) to inform
Please notify us of your change of address.

merchandise (n) goods
The store has a very good selection of merchandise.

prefer (v) to like one thing more than another
I prefer pop music.
I would prefer if we could put it off till this evening.

press (v) to use an iron to remove creases or wrinkles from clothing and get them ready to wear
Could you clean and press these two shirts?
The hotel staff can press your suit pants if required.

recommend (v) to make a suggestion as to a particular choice
Would you recommend it?
I recommend the fish – it is very fresh and delicious.

suitable (adj) a good match for the person concerned, acceptable for the purpose
There are no suitable places left.
I don't know of any suitable hotels that the president can stay at.

Quiz 24

1 Read the definitions and write *true* or *false*.

1 To *allow* someone to do something means to give them permission.
2 An *awkward* situation makes you feel amused.
3 You have to write an *appliance* to get a job.
4 You probably appreciate it, if someone does you a *favor*.
5 To *locate* means to lose.
6 To *notify* means to inform.
7 People who work 100 hours a week do not have a *reasonable* work–life balance.

2 Complete the sentences with the following words.

aisle merchandise prefer pressed recommended suitable

1 We chose a local company to do the work because they were .... by a neighbor.
2 The picture is not .... for the brochure; we need something more colorful.
3 I can't wear this shirt – it hasn't been ....
4 Which wine do you .... ? Red or white?
5 On a long-haul flight, it's a good idea to walk up and down the ....
6 I am returning the enclosed .... because it is faulty.

Unit 25

affordable (adj) not too expensive, at a price that the customer can pay
We are focused on keeping prices affordable.
The property in that area is generally quite affordable.
attendee (n) a person that is joining an event, usually having been invited to do so
Why must attendees wear their identification tags?
All attendees must register at the entrance.
constant (adj) not changing, staying the same over time
The price has remained constant despite tax rises.
He is the only constant member of the team.
ensure (v) to make certain of something
To ensure safety...
Keep wallets hidden to ensure they are not stolen.
impression (n) how something makes you feel, your initial feeling about it
They can create the right impression.
I get the impression he is not interested in the project.
organize (v) to make plans for an event, or be responsible for its completion
I'm helping to organize the shareholders' meeting.
Can you organize the food for the party?
outlook (n) a prediction for how the future is likely to be
The outlook for the weekend, cold, with showers...
The outlook for this project is not so good.
patented (adj) an idea or invention protected from being copied by government recognition
You know it's a Seymour suit by the patented breathable lining.
It has a patented anti-lock braking system.
reasonably (adv) fairly, at an acceptable level; or to some extent, quite
They are reasonably priced.
It is a reasonably long walk.
remind (v) to help someone else to remember something
The organizers would like to remind attendees...
She reminded me to bring my laptop to the presentation.
slump (v) of people, to lie or fall to the ground because you are very tired or fell ill; of prices, to drop suddenly
Sales have slumped in the last year.
He slumped to the floor.
stable (adj) not likely to break, fail to operate, fall over or have any other problems
The new software is much more stable than the previous version.
Make sure the ladder is stable before you climb up it.
suspicious (adj) appearing to be dangerous or illegal
To report a suspicious package.
A suspicious-looking man has been waiting near the bank all day.
toiletries (n) products used for personal cleaning or making the user look beautiful
To purchase toiletries...
I get all my toiletries at the drugstore around the corner.
(in) transit (n) when traveling, changing from one plane to another to continue a journey
We were in transit to Paris.
The goods are currently in transit.
unattended (adj) left without an owner present
To collect his unattended bag...
Unattended bags will be taken away and destroyed.

Quiz 25

1 Complete the sentences with the following words.

impression patented reasonably suspicious toiletries transit unattended

1 Passengers flying on to other destinations please make your way to the .... lounge.
2 Essential .... are provided and can be found in the bathroom of your hotel room.
3 Passengers are reminded not to leave their baggage .... at any time.
4 Did you notice anything .... last night? Our neighbor's car was stolen.
5 Products that are .... cannot be produced or sold by other companies.
6 The price slump has resulted in more .... priced electronic goods.
7 At an interview, the candidates clothing gives an initial .... of the type of person he or she is.

2 Read the definitions and unscramble the words.

1 to make certain (senrue)
2 a person joining an event (etendate)
3 a prediction about the future (koolout)
4 to drop suddenly (lumps)
5 regular, without changing (stocantn)
6 to make people remember (demirn)
7 to be responsible for arranging an event (zogirane)
8 unlikely to have any problems (tables)
9 reasonably priced (dofarfaleb)

Unit 26

attend (v) to go to or be present at a function (usually formal)
I attended my sister's wedding.
Jane and her new assistant attended the conference.
capital (n) money used to start a business, buy a house, etc.
The failed project has left us without working capital.
Selling the property will help to release some capital.
(high) demand (n) very popular, wanted by many people
The things the local people make are in high demand.
The latest games consoles are in high demand just before Christmas.
function (n) a large formal dinner or other party
Ms. Smithers will attend the function.
All guests at the function were given a gift.
particularly (adv) specially, more so than others
The candidate is particularly suitable for the position.
He is a particularly interesting man.
properly (adv) correctly, done the right way
The watch didn't fit properly.
Be sure to fasten your seatbelt properly to avoid injury.
realize (v) to understand something (often suddenly)
I realize that this is a non-working day.
The staff realized the amount of time that had gone into the job.
reception (n) the place in a company where guests are greeted
You have to sign in at the reception.
I'll come down and meet you at the reception.
receptive (adj) open and willing to listen to something
The director was very receptive to your ideas.
The marketing section is always receptive to suggestions.
repayment (n) paying money back that was previously borrowed
The bank has requested immediate repayment of all outstanding debt.
It is possible to spread repayments over two years.
submit (v) to give a required document to the person that needs it
I had to submit the request three weeks in advance.
Please submit three photographs with each application.
(in) transit (n) when traveling, changing from one plane to another to continue a journey
We were in transit to Paris.
The containers were damaged in transit.
upset (adj) to feel unhappy or angry about something
The members were upset that dinner hadn't been arranged.
I think he was very upset by the news.

Quiz 26

1 Complete the sentences with the following words.

capital demand particularly properly realize reception submitted

1 The company needs more .... to be able to complete the project successfully.
2 All guests will be met by the manager at the ....
3 Experienced engineers are in high ....
4 Three applications for the post of manager have been .... already.
5 I .... it's a good promotion, but I don't want to live abroad right now.
6 I didn't do the report .... so I had to do it again.
7 I think Tina is .... suitable for the job because she is so experienced.

2 Read the definitions and write *true* or *false*.

1 A *function* is an event.
2 If you are *upset* you are feeling very happy.
3 A *repayment* is the return of an amount of money.
4 If something is in *transit* it's moving.
5 If you *attend* an event you don't go to it.
6 If you *renew* something you start again.
7 A *receptive* person listens to new ideas.

Unit 27

agricultural (adj) connected to farming
The waters will be channeled for agricultural purposes.
delivery (n) carrying or transporting something, by mail or courier
This has caused a delay in the delivery of replacement parts.
developer (n) the person that comes up with an idea and produces it
We are all excited to hear about your proposals for the solar electric generator at the developers' conference on the 25th.
The site was bought by a property developer.
effectiveness (n) quality of working well
A major goal is to maximize the effectiveness of our recruiting decisions.
fail (v) to not succeed to do something
He passed the initial interview but failed the second interview.
Only 5 percent of test-takers fail to reach the required level.
guideline (n) advice
Following these simple guidelines can improve hiring procedures.
hesitate (v) to pause or stop before doing something
Don't hesitate to contact me.
keen (adj) interested and excited, very much wanting to do something
I'm sure you will be keen to attend.
We are keen to show him the new production line.
landscape (n) the features of an area, usually countryside
Channeling the waters of the Wan Hei has led to a major change in the landscape.
luxury (n) an expensive and high quality item, not usually something needed
We have the service to suit you if you want to travel in luxury...
Enjoy the luxury of real silk next to your skin.
manufacture (v) to produce a large number or amount of something, usually in a factory or plant
Our principal supplier has been experiencing difficulties at one of their main manufacturing plants.
The parts are manufactured overseas, but assembled in our factory here in the US.
plant (n) a factory, or the place where goods are manufactured
A fire damaged one of their main manufacturing plants, and this has left us with a deficit of replacement parts.
The shoes are made at our Asian plant.
recruitment process (n) way of hiring new employees
A major goal is to maximize the effectiveness of our recruitment process.
solar (adj) powered by sunlight
We are all excited to hear about your proposals for the solar electric generator at the developers' conference on the 25th.
The calculator operates on a solar cell, so no batteries are required.
suit (v) to match or fit somebody well
We have the service to suit you...
That new hairstyle really suits you.
transformation (n) change
The region has undergone a transformation in the last 50 years.

Quiz 27

1 Use the definitions to find the words in the puzzle.

1 To produce
2 Advice
3 Hiring
4 Countryside
5 Factory

2 Choose the correct word.

1 There should be a(n) .... of parts to the factory this Friday.
(A) delivery
(B) developer
(C) industry

2 There are several .... who have new plans and ideas for the company.
(A) plants
(B) industries
(C) developers

3 A job as a receptionist would really .... me right now.
(A) confirm
(B) fail
(C) suit

4 I'm not so .... going to the movies; I prefer going to the theater.
(A) keen
(B) keen on
(C) keen to

5 We assemble the monitors at this ....
(A) environment
(B) investment
(C) plant

6 The prize is a fourteen-day .... cruise around the Mediterranean.
(A) deficit
(B) luxury
(C) solar

7 Please don't .... to ask me any questions.
(A) hesitate
(B) seek
(C) suit

8 We need to improve the .... of our decision making.
(A) effect
(B) effectiveness
(C) effective

Unit 28

appreciate (n) to feel grateful to somebody because of what they have done for you
I really appreciated your help.
I would appreciate some compensation.
compensation (n) money paid to apologize for disappointment with goods or services
I would appreciate some compensation.
We demanded compensation for our lost luggage.
confirm (n) to state that something is definitely correct
I am just writing to confirm...
I've received replies from almost all of you confirming attendance, but...
constant (adj) not changing, staying the same over time
He was the only constant member of the team.
The number of rehires remained constant.
enthusiastic (adj) very interested, keen and excited about something
You should be enthusiastic and knowledgeable about the movie business.
Enthusiastic students can hope to learn in as little as four weeks.

knowledgeable (adj) understanding something to a great degree
You should be enthusiastic and knowledgeable about the movie business.
He is very knowledgeable about cars.

(be) led (v) caused to think something, persuaded
Firstly, I was led to believe that all rooms in the hotel...
I was led to think that there was no future for me in the business.

mere (adj) only, a smaller than expected amount
...a mere five minutes from the beautiful blue waters of the Aegean.
He wrote his first piece when he was a mere seven years old.

misrepresent (n) not show, or indicate correctly
The advertisement misrepresented the hotel.

recruit (n) a person hired by a company to do a job
Recruits from other companies.
The number of recruits fell last year.

rehire (n) a person hired again to do the same job
The number of rehires remained constant.
Rehires are often sought after, as they require less training.

renovate (n) to repair something to a condition as good as new
The house really needs to be renovated.
Stay at the recently renovated Casa Stanoupolos Hotel.

secretarial (adj) associated with the work of secretaries, administrative work
Secretarial position available starting March.
Secretarial skills are essential in this line of work.

unspoiled (adj) not damaged, altered or affected (especially by tourists)
...visit the unspoiled island of Kefalonia.
It is an unspoiled area with few hotels.

Quiz 28

1 Complete the sentences with the following words.

confirm knowledgeable led mere rehires renovated misrepresents secretarial

1 I'd like to apply for the .... position. I have good computer skills and can communicate well.
2 The farm buildings have been .... at last.
3 We were all .... to believe that there would be an increase in our salaries this year.
4 The hotel is a .... five-minute walk from the beach.
5 There have been several .... this month. It's great to bring their experience back into the company.
6 Helen is very .... She has researched the company well.
7 The brochure .... the holiday.
8 Can you .... that the order will arrive on Friday?

2 Find six words in the puzzle. Then match them with their meanings.

C	O	M	P	E	N	S	A	T	I	O	N	L
T	A	P	P	R	E	C	I	A	T	E	W	E
M	N	S	E	U	D	B	Y	W	D	F	U	P
A	E	J	R	S	G	W	A	E	O	Y	M	O
B	K	I	Z	W	A	N	L	P	L	Q	E	V
R	D	H	N	E	P	I	F	E	P	S	L	E
E	A	F	T	K	O	B	S	V	E	C	O	R
C	O	L	J	P	N	N	I	J	R	U	L	A
R	V	G	S	C	E	T	V	A	I	S	M	L
U	C	N	O	M	A	B	T	Z	O	G	A	L
I	U	X	M	V	F	O	R	F	D	A	B	M
T	B	I	H	A	E	W	O	D	R	C	S	E
A	C	O	N	S	T	A	N	T	O	F	Y	A
E	N	T	H	U	S	I	A	S	T	I	C	X

1 payment
2 new employee
3 keen
4 be thankful for
5 untouched, perfect
6 regular

Quizzes key

1
1 keyboard 2 briefcase 3 pick (it) up
4 discuss 5 workshop 6 waved
7 presentation 8 documents

2
1
1 C, 2 B, 3 C, 4 A, 5 A, 6 C

2
1 goods 2 parcel 3 customer 4 notice
5 repairs 6 cheap 7 terrible 8 decide
9 arrange

3
1
1 label 2 plug 3 purchase 4 courier
5 improvement 6 branch 7 stock
8 replacement 9 appreciate
10 participant 11 practical

2
1 included 2 socket 3 block 4 feedback
5 company 6 adapter 7 assistance
8 criticized 9 theoretical 10 requesting

4
1
1 C, 2 B, 3 B, 4 B, 5 B, 6 A, 7 A

2
1 false 2 true 3 false 4 false 5 true
6 false 7 false 8 true 9 true 10 false
11 true 12 false 13 false

5
1
1 considered 2 retirement 3 credit 4 downturn
5 impact 6 distribution 7 immediate
8 accommodation 9 recommendations
10 advantage 11 roughly

2
1 false 2 false 3 true 4 true 5 true
6 true 7 false 8 false 9 true 10 false
11 false 12 true

3
1 significant 2 suggest 3 improve
4 influential 5 intently 6 convince 7 donation
8 efficiently

6
1
1 B, 2 C, 3 A, 4 A, 5 A, 6 B, 7 C, 8 C, 9 A

2
1 audit 2 fail 3 consignment 4 specification
5 customer 6 invention 7 monument

7
1
1 facility 2 termination 3 failure 4 barcode
5 nonpayment 6 reservation 7 certification
8 inquiry 9 intend

2
1 nominate 2 applicants 3 intention
4 benefit 5 enable 6 anticipate 7 assist
8 potential 9 intended 10 responsible
11 promptly 12 tag 13 consignment
14 administrative

8
1
1 overpass 2 skyscraper 3 passenger
4 harbor 5 collect 6 revise

2
1 withdraw 2 guardrail 3 lie 4 monitor
5 tower over 6 customer 7 shining 8 holding
9 tent

9
1
1 A, 2 A, 3 C, 4 B, 5 B, 6 C, 7 B, 8 B, 9 B, 10 A,
11 B

2
1 depart 2 drive 3 upstairs 4 invite
5 probably 6 handy 7 member 8 detailed
9 venue

10
1
1 refund 2 attend 3 file 4 pushy 5 discount
6 receipt

2
1 seminar 2 disagreement 3 shipping
4 turnover 5 document 6 suggest 7 recent
8 satisfied

3
1 situation 2 inexperienced 3 argument
4 carelessness 5 definitely 6 mileage
7 demanding 8 drastically

11
1
1 B, 2 C, 3 B, 4 A, 5 B, 6 A, 7 C, 8 A, 9 B

2
1 false 2 true 3 true 4 false 5 true 6 true
7 false 8 true 9 true 10 true 11 false
12 true

12
1
1 B, 2 C, 3 A, 4 B, 5 A, 6 C, 7 A, 8 A, 9 C

2
1 false 2 false 3 true 4 true 5 true 6 false
7 false 8 true 9 false

13
1
1 convenient 2 highly 3 invaluable 4 serious
5 comfortable 6 consistently 7 grueling
8 restored

2
1 C, 2 B, 3 B, 4 A, 5 A

14
1
1 campaign 2 withdrawals 3 cancelation
4 participants 5 complaints 6 remittance
7 alumni 8 bulletin 9 applications
10 cardiovascular 11 strategy
12 memorandum 13 refund

2
1 false 2 false 3 true 4 true 5 true 6 false
7 true 8 true 9 true 10 false 11 true
12 true 13 true

15
1
1 C, 2 A, 3 A, 4 A, 5 B, 6 C, 7 C

2
1 chef 2 valley 3 grill 4 draw 5 studio
6 brush 7 plow

3
1 wooden 2 fixed 3 backpack 4 yard
5 forest 6 figurine 7 pier 8 scene

16
1
1 blocks 2 drawer 3 bank 4 ordered
5 cafeteria 6 kept 7 several 8 actually
9 polite

2
1 false 2 true 3 false 4 false 5 false
6 false 7 false

17
1
1 B, 2 C, 3 C, 4 A, 5 B, 6 A, 7 A, 8 A, 9 A,
10 A, 11 B

2
1 celebration 2 heel 3 right away
4 concern 5 stadium 6 disappointing
7 withdrawal 8 reservation

18
1
1 spectator 2 schedule 3 delighted 4 salvage
5 realize 6 feature

2
1 condition 2 apprentice 3 target
4 ambitious 5 latecomers 6 support
7 imaginative 8 adjust 9 waterproof
10 background

19
1
1 investigation 2 repetitiveness 3 intercom
4 document 5 bankrupt 6 impatient
7 non-refundable 8 internship 9 dependence
10 criticize

2
1 C, 2 B, 3 C, 4 A, 5 A, 6 C, 7 B, 8 B, 9 C, 10 A

20

1

1 true 2 true 3 true 4 true 5 true 6 false 7 true 8 false 9 false 10 false 11 true 12 true

2

1 retirement 2 situation 3 foreign 4 invoice 5 employed 6 refuse 7 report 8 rare 9 rescued 10 surrounding

21

1

1 A, 2 C, 3 B, 4 C, 5 C, 6 A, 7 B, 8 B, 9 A

2

1 culinary 2 vendor 3 ensure 4 festivities 5 tradition 6 explorer 7 orienteering 8 elderly 9 personalized 10 revised 11 host

22

1

1 keyboard 2 outfit 3 counter 4 set 5 deserted 6 decorate 7 harbor 8 Cycling 9 display 10 control panel 11 raise 12 pointed

2

1 commuter 2 flight attendant 3 sweep 4 locker 5 customer 6 walkway 7 hiding 8 lean

23

1

1 C, 2 B, 3 C, 4 B, 5 C, 6 A, 7 C, 8 A, 9 B

2

1 quote 2 book 3 policy 4 license 5 amusing 6 frankly 7 appreciate 8 borrow 9 motivate 10 terrific 11 maintenance

24

1

1 true 2 false 3 false 4 true 5 false 6 true 7 true

2

1 recommended 2 suitable 3 pressed 4 prefer 5 aisle 6 merchandise

25

1

1 transit 2 toiletries 3 unattended 4 suspicious 5 patented 6 reasonably 7 impression

2

1 ensure 2 attendee 3 outlook 4 slump 5 constant 6 remind 7 organize 8 stable 9 affordable

26

1

1 capital 2 reception 3 demand 4 submitted 5 realize 6 properly 7 particularly

2

1 true 2 false 3 true 4 true 5 false 6 true 7 true

27

1

1 manufacture 2 guidelines 3 recruitment 4 landscape 5 plant

2

1 A, 2 C, 3 C, 4 B, 5 C, 6 B, 7 A, 8 B

28

1

1 secretarial 2 renovated 3 led 4 mere 5 rehires 6 knowledgeable 7 misrepresents 8 confirm

2

1 compensation 2 recruit 3 enthusiastic 4 appreciate 5 unspoiled 6 constant

Alphabetical Word list

Word	Unit
A	
accommodation (n)	5
actually (adv)	16
adapter (n)	3
adjust (v)	18
administrative (adj)	7
advanced (adj)	12
advantage (n)	5
advise (v)	12
affordable (adj)	25
agricultural (adj)	27
aid (v)	5
aisle (n)	24
allow (v)	24
alternative (adj)	12
alumnus (plural alumni) (n)	14
ambitious (adj)	18
amusing (adj)	23
anticipate (v)	7, 14
apologize (v)	4
appliance (n)	24
applicant (n)	7, 12
application (n)	14
appointment (n)	3
appreciate (v)	3, 23, 28
apprentice (n)	18
argument (n)	10
arrange (v)	2
arrangement (n)	2
assist (v)	7
assistance (n)	3
attend (v)	10, 26
attendee (n)	25
attentively (adv)	13
audit (n)	6
available (adj)	9, 17
awkward (adj)	24
B	
background (n)	18
backpack (n)	15
bank (n)	16
bankrupt (adj)	11, 19
barcode (n)	7
benefit (v)	7
beverage (n)	21
block (n)	16
block (v)	3
boardroom (n)	16
boast (v)	11
book (v)	23
boost (v)	4
bored (adj)	16
borrow (v)	23
bother (v)	2
branch (n)	3
briefcase (n)	1, 9
brush (v)	15
bulletin (n)	14
C	
cafeteria (n)	16
calculator (n)	23
campaign (n)	14
cancel (v)	4
cancelation (n)	14
capital (n)	26
cardiovascular (adj)	14
careless (adj)	12
carelessness (n)	10
cautiously (adv)	13
celebration (n)	17
certification (n)	7
chairperson (n)	20
charity (n)	20
cheap (adj)	2
chef (n)	15
closure (n)	11
coach (adj)	17
collect (v)	8
commuter (n)	22
company (n)	3
compensation (n)	28
complain (v)	6
complaint (n)	2, 14
complimentary (adj)	4, 21
comprehensive (adj)	14
concern (n)	17
condition (n)	18
confirm (v)	6, 28
considerable (adj)	5
considered (be) (v)	5
consignment (n)	6, 7
consistently (adv)	13
constant (adj)	25, 28
control panel (n)	22
convenient (adj)	13
convince (v)	5
cordless (adj)	11
co-supervise (v)	19
counter (n)	22
courier (n)	3, 5
credit (n)	5
criticize (v)	3, 19
crowded (adj)	17
culinary (adj)	21
custom (n)	9
customer (n)	2, 8, 22
cycle (v)	22
D	
damage (v)	6
deadline (n)	4
debt (n)	11
decide (v)	2
decorate (v)	22
definitely (adv)	10
delighted (adj)	11
deliver (v)	15, 23
delivery (n)	27
demand (high) (n)	26
demand (v)	12
demanding (adj)	10
depart (v)	9
dependence (n)	19
deposit (n)	17
deserted (adj)	22
desperate (adj)	17
detailed (adj)	9
developer (n)	27
(have) difficulty doing something (expression)	17
disagreement (n)	10
disappointing (adj)	17
disconnect (v)	18
discount (n)	10
discuss (v)	1, 15
display (n)	22
disposal (n)	14
distribution (n)	5
document (n)	1, 10, 19
donation (n)	5
double (v)	11
downturn (n)	5
drastically (adv)	10
draw (v)	15
drawer (n)	16
drive (v)	9

pick up (v) 1
pier (n) 15
plant (n) 27
pleasantly (adv) 4
plow (v) 15
plug (it) into/in (v) 3
point (v) 22
policy (n) 23
polite (adj) 16
politician (n) 11
popular (adj) 15
potential (adj) 7
practical (adj) 3
prefer (v) 9, 24
prepare (v) 9
presentation (n) 1
press (v) 24
principal (adj) 12
probably (adv) 9
process (v) 5
profit (n) 2
profitability (n) 20
prohibit (v) 21
prompt (adj) 6
promptly (adv) 7
properly (adv) 26
purchase (v) 3
pushy (adj) 10

Q

questionnaire (n) 12
quote (n) 23

R

raise (v) 20, 22
rare (adj) 17, 20
read through (v) 9
reach (v) 5
realize (v) 18, 26
rearrange (v) 9
reasonably (adv) 25
receipt (n) 10
receive(d) (be) (v) 2
recent (adj) 10
reception (n) 26
receptive (adj) 26
recommend (v) 24
recommendation (n) 5
recruit (n) 28
recruitment process (n) 27
reduction (n) 4
re-enactment (n) 21
refrigerator (n) 16
refund (n) 4, 10, 14
refuse (v) 20
regardless (adv) 14
regret (v) 12
rehire (n) 28
remarkable (adj) 11
remind (v) 25
remove (v) 19
remittance (n) 14
renovate (v) 11, 19, 28
repair (v) 20
repairs (n) 2
repayment (n) 26
repetitiveness (n) 19
replacement (adj) 3
report (v) 20
representative (n) 4
request (v) 3
reschedule (v) 20
rescue (v) 20
reservation (n) 7, 17
reserve (v) 23
respond (v) 11
responsibility (n) 2
responsible (for) (adj) 7, 11
restore (v) 13
retirement (n) 5, 20, 23
revise (v) 8
revised (adj) 21
right away (adv) 17
rivals (n) 12
road conditions (n) 4
roughly (adv) 5
run out (v) 17

S

salvage (v) 18
satisfied (adj) 10
scene (n) 15
schedule (v) 18
seaside (n) 15
secluded (adj) 4
secretarial (adj) 28
select (v) 5
seminar (n) 10
senior citizens (n) 21
serious (adj) 13
set (v) 22
several (adj) 16
shareholders (n) 11
shine (v) 8
shipping (n) 10
significant (adj) 5
simplify (v) 5
situation (n) 10, 20
skyscraper (n) 8
sleeve (n) 17
slump (v) 25
socket (n) 3
soften (v) 19
solar (adj) 27
spacious (adj) 11
specification (n) 6
spectator (n) 18
stable (adj) 25
stack (v) 15
stadium (n) 17
stare (v) 16
steep (adj) 15
stock (n) 3
strategy (n) 14
studio (n) 15
subdivide (v) 19
submit (v) 26
suggest (v) 5, 10
suit (v) 27
suitable (adj) 24
support (v) 18
surrender (v) 20
surrounding (adj) 20
suspicious (adj) 25
sweep (v) 22

T

tag (v) 7
takeover (n) 12
target (n) 18
target (v) 4
tent (n) 8
termination (n) 7
terrible (adj) 2
terrific (adj) 23
theoretical (adj) 3
through (read/go) (adv) 9
tidy (adj) 6
toiletries (n) 25
top (n) 9
tower over (v) 8
tradition (n) 21
transformation (n) 27
transit (in) (n) 25, 26
tremendous (adj) 4
triumph (n) 13
turnover (n) 10

U

unattended (adj) 14, 25
unconditional (adj) 21
underprivileged (adj) 5
understand (v) 9
unfavorable (adj) 11
unfortunately (adv) 9
unspoiled (adj) 28
unwrap (v) 19

OXFORD
UNIVERSITY PRESS

Great Clarendon Street, Oxford OX2 6DP

Oxford University Press is a department of the University of Oxford. It furthers the University's objective of excellence in research, scholarship, and education by publishing worldwide in

Oxford New York

Auckland Cape Town Dar es Salaam Hong Kong Karachi Kuala Lumpur Madrid Melbourne Mexico City Nairobi New Delhi Shanghai Taipei Toronto

With offices in

Argentina Austria Brazil Chile Czech Republic France Greece Guatemala Hungary Italy Japan Poland Portugal Singapore South Korea Switzerland Thailand Turkey Ukraine Vietnam

OXFORD and OXFORD ENGLISH are registered trade marks of Oxford University Press in the UK and in certain other countries

First published 2007
2011 2010 2009 2008
10 9 8 7 6 5 4 3 2

ISBN: 978 0 19 452953 2

Printed in China

ACKNOWLEDGEMENTS

The publisher would like to thank the following for reviewing/piloting the material in this course: Mr JOE Dae-ho, Testwise SISA, Jongno, Seoul; Ms YANG Soh Jeong, Korea University, Seoul; Ms SEO young-ja, Korea Foreign Language University, Seoul; Ms. Jo Kirihara, Ritsumeikan University, Kyoto; Mr. Nobuo Tsuda, Konan University, Hyogo; Ms. Rena Yoshida, Obirin University, Kanagawa; Ms. Keiko Slaybaugh, Showa Ongaku Daigaku, Kanagawa; AIT Foreign Language Center, Tokyo; Tsuda Jukukai Institute, Tokyo; Nichibei Kaiwa Gakuin, Tokyo; International Language Centre, Tokyo; Graeme Petrie, Tokyo; Steven Yoell, Mark Barrett, Osaka.

Cover images courtesy of: Digital Vision/Getty Images (portrait), Corbis UK Ltd (meeting).